Slings & Arrows

Slings & Arrows

How Toxic Narratives Perpetuate Poverty in Indian Country

David W. Bland

Washington, DC

Copyright © 2019 by David W. Bland
New Academia Publishing, 2020

All rights reserved. No part of this book may be reproduced or transmitted in any form or by any means, electronic or mechanical, including photocopying, recording, or by any information storage and retrieval system.

Printed in the United States of America

Library of Congress Control Number: 2019916011
ISBN 978-1-7330408-9-1 paperback (alk. paper)
ISBN 978-1-7333980-5-3 hardcover (alk. paper)

 An imprint of New Academia Publishing

 4401-A Connecticut Ave., NW #236 - Washington DC 20008
info@newacademia.com - www.newacademia.com

For more information visit www.davidwbland.com

Contents

Foreword	vii
Introduction	1
Part I – The Backstory	7
Chapter 1 Winchester, City Light, and Indian Country	9
Chapter 2 Richard Bland, Harry Byrd, and Narrative Economics	23
Chapter 3 The Poor Will Always Be With Us	35
Chapter 4 Why is Doing the Right Thing So Hard?	45
Chapter 5 Moving On	61
Part II – Building the Foundation	77
Chapter 6 Shivs and Arrows	79
Chapter 7 Have I Got a Deal for You	93
Chapter 8 Great Falls and Great Ambitions	109
Chapter 9 Wounded Knee and Cannon Ball	119
Chapter 10 Not an Auspicious Beginning	133
Photo Gallery	149
Chapter 11 Big White Ugly $#@%&	165
Chapter 12 The Duke and Kareem	181
Chapter 13 There is No Such Thing as No Risk, But We Come Close	195
Part III – Slowly Becoming Mainstream	209
Chapter 14 Grim Reality Check	211
Chapter 15 A Wobbly Stool and Driving While Black	229

Chapter 16 The Dunning Kruger Twins 243
Chapter 17 Swimming Pools and Smurfs 259
Chapter 18 Demons and Prayers 267
Chapter 19 A Good Time to Go 277

Acknowledgments 283
Notes 285
Photo Credits 293
Bibliography 294
Index 297

Foreword

My first thought after David asked me to write a foreword – my first ever – was that I'm just not the right guy. I'm putting that aside for a couple of reasons. First, after 40 years, I know the author better than most. And second, I "lived" much of the story he tells in this work.

I hired David for a position at the Norfolk, Virginia, Redevelopment and Housing Authority (circa 1976) – his first job out of Wake Forest University. I watched an amazing career develop and made a most valued friend. Our careers in housing and community development have run somewhat parallel, working together from time to time. While in Norfolk, David saw firsthand the realities of slums, poverty, early urban renewal and public housing. I think this formed a resolve in David to do better for communities – and people. In his roles with the Urban Reinvestment Task Force, the Federal Reserve, and his City Light Development nonprofit, it was about making change, often where the odds were against that. It's fair to say, David won a few and lost a few. We would joke that, in the affordable housing and community development business, "folks don't always want what we got." But that never bothered David, and the challenges he took on seemed to get more daunting over the course of his career.

David presents the fascinating story of a career that begins with failing urban renewal and public housing programs and ends with arguably the most significant advancement of the Native American housing cause in our history. To David, the Native American housing issue was the ultimate in a need and a people underserved. At the same time, David considered this an untapped market – one that had little access to the more progressive affordable housing and community development tools that he knew – and even less access to capital. With Travois, Inc., he was determined to make that change. In the early days of Travois (i.e., David and wife Marianne), I would talk with David periodically as he personally covered the remote Indian Country. I'm thinking this may not have a good ending. But perseverance combined with technical and interpersonal skills earned David hard-to-get respect in Indian Country. Travois began to create some traction. To say David and Travois made the market in Native American affordable housing is an understatement.

As much as I enjoyed David's career story, there's much more going on here. Throughout his career, David confronted different narratives, most of them working against him and those he was serving, particularly Native Americans. Influenced by Nobel Laureate Robert Shiller, David takes 45 years of experience and develops an important theme around narratives – the "stories" we tell: "It is the stories we tell and the stories we hear that validate the actions we take when we might otherwise be more rational, more reasonable, more just."

When David's pen first put this to paper, he had little idea how much this notion would be in play today. David combines other theories that support how viral narratives cook up a "toxic stew" that perpetuate misguided public policy, among other things.

David has devoted 45 years to his passion, with remarkable results achieved where others would not go, did not care, or had questionable motives. Of all my friends and industry colleagues, no one created something of greater economic, social and moral importance. Now, David takes this experience, gives us a good story, great vignettes, and serious things to think about the impact of the stories we tell and the stories we believe.

Evan Becker, San Diego, CA

Introduction

TODAY, INDIAN COUNTRY is at once a romantic and mysterious place. It is in conflict with itself, with breathtaking beauty and heartbreaking misery. It is teepees against a setting sun and rusting cars on cinder blocks. It is elegant women clothed in beaded dresses lined with elk teeth, their dresses as colorful as a rainbow and every bit as majestic. It is coal black eyes and high cheekbones, lined skin and braided hair, anger and frustration. It is dirt roads and septic tanks, spent water wells and LP tanks. It is too-thin teenagers riding ponies bareback, bare feet dangling loosely astride their mounts, unaware of the incongruity of their mode of conveyance. Indian Country is all of these things. It is abject poverty and unwavering devotion to family and homeland.

Mostly, it is deserving of better. As Chief Joseph wrote, "Good words do not last long unless they amount to something." This book stands as testimony to hard-won insights and is a how-to manual of sorts for the work we all have left to do.

In August 1993, on the first Sunday following my first week as the new manager of community affairs for the Minneapolis Federal Reserve Bank, I was unceremoniously informed that a long-planned expedition, via Fed car, to every major Indian Reservation in the Ninth Federal Reserve District, the Minneapolis Fed's domain, could be put off no longer. I was dragooned into this little adventure. Along with two long-term Fed employees, my boss Kathy Erickson and my assistant, Liz Wahlstrand, I left for Montana and the Dakotas and would return two weeks later. It was a memorable trip, not the least because I was destined to spend about a hundred hours in a car with two women I barely knew, but also because I had little understanding of Indian Country or the role of the Federal Reserve Bank in meeting the needs of tribal people. I was way out of my comfort zone, a feeling soon to be exacerbated by the fact that my two travel companions had starkly different eating habits than I did.

I was used to three meals a day with some regularity, while my two car mates seemed to view mealtime as fungible and mostly a nuisance. Kathy was a long-time Fed employee, a vice president whose responsibilities included the community affairs division which I now managed. Liz was a young woman who was industrious but reserved and very private. They were close and I was the outsider, not in on the jokes. They had an odd habit of putting old fashioned Tootsie Pop candies on the dashboard of the car, in direct sunlight, to soften them into a sort of hard candy-coated but slightly mushy popsicle. They lined them up on the dashboard like little road warriors and ate them throughout the long drives, which I thought was weird. Otherwise they proved to be congenial travel companions.

Our first night was spent in Winner, South Dakota, at the Buffalo Trail Motel. We arrived after dusk and the neon sign of the motel was misfiring. The "r" in Trail was out of order and seemed to be advertising the Buffalo "Tail" Motel. The motel rated a zero on a one to five scale on its best day. That uncomfortable first night preceded a stressful two weeks of meeting tribal leaders who were about as much in the dark as to the purpose of the trip as I was. Having the imprimatur of the Federal Reserve was a big help in getting the attention of the tribal leaders. Kathy had apparently spent months arranging to meet each one on a timetable that she did not share with Liz and me. Instead, upon embarking on the next part of our road trip each day, Kathy would announce where we were going as though the information had been proprietary in some way.

We did not hit every reservation in the District on this trip, but we made it to the largest and some of the poorest reservations, including Rosebud, Pine Ridge, Northern Cheyenne, Crow, Rocky Boy's and a few others. My introduction to Indian Country via this trip was later to take on mythic proportions at the Fed, with anecdotes of hotel rooms without windows and a flat tire somewhere east of Malta, Montana, with a storm blowing in from the west threatening to scatter us all into North Dakota. I changed the tire, in good manly fashion, and Kathy bribed the only tire store within a hundred miles to stay open and repair the flat so that we could make it to our next destination. The trip became known as the "Trip from Hell" at the Fed and I was granted some well-deserved streetcred for having endured it in only my second week on the job.

At each stop at a different reservation I learned not only about life on that reservation, but I learned about some peculiar aspect of the legal structure of Indian reservations and the sometimes-conflicted relationship tribes had with the states in which they were situated. I also learned that every reservation and every tribe is unique, with its own cultural heritage, and a proud and honorable history peculiar to that tribe. I learned about the self-defeating actions that tribes all too often took. At every reservation, we met with the tribal president and usually several members of the tribal council. They were earnest and forthright in discussing the needs on the reservation, including the problems they typically had with local banks unwilling to lend to tribal members or sometimes even unwilling to extend credit to the tribes themselves. The only consistent and uniform complaint that we heard at every reservation we visited was that there was a true crisis in affordable housing. Banking services were needed to one degree or another, capital was scarce for new businesses or expansions of existing businesses on some but not every reservation. But affordable housing was the greatest need on every reservation and it was here that the Federal Reserve Bank of Minneapolis and its newly minted manager of community affairs had the least to offer.

Right from the start of my new job I was confronted with a dilemma. The thing I knew the least about—capital formation and banking services in rural areas—was what we could offer, but the thing I knew the most about—affordable housing and how to get it financed and built—was the one thing the Fed could do almost nothing about. This began to gnaw at me from the outset of my work at the Fed and I had no choice but to sublimate my own set of skills and learn as much as I could and do as much as I could in the areas where the Federal Reserve Bank might actually be able to help. I started on an effort to learn about why banks would not or could not provide the same kinds of banking services to tribes as they do to majority communities. I started reading about micro-loan programs and peer lending. I wanted to find out why banks were so reluctant to lend to Indians and what we could do to help out. I put my affordable housing hat in the closet and began the process of becoming a banker, of sorts.

When the Minneapolis Federal Reserve Bank asked me to manage their community affairs office I was excited. I had no clue, mind you, what it meant to manage community affairs for one of the federal reserve banks, but it sounded right up my alley. Ultimately, I realized that I was not very good at it, and they were pretty glad to see me go when the end finally came. But I got something unexpected out of the time I spent struggling in the wood-paneled and money-scented trenches of the Federal Reserve Bank. I learned about Indian Country.

Indian Country is the term used to define the land where most Native Americans now live as well as the lands they once controlled. There are 573 federally recognized Indian tribes in the United States. There were fewer than that when I started in Minneapolis in 1993, but only by a handful. There are, of course, the iconic tribes that we remember from John Ford and John Wayne movies—the Apaches, Shoshones, Sioux, Cheyenne and Arapaho. But there are others that too few of us have ever heard about, such as the Modoc, the Pomo, the Tulalip, the Confederated Tribes of the Colville Reservation and the Ak-Chin Indian Community. They have histories and traditions that enrich our lives and define who we are as a nation. And all too often, the white people who live on or near Indian reservations display a mean-spirited vindictiveness toward their Native American neighbors.

This is the story of how I got to Indian Country; how a company I started made a big difference in the lives of very poor Native American families and is still at it. And it is a story of the things we do collectively and individually to perpetuate the poverty we find on too many Indian reservations. It is a book about the disheartening stories I heard, about the negative narrative of Black and Native American lives, and how I worked to create a new narrative. Robert Shiller, the 2013 recipient of the Nobel Prize in Economic Sciences, has a theory he calls *Narrative Economics*, with the premise that the stories we tell, the myths we invent and repeat, have economic impact. And the stories we tell can become contagious. We all know of some ridiculous story that has gone "viral" on the internet. Shiller's theory is that stories, like diseases, can be contagious and spread throughout a population, and that these stories can have good and, all too often, bad results.

Shiller's research explains why people think the way they do and tell the stories they tell, and this helps me understand why poverty is so intractable on Indian reservations and in the Black community. The crux of my hypothesis is that people are inordinately receptive to mean-spirited and grossly unfair stories about why Black and Native American families are poorer, on average, than white families. And this vulnerability to offensive stories is abetted by the deeply flawed behaviors we engage in. The decisions people come to via these flawed processes and the scornful stories told and retold are a recipe for dogma. We need a way to replace the damaging dogma with a more tolerant and respectful canon.

I believe my 40 years or so of working in Black and Native American communities have given me insights that few others have. I believe that our words and deeds have perpetuated the unconscionable circumstances imposed upon Black and Native Americans, and we must hold ourselves accountable. We must learn to overcome our illusions. It will not be easy. As William Faulkner wrote "Your illusions are a part of you like your bones and flesh and memory."[1] It's time we examined the policies we promote and the behaviors we tolerate that leave a lasting impression on families and communities. We besmirch and defame and the smudge on our psyches and souls must someday be wiped away, but only if we take an honest look at how and why we tell the stories we tell and do the things we do.

Part I
The Backstory

Chapter 1

Winchester, City Light, and Indian Country

WINCHESTER IS NESTLED at the top of the Shenandoah Valley in far northwest Virginia, very near the border with West Virginia. From Washington DC, you can get there by taking Route 50 through the horse country towns of Middleburg and Upperville (which we jokingly called Upper-income-ville) where the Mellons and Firestones and other similarly wealthy families settled after leaving Pittsburgh or Akron or wherever they originally made their fortunes. Middleburg is so named because it was midway between Alexandria and Winchester, Winchester being the largest city on the western frontier in colonial days.

Nowadays Winchester can't seem to make up its mind which is more important: its history as a western frontier city during the 17th and 18th centuries with ties to George Washington, Lord Fairfax, and Daniel Morgan; its dubious history of being captured and released, like some hapless rainbow trout, 72 times during the Civil War; or its self-proclaimed distinction as the Apple Capital. It is the home of the Byrd family, of Governor and Senator Harry Flood Byrd, Jr. and Sr., was the home of Patsy Cline, and is still home to the annual Shenandoah Apple Blossom Festival.

Winchester welcomed my wife Marianne Roos and me and that counted for something. Our fledgling consulting company, Bland, Roos and Associates, had completed a market study for the National Trust for Historic Preservation's Main Street program in Winchester and we fell in love with the beautiful and historic downtown, moving there in 1985. Winchester became our home and the place where we fought a few battles of our own and learned a thing or two about ourselves and about what it was like to live in a city whose image of itself did not necessarily fit its reality. We dove into community life, joining the First Presbyterian Church, becoming youth group advisors and serving on countless committees. We volunteered for the local historic preservation group, putting our house on the Christmas tour to help them raise money. Marianne joined the Rotary Club. I helped the City win an All-America City Award from the National Civic League, "recognizing communities that leverage civic engagement, collaboration, inclusiveness and innovation to successfully address local issues."

We were fortunate enough to find a spacious office above a quaint book store in downtown Winchester where we set up our own childcare center for Elizabeth, our firstborn, and for the children of an assistant we had hired. Because our jobs required so much travel, which we shared between us, we wanted to have Elizabeth and our soon-to-be-born son, Gregory, close at hand as much as possible. Sometimes we found the balance hard to strike and I adopted a lighthearted plea to Elizabeth to play by herself and just please leave me alone so that I could get my work done. I would say, "I love you, GO AWAY." The first time I said this to Elizabeth she looked positively stunned, but then she laughed and went away to play on her own. It became a sort of mantra for Marianne and me whenever we were feeling a bit overwhelmed, which was often.

Making Applesauce Out of Apples

Winchester would eventually gnaw through the bonds that held us to it. It is a city that always had trouble with its place in the world, unsure of its narrative. It has, for example, always had ambitions for the Apple Blossom Festival, its celebration of the local apple orchards and canning industry and the most important social event of the year. For over ninety years it has occasionally attracted big name celebrities to be the grand marshal for the festival. Notably, Bing Crosby was the grand marshal in 1948, followed naturally by Bob Hope in 1949. But more recently they have scored the likes of Kevin Jonas, one of the less famous Jonas Brothers, and Val Kilmer, a decade or so after his sell-by date. Far worse, Winchester seemed not to be the least embarrassed by having Lillian Somoza, daughter of the ill-fated dictator of Nicaragua, as the Queen of the Festival in 1940. You do have to wonder what they were thinking back in 1940, sitting around the table throwing out possible names for the coming parade's crown, deciding whom to pick, who could be the most heart-warming candidate to represent a wholesome family festival. What sort of flawed decision-making process did they follow? Why would someone suggest the daughter of a brutal banana republic dictator?

The apple-growing first families of Winchester were still running the town in the 1980s from their positions in local government, real estate, law, medicine and banking. The Byrd Family controlled the local newspaper, The Winchester Star. The town fathers and mothers did not brook criticism and did not want anyone pointing out that there might be monsters under the bed. We did not shy from the fight but we did not have a lot of firepower, either.

An Introduction to Inequality

My preparation for the battles we fought in Winchester began in 1976. I graduated from college and landed my first job at the Norfolk Redevelopment and Housing Authority. I found there a comforting balance of pragmatism and idealism, a true yearning to improve the life of the city and its poorest residents, something I very much wanted to be a part of. I also had the good fortune to find a patient mentor, Evan Becker, my first boss. Evan was director of communications and he and I were responsible for explaining the actions of the Housing Authority, a place with a misguided optimism that things could be made better by tearing down the old under the rubric of "urban renewal" or sometimes simply called blight removal.

Urban renewal was tragically powered by a callous disregard for the places Black families lived, fostered memories, and cared for one another. "Blight removal" largely meant tearing down entire Black neighborhoods and replacing them with public housing. All too often new highways cut through the heart of Black neighborhoods but for some reason never seemed to go through middle class white neighborhoods. Of course, the intentions were mostly good even while the policies were grossly misguided. The federal 1937 Housing Act was intended to cure overcrowding and the social ills that go along with slums and tenements. But in tearing down whole neighborhoods of neglected buildings, some with handsome facades and some with historic character and all rich with memories, something crucial was lost.

What was lost was the sense of community which those bustling neighborhoods had in abundance. Those buildings marked for destruction were crowded and crooked, but they were the scene of countless games of hide and seek while parents and grandparents kept an eye on the street. That sense of community could not be recreated in the sterile, nondescript public housing buildings that were built in their place. This slow-moving tragedy struck Norfolk like it did nearly every large city in the US and reinforced in my young mind the sense that fairness and justice were not equally distributed in society. Poor families, but especially Black families, saw little of the fairness in Norfolk that was demanded and expected by everyone else. Good intentions gone awry would be a theme throughout my life in Norfolk and later in both Winchester and Indian Country.

After learning as much as I could from Evan, in 1978 I left for Washington to work at the national Urban Reinvestment Task Force, the predecessor of the Neighborhood Reinvestment Corporation, also known as NeighborWorks, now one of the largest non-profit housing corporations in the country. I traveled throughout the country assisting where I could but mainly learning about the many innovative ways communities were dealing with housing and community development problems.

In 1979 my boss at the Task Force recruited me to move with him to the Rouse Company, the most highly respected development company in the nation. We worked for a Rouse Company subsidiary, the American City Corporation, trying to build vibrant downtowns and create new opportunities in neglected neighborhoods. It was there that I learned about development finance and how cities ebb and flow over time.

In 1979, I had quite fortuitously met Marianne Roos through a blind date arranged by mutual friends. Neither of us had much money so our dates were pretty modest affairs. We spent a lot of our Saturdays walking along the mall in Washington and visiting the museums of the Smithsonian Institution, Kramerbooks & Afterwords, or walking along the tow path of the old C & O Canal. Over the weeks, I was falling deeply in love with Marianne. She was a manuscript reference librarian at the Library of Congress and had been working for months with Edmund Morris, the Pulitzer Prize-winning author of the highly-acclaimed Theodore Roosevelt series. His first book on Roosevelt had just been published and Morris later inscribed my copy of the book with "Thanks for your wife's charming assistance in my research!" Marianne became friendly with Edmund and his wife Sylvia, who also did research at the Manuscript Division as she was writing a book on Clare Booth Luce. I was fairly intimidated by Marianne's easy rapport with these giants of the literary world and could not be anything but captivated by her. Marianne was not the least impressed with herself and was so sweet and charming that everyone fell for her, but I was determined to stake my claim. We married in 1980.

After learning as much as I could at the Rouse Company I took the leap and started a small market research consulting company to help small cities (those with populations of under 50,000 or so) revitalize their historic downtowns. After a few years, Marianne agreed to leave the Library to work with me in Bland, Roos and Associates. We struggled for a time but had some remarkable experiences, including the plan for the revitalization of Manteo, NC, in anticipation of the 400th anniversary of the first English settlers in the New World.

We were the classic mom and pop business. When we had work, we worked very hard to complete the assignment for our customers to the absolute best of our ability. And the best of our abilities was considerable. Marianne had impressive research and organizational skills she learned in graduate school at UCLA and while assisting some of the very best historians and writers in the country. I brought my public and private sector redevelopment experience to bear for small cities and towns who could never have afforded the Rouse Company but needed help competing with the Walmart on the bypass. We made some progress and did some good but being consultants could only take us so far. Telling someone what they ought to do is one thing; doing what ought to be done is a whole 'nother animal. We started to yearn to actually do what ought to be done.

City Light

Even though our consulting business was thriving, we both wanted more. So, in 1987 I started a housing non-profit in Winchester called City Light Development Corporation and Marianne returned to librarianship, becoming the director of the Handley Library, the combined city and county library.

At the core of our work in Winchester was fighting the injustice of neglect, fighting the sense that conditions among the poverty stricken and largely Black residents on the north side of town, literally on the wrong side of the railroad tracks, could be addressed in the routine course of business over the (very) long run and required no sense of urgency. Winchester ran with a persistent, overwhelming narrative that the political leaders and business leaders shared with one another that the town's image mattered more than its day-to-day reality of stark inequality. Our little non-profit, City Light, worked in a town steeped in a history of racism from the days of the Byrd machine and massive resistance, a town struggling to define a new identity not burdened with that history. We built houses for some very low-income families, almost all African American. More importantly, we tried to change the narrative, to change the attitudes and perceptions about the lives of Black families in a Southern city that had spent decades marginalizing those people and families.

City Light Development Corporation emerged from Winchester's shameful willingness to simply look the other way, to assume the worst about poor people. It made me question the town we had chosen as our home and compelled me to change the trajectory of my career. We fought with the city and made more than a few enemies, and I left with the work undone. The resistance to change, the comfort with the way things were, was too hard to fight. We did not transform Winchester, or even the neighborhood where we did most of our work. We did make a difference though. We put under a spotlight some of the hide-bound policies that hampered our efforts to provide affordable housing. We exposed some of the hurtful attitudes that were barely beneath the surface of life in Winchester. Because of our work the city could not ignore its complicity in the deterioration of a whole neighborhood and the lives of the families fighting every day against willful ignorance.

I could not overcome Winchester. But that experience left a fire in my belly and it gave me insights that helped prepare me for what lay ahead. Black families aren't the only grossly and systemically stigmatized and disregarded minority. As I uncovered more and more evidence of our city, state and federal apathy and mismanagement, I discovered my own life's work.

The Start of a New Narrative

The Indians of the Great Plains used the *travois*, a frame slung between poles and dragged behind a horse or dog, to move their belongings. *Travois* was the perfect name for a company whose slogan, "You know where you want to go. Let us pull some of the weight for you," expressed what Bland, Roos and Associates became: a firm committed to helping Native American tribes access funding and opportunities to enrich the lives of their people.

Travois, Inc. is a tiny company compared to the great industrial and financial behemoths astride the American corporate landscape. But by nearly every measure, Travois is an extraordinary company. We have maintained a market share of over 90% or better for most of our 24 plus years in business, admittedly in a small market. More importantly, this small family company developed a how-to manual for Indian Country. We needed to convey a new story, starting with housing and community development. Changing the story, telling a different tale, helped us to create, virtually from thin air, a robust, multi-million-dollar trading market in an unfairly neglected segment of the financial and real estate marketplace: affordable housing and economic development on Indian reservations.

Travois works on Indian reservations in some of the most inhospitable places you can imagine. Because of what our company has done, some of the poorest families in the country have a decent place to call home in one of over 5,400 affordable housing units we financed, have safe drinking water, have electricity for the first time in their lives, have a place to see a doctor or a dentist that isn't an airplane ride or an eight-hour truck ride away, and their kids have someplace safe and stimulating to go after school.

Travois is powered by a strong sense of purpose to see, hear, and address the tragic invisibility of Indian reservations, the racism that still permeates the Northern Plains and the Southwest, the wild tales people tell, and the indifference from people who ought to know better.

Doing business on Indian reservations takes more than just a good idea, fortitude, and persistence, though it takes all of that. There are laws and customs that must be understood and honored. From the very beginning we faced what seemed like insurmountable resistance from every corner, including sometimes from the tribes themselves. The hostility and racism that persists against Indians is deplorable. There was also ignorance, and this ignorance seemed especially concentrated among people with money and power—bankers, investors, credit-ratings firms, even government agencies. And here again the eagerness of people to perpetuate the stories that hurt people, that leave people less than whole, unwilling to consider what life is really like on Indian reservations and why it is so, contributed to an easy willingness to assume the worst.

We eventually found a way to tell a different story. Over the first twenty years of Travois' life, we have coaxed more than a billion dollars from investors and government agencies for decent houses and economic development projects on Indian reservations that doubtlessly would not have happened without our efforts. As of today, this company of only fifty employees, nine of whom are family members, is second only to the US government in the amount of capital brought to Indian reservations for affordable housing and for the development of such things as health clinics, waste water treatment facilities, wellness centers, and even broadband services. We are what has become known as "social entrepreneurs" who created a thriving market where none had existed.

Travois works in places that most Americans associate only with movie sets or history books. Places like Wounded Knee, Fort Apache, Wind River, Lame Deer. We work with people whose names most Americans think died out long ago. People like Dani Not Help Him, Ron His Horse Is Thunder, and Herman Bear Comes Out. We work in places where great and terrible things happened in the past, but where great and wonderful things are happening now. Places like the Blackfeet Reservation in Montana, where high levels of childhood poverty will be found, but where the Blackfeet Community College is training nurses and teachers. And we work at the White Mountain Apache Reservation in Arizona, home of the historic Fort Apache, where Kareem Abdul-Jabbar coached the local high school basketball team. We worked on the Standing Rock Sioux Reservation, where the resistance to the Dakota Access Pipeline (DAPL) riveted the country for months, with on-again, off-again approvals of an oil pipeline that runs beneath the Missouri River, the sole source of drinking water for the Standing Rock Tribe. We have done housing projects in Cannon Ball, the center of the daily demonstrations against this pipeline. We know this place, we know these people, we know their struggles.

This is a story about perseverance and persistence. But this is also a story about how the better angels of our nature are still too often drowned out by the bitter forces of indignity, inequality, injustice and unfairness. We learned dispiriting things about Indian Country. We learned about things that are but ought not to be. We learned that Indian Country is mostly disregarded when it comes to the collective consciousness of this country.

Consider the Great Recession of 2008 and 2009. According to Ben Bernanke, the then chairman of the Federal Reserve Board of Governors, "During a recession, banks lend more cautiously as their losses mount, while borrowers become less creditworthy as their finances deteriorate. More cautious banks and less creditworthy borrowers mean that credit flows less freely, impeding household purchases and business investment. These declines in spending exacerbate the recession."[2] Everyone, it seems, felt the effects of the Great Recession of 2009 and beyond, and we all, presumably, enjoyed the recovery, slow though it may have been. Banks were bailed out, credit and capital were freed from the shackles that had bound them, and employment rebounded, perhaps not to everyone's satisfaction, but to levels far above the levels before the stimulus was enacted. But not everyone fell into the recession and not everyone came out of it. Indian reservations, most of them anyway, did not *fall* into the recession because they were already in one; they are in a perpetual recession that has no beginning and has no end. At the height of the Great Depression during the 1930s, overall unemployment hovered between 25% and 33%--devastating rates of unemployment to be sure. There are Indian reservations that have never had unemployment *below* those numbers.[3] Ever. There is the occasional upturn on some reservations, but they amount to a "dead cat bounce."[4] Too many tribes have no banks on or near the reservations. The classical response to a banking crisis is to increase credit to encourage borrowing by creditworthy borrowers and lending from solvent lenders. But what if there are too few banks and far too few creditworthy borrowers? Of course, this is not true of all reservations. But it is true on the reservations where we have chosen to work, and they number in the hundreds, where hundreds of thousands of families try to eke out a better life for themselves and their children.

One response to the recession was to allow banks to make more "character loans." These loans, as the name implies, are made based on the character of the borrower rather than on the collateral offered. Since most land on Indian reservations is held in trust by the federal government and cannot be used as collateral (more about this later), Indians are more dependent on the availability of character loans. Yet banks are inordinately reluctant to make character loans in Indian Country, whether it is because of cultural misunderstanding or outright hostility (more about this later, too).

There are many reasons that Indian reservations persist in a constant state of economic stagnation, with virtually no manufacturing jobs, where even service jobs are scarce. But one reason, perhaps even the most important reason, is the character-blighting myths that get told and retold. "You know, Indians get a check every month from the federal government, just for being Indian," is a common false refrain heard in states with large Indian reservations. "If you have to go to tribal court, look out, you'll never get a fair trial," is another fairytale you hear about Indian Country. These hurtful myths cover up longstanding patterns of discrimination. And the federal policies that impose limitations on Indian Country perpetuate the dysfunctional dynamic generation after generation.

Most Indian reservations are isolated physically, culturally, and economically from the rest of the country, a legacy of the Indian Wars and the US government's desire to claim for white settlers the most productive agricultural lands adjacent to cities and towns. The primary employer on most reservations is tribal government, the schools, and the Bureau of Indian Affairs. There is farming and ranching, but on most farms in Indian Country the main crop is despair. Reservations were purposefully situated in remote and almost unreachable areas on dry land far from rivers or lakes where wells descend hundreds of feet for negligible returns. The status of tribes as dependent sovereign nations, with different laws and customs, contribute to the perpetual economic malaise in Indian Country. But these differences are only part of the reason that Indian reservations are persistently poor. The absence of a traditional commercial code, the fear of tribal court, can both be overcome. Fixes can be found for legal and even cultural barriers. The real barriers, the biggest roadblocks, are the things people say about Indians, about tribes and reservations. The things people say, the apocryphal tales of lost investments and foolish behavior engender a suspicion, prolong the distrust, enliven the discrimination.

The Myth of Casino Profits

Let me put to rest the perception that casino gaming on Indian reservations has solved the economic problem. There is a persistent delusion, especially in California, that through gaming, through the development of casinos, tribes have become wealthy. It is another one of those myths that is difficult to disprove because so few people know anything else about Indians. All they see are the roadside casinos. All they hear about are the considerable profits generated by Indian gaming. The reality is quite different. Casinos have indeed made some Indians prosperous, have made some tribes wealthy. It is not true across the vast majority of Indian Country. If people just thought about it for a minute they would realize the contradiction.

Reservations are remote (think of Lame Deer, Montana, one hundred miles from Billings, the nearest city), and hard to get to (think of Belcourt, North Dakota, hundreds of miles from any city, just south of the Canadian border). They are mostly in regions of the country with a very low population. Montana, Wyoming and North and South Dakota together have fewer people than the population of Oklahoma alone. How would it be possible for casinos in such remote areas to be successful enough to make anyone wealthy? Are tribal casinos immune to the forces of the marketplace and have they a mysterious ability to attract millions of gaming devotees in spite of their remote location and low population?

The National Indian Gaming Commission tells us that there are approximately 230 tribes and Native Alaskan Villages with casinos. Collectively they operate about 460 casinos because some tribes have more than one casino. These casinos nationally have gross revenue of about $28 billion every year, so that works out on average to be about $62 million per casino. Not bad. But the revenue is not distributed evenly among the 460 casinos. Only about 50 casinos, 11% or so, generate over 70% of the gross revenues of all Indian casinos. California alone accounts for over 25% of all Indian gaming revenues.[5] Those few casinos, as you would expect, are located near major metropolitan areas, near established tourism centers or are situated on major transportation routes. This is not the "real" Indian Country. The casinos on tribal lands outside of major metropolitan areas mostly trade Indian dollars, with the occasional presence of a white patron. These tribes are lucky if the casino is an employer of local Indians, able to pay a modest wage, and maybe brings in some visitors to the smoke shop or gas station.

The bulk of Indian Country is composed of reservations that have frail economies, failing schools, and where a decent place to sleep is never taken for granted. The tribes where Travois works have dwellings with incomplete plumbing at a rate that is ten times the national average, where the share of households without complete kitchens is seven times greater than the national average, where the share of housing units that are overcrowded is double the national average.[6] This is where Travois works and has made a difference.

Here's the thing: Marianne and I did not just decide, out of the blue, to work with Indian tribes and tribal people. We knew as little about Indian Country as most middle-class Americans growing up in the latter half of the twentieth century. We undertook a rite of passage, we traveled to the reservations, listened to native people, persuaded a few of them to trust us and then more and more of them to work with us to help them take advantage of federal programs that had been there for years but had never been used successfully by tribal nations to address their chronic and persistent housing crisis. Winchester was our crucible. Working with poor African American families in Winchester, in Norfolk and with the Urban Reinvestment Task Force, laid the foundation for understanding. Indian Country became the framing timbers on our national housing project.

Chapter 2

Richard Bland, Harry Byrd, and Narrative Economics

MY ANCESTOR, GOING back seven generations, is Richard Bland. He was born in 1710 and died in 1776. Richard inherited Jordan's Point from his grandfather Theodoric Bland, one of the great landowners in colonial Virginia and a man with a great first name. The Jordan's Point plantation in Virginia (sometimes called Jordan's Journey) was about 30 miles from Williamsburg, where Richard Bland served in the Virginia House of Burgesses along with his young cousin, Thomas Jefferson. (Yes, I am related to old Tom Jefferson.) As the colonies debated their future, Richard Bland served in the First and Second Continental Congresses. My grandfather, Haywood Gilbert Bland, Sr., in addition to being a mean old SOB, was certain of his proud Richard Bland lineage and his wife, my grandmother, was herself a Bland, Elizabeth Bland Roane, who became Elizabeth Bland Roane Bland when she married my grandfather. She was also a direct descendant of Richard Bland. Elizabeth and Haywood were second cousins. (I don't recommend this.)

Theodoric Bland's original land holdings once included the land on the banks of the James River that became the great Westover Plantation, the ancestral home of William Byrd, from whom the Byrd family of Winchester directly descended. Theodoric sold the Westover Plantation to William Byrd. Theodoric also surveyed and platted the land that later became the City of Williamsburg.

Richard Bland, in concert with his young cousin Thomas Jefferson, introduced legislation in the Virginia colony's House of Burgesses to allow slave-owners to free their slaves. He was roundly condemned for this unsuccessful attempt at legislating more humane treatment of slaves, but that is a story for another day.[7] I like to think that, given my relationship to Richard Bland, I have a genetic inclination to fight for the underdog.

In a quirk of fate, Richard Bland was asked by the First Continental Congress to seek out the cooperation of the Indian Nations, whose lands the first thirteen colonies usurped. Richard Bland became the leading advocate for improving general relations and trade with Indians prior to the revolution and then again at the very outset of hostilities with Great Britain. His frustrations in dealing with sometimes reluctant colleagues and representatives from the other colonies weirdly foreshadows the frustrations and difficulties that Travois encountered as we sought to increase trade with tribes, some 250 years later. Richard was joined in this effort by none other than the fiery Patrick Henry of "Give me liberty or give me death" fame. But it was Richard Bland that the First Continental Congress looked to for help from Indians as they foresaw the difficulties of winning a war against Great Britain.[8]

Things that Run in the Family

The Byrd family was one of the most powerful and wealthy of all Virginia planters and slaveholders. Westover Plantation signified the exalted position of the Byrd family before and just after the revolution, but later generations of the Byrd family fell onto hard times and lost the family wealth. Apparently, gambling was involved. The descendants, including the first Harry Flood Byrd, worked their way back into wealth and power and became the most dominant political force in Virginia by 1922.[9] They settled in Winchester, grew apples on the largest orchard in the state, and became governors and senators and ran what became known as the Byrd Machine.

Senator Harry F. Byrd, Sr. feverishly fought efforts to desegregate schools and institutions and became a stalwart opponent of the Brown v. Board of Education decision in 1954. The Byrd family legacy of racial intolerance became an insidious force in Winchester. When Marianne and I first came to the city, we were lulled into a belief that it had overcome the Byrd legacy, despite the control the Byrd family still exerted through their ownership of the only newspaper in town. We learned that the legacy had taken on a more devious and subtle form, but was nonetheless real and continued to stifle the lives of African Americans trying to make a home in Winchester.

There are many things to love about Winchester. Its beauty is understated and unassuming. Winchester sits at the top of the Shenandoah Valley, which was known as the breadbasket of the Confederacy for good reason. It is lushly green and its soil is rich and fertile. As you approach Winchester from the east on Route 50, at the border of Clarke, Loudoun, and Fauquier Counties, you cross Ashby's Gap at an elevation of about 1,100 feet in the heart of the Blue Ridge Mountains. This little wind gap was an important junction during the Civil War. But its lush beauty today beguiles you into forgetting the truth of what transpired there little more than 150 years ago. There was much to like about life in Winchester. It was especially nice if you were white. Maybe not so much if you were Black.

On the northeast side of downtown, literally on the other side of the railroad tracks, is the North Kent Street neighborhood, the predominately Black neighborhood of Winchester. This is a neighborhood of bruised and beaten houses with sagging window sills, mismatched siding and leaking roofs. Marianne and I got to know this neighborhood because our daughter, Elizabeth, attended Frederick Douglas Elementary School, the once segregated school in North Kent.

The differences between the North Kent Street neighborhood and the rest of the downtown, divided as they were by the railroad tracks that ran right between them, were more than physical. They were deeply psychological and emotional. North Kent was a forgotten neighborhood. The buses did not go down any of the side streets of this neighborhood because the streets were too narrow, or so it was said. There were virtually no sidewalks and precious few street lights. Aside from the school grounds, there were no parks and no benches to lighten an old man or old woman's weary legs and no place for children to play other than their meager yards. But strangely, this was also a neighborhood that had many of the things that help some neighborhoods thrive. It had aunties and grandmas in abundance to watch over the children before and after school. It had corner stores that sold exotic Caribbean spices and foods that gave life to the street. It had multiple generations in single households providing the glue that sociologists say is so important for family health. But it was not enough.

It also had grinding poverty and too many moms and not enough dads. It had unpainted walls inside and out and the windows of these houses were like sad and heavy-lidded eyes that longed to see better days. Even in 1988, unbelievably, some of the houses still had only dirt floors. Somehow though, the children made it to school and the moms went to work and the dads, few though they may be, made it to work. They were the janitors and lunchroom workers at the schools and the Winchester Medical Center. They labored at the non-union construction companies and, yes, some of them hung out at the corner store. But there was a strong professional class too, as close to a Black middle class in this neighborhood as Winchester would acknowledge, with tidy houses and churches that were full every Sunday. Marianne and I never once felt uneasy as we took Elizabeth to school, but the neighborhood was nonetheless considered, by those who couldn't possibly know, unsafe, unsound. As Marianne and I were wrestling with what we were doing with our lives and our place in the world, we could not help but notice the deplorable conditions in the North Kent Street area as compared to the relative wealth in the city's other neighborhoods.

It Starts with a Narrative

Maybe it is in my DNA. Maybe the outrage at the unfairness and the shame of slavery and the inequity of the treatment of the real first Americans was passed on through our family by Richard Bland and his fight became our fight. Maybe we were persuaded by facts and logic to see the meanness inflicted on the "have nots" in our communities. Whatever the reason, my family fought hard to bring about change, and we were met by intractable barriers and sometimes insurmountable obstacles as we worked to make a difference. As we fought on the front lines, in Winchester and later in Indian Country, academics unbeknownst to us were studying the forces that made it so difficult for facts and logic and rational decision making to influence human behavior. The poor Black and

American Indian families with whom we worked were victims of this human tendency to favor stories that put them in a bad light with bankers, government officials, and others in a position to help or harm them. The impact of these stories reverberates to this day.

Robert Shiller introduced his newest economic theory, *Narrative Economics,* to the world in January 2017. The abstract for his paper says, in part:

> The human brain has always been highly tuned towards narratives, whether factual or not, to justify ongoing actions, even such basic actions as spending and investing. Stories motivate and connect activities to deeply felt values and needs. Narratives "go viral" and spread far, even worldwide, with economic impact.

Shiller's paper and his proposition regarding narrative economics serendipitously and scientifically explains everything I witnessed over my 45-year career. It is the stories we tell and the stories we hear that validate the actions we take when we might otherwise be more rational, more reasonable, more just. And these actions have consequences. Schiller further states:

> I use the term "narrative" to mean a simple story or easily expressed explanation of events that many people want to bring up in conversation or on news or social media because it can be used to stimulate the concerns or emotions of others, and/or because it appears to advance self-interest. To be stimulating, it usually has some human interest either direct or implied. As I (and many others) use the term, a narrative is a gem for conversation, and may take the form of an extraordinary or heroic tale or even a joke. It is not generally a researched story, and may have glaring holes, as in "urban legends." The form of the narrative varies through time and across tellings, but maintains a core contagious element, in the forms that are successful in spreading. Why an element is contagious, when it may even "go viral" may be hard to understand, unless we reflect carefully on the reason people like to spread narrative. Mutations in narratives spring up

randomly, just as in organisms in evolutionary biology, and when they are contagious, the mutated narratives generate seemingly unpredictable changes in the economy.[10]

Examples of Shiller's "mutated narratives" abounded in my career. Soon after I started City Light Development Corporation to build affordable housing for the largely African American residents of the North Kent Street neighborhood in Winchester, I was asked to have lunch with a city councilman. This councilman owned a small office supply store in Winchester. He spoke with a self-assurance and moral certainty that might be bearable in someone who had accomplished great things or managed great enterprises. It was odd in someone of such modest achievement. Virtually everything he said to me while I was trying to enjoy my lunch had been marinated in stories which told of presumed entitlement of Black households, their ingratitude, and, of course, their impatience with racial progress. He talked about individual responsibility, something he felt was largely missing in the Black community, and a lot about pulling yourself up by your own bootstraps, just like he had, of course. He was trying to convey to me the sense of the city council, taking pains to point out that this was not an official position of the council, just the "sense" of the council, whatever that meant. Apparently, he and they were concerned that City Light Development Corporation might, I AM NOT MAKING THIS UP, encourage "welfare queens" from New York and Washington, DC to move to Winchester when they heard about all the new affordable housing we intended to build for poor Black folk.

How do you counter an argument like that? Aside from the fact that the whole "welfare queen" thing was an excellent example of false narrative, an invention of Ronald Reagan's that was thoroughly debunked, it was more than just implicitly racist. The idea of someone uprooting herself from New York City, much less from Washington, DC, and moving to Winchester on the hope of an affordable housing unit in a small neighborhood was so laughable as to be, well, laughable. I told him so and things went swiftly downhill from there. They actually sort of careened downhill. I asked the councilman if he thought that folks in Brooklyn or maybe in Harlem regularly read the Winchester *Star*, the local newspaper. Was that how they would find out about the new affordable housing units in Winchester? Or maybe there was some sort of super mysterious communications network, like poor people's smoke signals, that only those below a certain income level could decipher that would let them know when affordable housing was suddenly available, wherever it might pop up?

He said I was being ridiculous and suggested that word of mouth would be enough. He went on to say that the council was also concerned that City Light seemed to be moving unnecessarily fast. In his words, "It took decades for North Kent Street to get in the condition it is in now, there is no reason to try to fix it in just a year or two." At that I said that maybe it was easy for him to say, "slow down, take it easy," since it was likely he did not often go to bed at night without the warmth of reliable heat, and that his children would likely not have to sleep four or five to a bed. I suggested that maybe that was why he did not think we should be in such a hurry. Some other folks might disagree with his "no need to hurry" hypothesis. I made no headway.

Mythology and Massive Resistance

The toxic narrative here is the long-ingrained myth that Black men and women, especially women, will go wherever there is a better handout. Ignoring the fact that people of limited means lack mobility, not to mention that it is a degrading and untrue stereotype, stories like these get dredged up whenever the teller needs to shore up a defense of the status quo. Ronald Reagan used the term "Welfare Queens" often as he ran unsuccessfully for president in 1976 and successfully in 1980, and the myth, the contagious story, took flight.[11] Yes, of course, there have been and always will be people who take unfair advantage of government programs. Think of Enron, Tyco, and Worldcom. Unfortunately, too few people think of corporate thievery when they think of people abusing government subsidies, they think only of Black men and women, or as I will describe later, Native Americans. This is what is known as "motivated reasoning," the "unconscious tendency of individuals to fit their processing of information to conclusions that suit some end or goal," as described by Yale law professor and social scientist, Dan Kahan.[12]

It was at this lunch meeting that the diaphanous curtain of innocence finally parted to reveal a seamier and rougher Winchester, to my great chagrin. We so loved our historic house. We so much wanted to be a part of a small-town business and political community, but we had failed to do our homework to understand the dark history of Winchester. This meeting brought to light what lingered just below the surface.

There was among the powerful in Winchester an almost absolutist resistance to the lingering, generational effects of poverty. There was a denial of institutional racism despite the near complete absence of Black political representation at that time in Winchester. There were no Black football coaches, no Black school principals, no Martin Luther King Boulevard. Winchester, after all, was the home of Harry F. Byrd Sr. who coined the term "Massive Resistance" and led the fight against school integration not only in Virginia, but nationally. He was the primary author of the "Southern Manifesto," the document that southern senators and congressmen signed and followed that spelled out in loathsome detail how the southern states would resist all efforts at integration.

With the shadow of Harry Byrd and Massive Resistance lingering in the background, I told Diane Sinclair, the president of my board of directors at City Light Development Corporation, and Judy Humbert, another of my board members, an unassuming, but fiercely determined Black woman, about my lunch with the city councilman. They came up with a brainstorm that helped me plant some seeds in a few minds. They suggested that we hold after-dinner "Teas" with notable (read: wealthy) women in town, wives of influential men in most cases. The goal was to refute the notion that City Light was going to be a "giveaway," or that it was going to move too fast, or whatever the trope of the moment happened to be. The idea was to guide these women so that they would see just how stacked the deck was, to see how tough it was for even the working poor to make ends meet.

Diane agreed to arrange the first few such meetings for me and to attend them with me, as my own personal bodyguard. Judy could not bring herself to attend, quite understandably. Judy was the first

African American woman to serve on the Winchester School Board and did not gladly suffer fools. She is not quite 5'4" tall, but you would not know it. She has stature beyond her height. She is quiet until she has something to say; she does not fill silence with inanities or happy talk but nevertheless remains relentlessly optimistic and cheerful. Diane warned me that the women she intended to present me to would be charming, but headstrong. They could also gut me like a deer on opening day of hunting season. I armed myself with flow charts and handouts and was as charming as I could possibly be. They were skeptical and suspicious and began sharpening their knives. After all, these women had heard the same stories, the same myths about welfare queens and food stamp frauds. It was so much easier to simply believe in the failures of "Black culture" and the misguided entitlement and welfare programs that sap initiative. We were determined to change the narrative.

In the first exercise, we described a typical household budget for a single mom with two children. She was presumed to earn minimum wage which was $3.35 per hour in 1988. In an unlikely scenario, we endowed her with a car and no car payment. We had a nice chart that showed that even if this hypothetical single mom had a job in which she was reliably able to get in a 40-hour work week at minimum wage, which is almost unheard of at that pay grade, she would have a monthly income before taxes of about $536. There are always payroll taxes, even if she would not be subject to state or federal income taxes, and in those days there was no such thing as the earned income tax credit.

The ladies I met with, to their credit, were shocked.

These ladies blew through $536 per month on clothes and lunches out. My City Light team wanted them engaged in the process, so we then asked them how much they thought a reasonable rent would be for a livable apartment for a single mom with two young children. They suggested $350 per month. We came prepared and brought out the newspaper with the listing of apartments for rent, including one-bedroom and two-bedroom apartments. There were none available at that price. Nothing. The cheapest was around $450. Then we asked them to estimate how much a single mom could get in food stamps in Virginia with two small children. Of course, you can't use food stamps to pay for any of your other household expenses, so we would assume, wrongly we pointed out, that this hypothetical mom would have enough food stamps to cover her entire food bill for her entire household. We did this just to be conservative. On to other expenses.

We asked the wives what other things a single mom would simply have to spend money on, no matter what. These wealthy women offered up diapers, which you cannot buy with food stamps, gasoline for the car, car insurance, telephone, and clothes, among other expenses. We presumed the kids' ages to be one year and three years. Of course, kids have a nasty habit of growing out of their shoes and clothes and occasionally you need to buy some stuff that cannot always be found in thrift stores. We tallied up the budget to see how much this diligent mom had left over at the end of the month and the wives were aghast to find that she had a negative $50 every month. And this assumes that she paid no payroll taxes, never missed a day of work, never got sick, never had to have her car repaired or had a flat tire and found that fairy tale apartment for rent for $350 per month.

Then we hit them with the surprise that we had been hiding. We purposely "forgot" all about utilities and the cost for child care. We then had to add in heat and light and some assumption about daycare costs for her children. These thoughtful women sat back in their well-upholstered chairs and were quiet for a while.

Diane Sinclair went on three or four of these meetings with me, each time there were five or six quite wealthy and prominent women in attendance. And at each one we found mostly the same reaction. We got better as we went along. After a while Diane said that I did not need her anymore and she set me free, sort of a solo safari. I was a bit anxious doing it on my own for the first time. These were intimidating women and I was not in my element. But the meetings went well. All in all, I think I went to about 20 of these little soirees over about a six-month period and it helped to put a little doubt in some minds. We had a few victories and created some staunch supporters and it helped with fundraising, too, even though that was not our intent. Our intent was simply to change at least a few minds, to change the narrative just a little. That is much harder to measure.

My city council antagonist was certainly not going to change his mind, nor were a few other members of the council and the planning commission. They had heard too many stories of laziness, welfare fraud, and the like. As Robert Shiller suggests, "It seems that the human mind strives to reach enduring understanding of events by forming them into a narrative that is imbedded in social interactions."[13] As he said, these ideas, these narratives, are enduring and have the weight of certainty.

This was going to take a while.

Far too many people in Winchester in positions of power suffered under this crushing weight of certainty. Nothing I could say, no facts I could provide, no heartfelt and passionate appeals could free them from this burden. Indeed, this burden gave them comfort. It was much easier to assign blame to laziness, stupidity, bad decision-making, lack of education, single-parenthood, anything other than individual and systemic racism, disenfranchisement, segregation, the socialization of inferiority, and, ultimately, institutionalized disparities in wealth.

The Winchester elite much preferred their version of life. It fit like an old shoe. In their version of life, poverty was a moral failing. It is so much easier to believe that and be done with it. Otherwise there'd be no choice but to think about the causes of poverty. The legacy of slavery and Jim Crow in Virginia, the fact that African Americans were unable to borrow money in redlined communities like North Kent Street, the fact that African Americans therefore own homes at far lower rates than white Americans, have miniscule amounts in savings when compared to white households, and have a fraction of the wealth of a typical white household of similar composition, education, and background was too disquieting. How would they reconcile such abounding evidence when, in their minds, it was simply a choice to be poor. Bad decisions led to such a lot in life.

Winchester's establishment loved to hear the stories and they loved to repeat them. It worked better than a train to keep them safely on their side of the tracks.

Chapter 3

The Poor Will Always Be With Us

ONE OF THE THINGS that has always vexed me is the seemingly insurmountable tendency of people to make snap judgments. Everyone is subject to this, including myself. But I try to question the dogma, to be skeptical of the assumption, when I can. Not often enough I am afraid. One of my Winchester acquaintances was well-educated and only modestly prosperous. He clung to an assumption, an assessment, that had no basis other than his personal, necessarily very limited experience. He insisted that Black women spend their food stamps, provided through a program now known officially as the Supplemental Nutrition Assistance Program or SNAP, on expensive cuts of beef. His firm opinion on the failures of the food stamp program was based solely on his experience in a grocery store checkout line as he was waiting to pay for his own inexpensive ground beef and canned tuna. He had done no research on the topic, had read no US Department of Agriculture reports, had read no large-scale random sample analytics about the use of food stamps and the purchase of expensive cuts of beef or seafood by SNAP recipients. He didn't know any of that, yet he knew what he saw, and that informed what he believed. Because he had seen a Black woman buy an expensive steak using food stamps, or more likely, he had been told by someone that they had seen this grave injustice, the availability of the story in his mind led him to the conclusion that it was a rampant misapplication of scarce federal dollars. He wanted this event to be true. It caught his attention and made him angry and it confirmed in his mind that people who use food stamps are not frugal, are not conscientious recipients of government aid.

If he had been better informed, and perhaps a bit more sympathetic to people of limited means, he would know that research shows that food stamp recipients, in fact, spend their food dollars pretty much the same way everyone else spends their food dollars, with the exception of a slightly (statistically insignificant) higher percentage of the food stamp "dollar" spent on nutritionally worthless sugary soft drinks and salty snacks.[14] SNAP funds are spent on soft drinks and chips at too high a rate to be sure, but that is a problem not confined to low-income households. We all spend too much on such lousy stuff. And while this is recent research, we have no reason to believe that people behaved differently in 1988.

Maybe the woman was buying an expensive cut of meat because it was a child's birthday or a once-in-a-blue-moon extravagance. My point is, my friend didn't know. He simply made a judgment and formed an opinion based upon a single occurrence. How many other firm opinions are formed in a similar way and can judgments made in this manner be dislodged? Daniel Kahneman (2002 Nobel Prize in Economic Sciences), Amos Tversky, and Richard Thaler (2017 Nobel Prize in Economic Sciences) pretty much single-handedly created the field of behavioral economics. Their research, observations, and experiments demonstrate our natural proclivities to make incorrect assumptions and draw incomplete conclusions. Kahneman, Tversky, and Thaler consider whether people make judgments haphazardly and whether they can be disabused of such notions. The three eminent scientists render their judgment: a lot and not so much.

But I had to try.

Despite my bad experience at lunch, I made it my mission to speak to every member of the city council and the planning commission individually over a period of months. I knew of innovative programs that the city of Winchester could employ, using federal funds through the Community Development Block Grant program offered by the Department of Housing and Urban Development (HUD) to help alleviate a variety of ills in the North Kent Street neighborhood.

So, with the unenthusiastic blessing of the planning director, who did not object nor endorse my efforts, I began advocating for very low interest loan programs for homeowners in the North

Kent Street neighborhood so that they could fix up their homes. I suggested that the loans have generous forgiveness provisions for the poorest homeowners. The decision-makers stonewalled with "What makes them so special?" "If we do this for them, why shouldn't we do this for middle-class homeowners in middle-class neighborhoods?" I countered that middle-class white homeowners had more resources and could borrow funds to repair their homes. I pointed out that some of the houses in the North Kent Street neighborhood had dangerous, life-threatening conditions, but I was hitting a brick wall: "Well, they should never have let them get in that condition in the first place."

I tried to explain that accumulating enough cash to make these kinds of repairs was nearly impossible for working-class folks, especially on the lower end of the working-class spectrum. It was hard enough for middle-class white homeowners but Black people in the North Kent Street neighborhood simply couldn't get loans on their houses. Banks wouldn't lend on the basis of the value of those homes. And the fact that so many of the houses were occupied by renters, not homeowners, was also a consideration.

I had no better luck with my suggestions for sensitive code enforcement programs that, by necessity, would be combined with landlord lending programs to alleviate the worst housing conditions. Studies have shown time and again that when cities offer some assistance to landlords who manage "problem" properties, in combination with consistently and predictably enforced health and safety codes, that improvements are made, slowly perhaps, but improvements nonetheless. My arguments were met with a maddening indifference. After all, these were nothing more than slum landlords, the board members explained. In some cases, they were indeed slumlords. But in most of those cases, the landlords had precious little money themselves and the little rent they collected barely covered their costs. It would never provide enough of a cash cushion so that they could make the kinds of improvements the houses desperately needed.

The Poor Deserve Their Poverty

The Winchester City Council and the Planning Commission concluded that disapproving such modest spending programs was a sensible business decision. As the commission saw it, the people living in the North Kent Street neighborhood should not be rewarded for having let the neighborhood decline to such a horrid degree. It would encourage future bad behavior, the so-called "moral hazard" argument. It was hard not to interpret their position as "Some people just don't deserve any help." To me, their decision was heartless and mean-spirited. To them, withholding funding was reasonable and justifiable because they did not want to waste taxpayer money, the certain outcome of such an investment.

The Winchester city leaders accepted the persistent belief that poor people make bad decisions and, therefore, merit their poverty. There is some truth to the notion that they make bad decisions, but less truth to the notion that they deserve their poverty. Being poor makes people more susceptible to overdrawing their checking accounts. They must own that mistake, without question. But they do not deserve to be further punished by the pernicious practice of re-sequencing bank overdrafts in order to maximize the banks' profits.

Overdraft fees hurt low-income depositors far more than others because they must, out of necessity, keep low balances in their accounts. Regulators have cracked down on these unfair overdraft fees, but despite million-dollar fines from regulators and strong public backlash from the practice, in a 2017 report it was found that nearly half of all banks continue to engage in what is called debit re-sequencing.[15] Debit re-sequencing is the practice in which a depositor's checks are presented for payment in such a way as to maximize the overdraft charges a bank can assess against an account, not in the order in which they were actually written. If, for example, a depositor has $100 in his account and checks come in for $20, $50, $5, and $60, in that order, the depositor should only be charged when the last $60 check is processed, leading to a single overdraft fee. But banks don't do that. They cash the checks for $60 and $50 first, out of order, meaning the depositor will have three overdraft fees instead of just one. And while re-sequencing applies to all bank customers, it has a disparate impact on poor depositors, the very people least able to afford the penalty. And it is a penalty that could be easily diminished simply by applying the penalty in the order in which funds are sought rather than in the order which provides the greatest benefit to the bank.

Also, there is strong evidence that poverty itself perpetuates poverty by inducing bad decision-making. In a robust study published in *Science* in 2013, the authors devised a series of experiments, using what they earnestly called "poor" people and "rich" people. The poor in the experiment had a median income of $20,000 and the rich had a median income of $70,000. They had each participant perform cognitive tests after imagining hard financial situations (for example, a car suddenly needing $1,500 in repairs) and easy financial situations (a car needing only $150 in repairs) and other such scenarios. The study was peer reviewed before publication and extensively scrutinized.[16] The results were striking.

The poor performed equally well compared to the rich on the cognitive tests when confronted with an easy financial situation. But they performed significantly worse after being confronted with a difficult financial situation. The authors demonstrated that the cognitive failures associated with the difficult financial situation for the poor amounted to a thirteen-point drop in IQ in what is known as Raven's *Progressive Matrices*, a common component in IQ tests used to measure "fluid intelligence." Fluid intelligence is the capacity to think logically and solve problems in novel situations, independent of acquired knowledge. The authors state that the "data reported here suggest a different perspective on poverty: Being poor means coping not just with a shortfall of money, but also with a concurrent shortfall of cognitive resources. The poor, in this view, are less capable not because of inherent traits, but because the very context of poverty imposes load and impedes cognitive capacity. The findings, in other words, are not about poor people, but about any people who find themselves poor." [17]

Is there any wonder that people who are constantly under financial stress make poor decisions, especially when so many things are stacked against them, not least re-sequencing, but also complex contracts, predatory pay-day lenders, indecipherable legal forms, and other dire challenges that require everyone to be at the top of their game all the time?

But it is worse than you might think. I am reminded of the words of F. Scott Fitzgerald:

> Let me tell you about the very rich. They are different from you and me. They possess and enjoy early, and it does something to them, makes them soft where we are hard, and cynical where we are trustful, in a way that, unless you were born rich, it is very difficult to understand. They think, deep in their hearts, that they are better than we are because we had to discover the compensations and refuges of life for ourselves. Even when they enter deep into our world or sink below us, they still think that they are better than we are. They are different.[18]

Indeed they are. According to Robert Sapolsky, a professor of biology and neurology at Stanford University, chronic stress, the kind you endure from worrying about having enough food for yourself and your children, about making the rent or the mortgage payment, the stress of just knowing that you are worse off than so many of your neighbors, increases the risks of memory impairments, sleep deprivation, adult-onset diabetes, hypertension, cardio-vascular disease, osteoporosis, reproductive decline, and immune suppression.[19] As if you didn't have enough to worry about, worrying itself can kill you. And if you are poor you suffer far greater than people whose lives are not as stressful. It isn't just the outward evidence of the rich being better off with fancier cars, bigger houses, and finer clothes, they are healthier too.

I suppose we have, nonetheless, come a long way, despite the persistent narrative that relegates the poor to second class citizenship. It's hard for us to imagine, but during the great potato famine in Ireland in 1846 the law required that no food could be given to anyone if they were starving for some reason other than the blight on potatoes. At that time some 2,385,000 people in Ireland were in a state of near constant starvation.[20] How exactly could John Bull determine if someone was starving because they did not have enough boiled potato rather than enough turnips? Was there a particular look that the British could somehow discern in the eyes or the skin of a poor Irish lad or lass that told them they suffered from too little potato rather than too little chicken? Must have been the eyes.

During the potato famine, the British sought Indian corn (maize), a commodity they did not ordinarily import, to prevent the starvation of millions in Ireland and at the same time avoid the collapse of the price of grain on the British market. In a display of monumental arrogance and incompetence, the greater concern was supporting the price of home grown corn rather the lives of Irish children. At the height of the famine, when thousands of Irish were dying each day, the British, who ruled all of Ireland at that time, begrudgingly agreed to import 350,000 bushels of Indian maize corn from the United States. But they didn't have a clue how to mill it or otherwise cook it or eat it. They just knew it would not likely compete with good old British corn.[21] Back then the Irish ate very little bread, and certainly not cornbread, which you couldn't make from maize anyway. Most of the maize spoiled and more people died needlessly because they wanted to prop up the price of British-grown corn rather than interfere with the marketplace.

In another ironic twist, the Choctaw Nation, one of the so-called Five Civilized Nations, remembered how they had suffered during the Trail of Tears and could not bear the thought of so much misery. Though desperately poor themselves, the Choctaw took up a collection and sent the generous sum of $170 to feed the hungry across the Atlantic Ocean. The British couldn't decide whether or not to allow the ships carrying the free grain to anchor for fear that their cargo would disrupt the flow of goods in the marketplace. It was finally decided that the Choctaw generosity could be received.[22] The sad history of British indifference in the face of Irish starvation fit a common theme of poverty and just desserts. Oddly, it was a British upper-class businessman who forever changed that attitude in the UK.

Seebohm Rowntree was the son of a wealthy business owner and a self-taught social scientist. At the turn of the last century, in 1899, he conducted a comprehensive study of poverty and housing conditions in York, England, literally interviewing every working-class household in York. He followed those studies in York with similar studies in 1935 and 1951. This study utterly transformed the minds of the British people about poverty and shaped public policy for most of the twentieth century. What this remarkable man did was make the United Kingdom understand that the working class of England was paid so poorly, worked so hard and so long, yet could not afford even the most basic features of a modern twentieth century life. Something had to be done. Both wage and hour laws were changed and housing improvements made life bearable for millions of English and Welsh and later Irish working class people. For the poor of England to survive at that time Rowntree found:

> A family living upon the scale ...must never spend a penny on railway fare or omnibus. They must never go to the country unless they walk. They must never purchase a halfpenny newspaper or spend a penny to buy a ticket for a popular concert. They must never contribute anything to their church or chapel, or give any help to a neighbor which costs them money. They cannot save, nor can they join sick club or Trade Union, because they cannot pay the necessary subscriptions. The children must have not pocket money for dolls, marbles, or sweets. The fathers must smoke no tobacco, and must drink no beer. The mother must never buy any pretty clothes for herself or for her children, the character of the family wardrobe as for the family diet governed by regulation, 'nothing must be bought but that which is absolutely necessary for the maintenance of physical health, and what is bought must be of the plainest and most economical description.' Should a child fall ill, it must be attended by the parish doctor; should it die it must be buried by the parish. Finally, the wage earner must never be absent from his work for a single day. If any of these conditions are broken, the extra expenditure involved is met, and can only be met, by limiting the diet; or, in other words, by sacrificing physical efficiency.[23]

Seebohm Rowntree may well have been the inspiration for Willie Wonka of Chocolate Factory fame. His father was a chemist and owned a chocolate factory; one of its more famous confections is the Kit Kat bar. More importantly, he pioneered many progressive labor practices, including living wages and a 40-hour work week. When Seebohm came to work at the family chocolate factory he instituted even more progressive policies, including having a company doctor provide on-site medical care, which later included dental care, and then a pension plan, which was simply not done anywhere at that time, among other remarkable human resource innovations. Seebohm Rowntree's early collaboration with the UK's prime minister David Lloyd George ushered in a long period of Labor Party power in the UK, but his most profound impact on the UK and the world is that he broke the back of the utterly entrenched and hopelessly mean-spirited idea that the poor are poor because they *deserve* it.

There have been countless studies in the US that have shown the same basic results as Seebohm's, just like City Light's little unscientific "Teas with the Ladies" demonstrated that the working poor in the North Kent Street neighborhood were indeed working and were indeed quite poor, but despite all their considerable efforts they could not lift themselves out of poverty. Minimum wage employees with kids, car payments, rent, utilities, medical expenses, and clothes to buy cannot pull themselves out of poverty. Their failure is not due to a lack of good heart or their strong moral fiber. It is a function of the insufficiency of income in the face of mounting expenses. And, of course, we compound it by confronting them every day in every imaginable form, on TV and radio, on billboards and magazines, in movies (and now the Internet) with the very life they want to have, the life it seems that everyone other than them seems to be enjoying, and we erect insurmountable barriers, barriers of status, income, education, and race that make this aspirational life unthinkable.

Attitudes changed dramatically in the United Kingdom at least in part, and maybe in large measure, as a result of the work of Seebohm Rowntree. In 1914 in a series of lectures on housing he went further and called for an expansion of the minimum wage to extend to what he called "casual labor" so that the lowest skilled person could afford a decent house. Minimum wages were already fixed for miners, bakers, tailors, even chain-makers. But the casual laborer had no wage protections. He called for a simultaneous effort at comprehensive housing code enforcement to be sure that every house was livable and met minimum standards of decency. And he called for a "statutory duty of all towns to see that their inhabitants are satisfactorily housed..."[24]

Nearly 80 years later in the US we still resist the idea that cities and towns have a "statutory duty" to ensure that everyone has a decent place to live and we continue to believe that somehow you are to blame if you cannot afford a warm, dry, safe place to live. Finally understanding this public policy intransigence in Winchester, I changed direction. First, I framed City Light's goals differently. Meeting such strong resistance to my poverty-is-complicated arguments, I stressed what the Winchester city leaders wanted to hear and what fit into a nice narrative of City Light's long-term goals: We set out to change the mix from mostly African American renters in the North Kent Street neighborhood to mostly African American homeowners. Because, of course, *homeownership* has a different connotation—one more consistent with the city's perceived values. To change the mix in the neighborhood, we had to build new homes rather than simply rehabilitate the decrepit old houses we had been devoting ourselves to so far. That new emphasis struck a nerve.

Chapter 4

Why is Doing the Right Thing So Hard

IT WAS MY GOOD fortune to start City Light at the same time as a new real estate financing mechanism was gaining ground and becoming popular after being inaugurated under the 1986 Tax Reform Act. The new program was known as the Low Income Housing Tax Credit program (LIHTC). Back then it was barely understood by anyone, including the states whose job it was to administer the program on behalf of the IRS. I had been reading about the program and became confident that this new federal housing opportunity was the right way for City Light to finance the reconstruction of the North Kent Street neighborhood.

I presented my ideas to the board of directors and they enthusiastically agreed. As Winston Churchill once wrote, "Chance is unceasingly at work in our lives, but we cannot always see its workings sharply and clearly defined."[25] Chance was clearly at work here. It was pure chance that the LIHTC program was becoming an industry-wide and acceptable practice just as I was starting a new real estate company whose goal was the development of affordable housing. It was pure chance that the program was complex enough that few people understood it, yet not loaded down by rules that later made it so formidable, so I was not intimidated. I didn't see any of this as chance at the time. It was just a choice and the time seemed right.

The underlying rationale for the legislation creating LIHTC was that the government was less efficient and less responsive than the private sector, and that the private sector would do a better job of delivering much-needed housing to the marketplace. The program switched the primary mechanism for the development of affordable housing from direct grants and loans made by the federal government to tax credits that can be used to directly reduce the taxes owed by those investing in the construction and rehabilitation of housing. These tax credits are also known as "tax expenditures" by the folks who pay attention to the federal budget. The cost to the US Treasury is the same, but the idea was that the private marketplace would produce more housing, faster and better, than a like amount of direct federal outlays to housing authorities.

They were right. Over time, the LIHTC program became perhaps the most successful delivery mechanism for high quality affordable housing the country had yet devised. Tax credits are allocated to every state according to the state's population and each state designated an agency to facilitate the distribution of the credits, following rules governing the LIHTC program. In practice, the way the LIHTC program works is that developers of affordable housing apply to state agencies like the Virginia Housing Development Authority that review the plan and determine whether or not it looks feasible from a financial and social perspective. The agency then grades the individual projects' applications for tax credits on a sliding scale, with more points in the competition going to projects that agree to provide housing for the lowest income families and fewer points for projects serving households with relatively higher incomes.

There are always more applications for the credits than there are credits, so it's a competitive process. The key to winning awards of tax credits is to tell a compelling story. If two projects have a very similar score and serve families with the same level of income, the project that has a more interesting, persuasive story will be the one awarded credits. I became good at telling the best stories about the families we served, the circumstances of their lives, and how our projects should be awarded credits instead of the other competing applications. It is often called the tax credit "beauty contest." I honed my skills in describing our projects as the contestants with the best talent (no hula hoop dancing in our beauty contest) who answered the questions in the least cliché-ridden manner (no "I just want world peace" for City Light). We wanted to improve the lives of hard working African American families who deserved a leg up and we told a good story. All of our projects were approved, without exception.

Show Me the Money

The developers who build housing projects through the LIHTC program rarely plan to use the tax credits themselves and rarely have enough tax liability to use up all of the credits. The developers are almost always "pass-through" entities, that is, partnerships or limited liability companies (LLCs) that do not themselves pay taxes. The pass-through partnerships or LLCs are created specifically for each project and function solely as the developer of that project. These partnerships and LLCs are composed of passive investors, typically banks, insurance companies and other highly profitable tax-paying corporations, that do not want to be involved in the day to day operations of the housing projects. They just want the tax credits so that they can reduce their tax liability. City Light, as a non-profit, had no tax liability and thus could not use the tax credits. Because we were not alone, a whole new "industry" was created to match developers who have tax credits with the people and businesses that had high tax liability and might want to partner with the developers in order to get ahold of the tax credits. The risk for the investor partners in such a transaction is that if the project does not follow the rules, if the project fails to live up to the promises it made to the state in order to be awarded the federal tax credits, the investor partners would have those tax credits recaptured by the IRS and would also face penalties for having paid too little in taxes, a potential double whammy.

The basic idea was that the discipline of the private sector combined with the fear of the loss of the tax credits would ensure that the projects stayed in compliance with the rules. It would be mostly self-policing but would have an adequate level of oversight by the states on behalf of the IRS. This oversight was slow in coming and as with most regulatory protocols, became ever more complex and unwieldy over time. At the very beginning of the program, it was easy to comply. That would not last.

The single most important requirement of the LIHTC program is that the people to be served must be low income. Specifically, they must have income no greater than 60% of the area median income, so the band for eligibility is pretty narrow, everywhere except as it turns out, in Indian Country, as we later learned. There are, however, other rules for eligibility and how the tax credits would be distributed.

In theory, every state has the right to adjust the federal LIHTC program a little bit to fit its own housing needs and conditions since the housing situation in Florida is going to be different than the housing situation in Wisconsin. Virginia's distribution plan for tax credits was straightforward. We easily met the distribution criteria, the goals that Virginia determined were in its best interests. Now all we had to do was find investors to buy the credits.

Investment pools known as syndicators were actively seeking projects with tax credits, so I began calling around. One of the biggest syndicators was one I already had an inside track with, having worked for the founder of its parent foundation, James Rouse. After Jim Rouse retired from the Rouse Company, he created the Enterprise Foundation, now known as Enterprise Community Partners. It had a for-profit subsidiary called Enterprise Social Investment Corporation, or ESIC, that pooled investment funds from large banks and other institutional investors and then bought tax credits on their behalf. I thought that they would be perfect for our first project, especially since they knew me and I had such respect for Jim Rouse. Not so much.

The price ESIC was willing to pay for each tax credit was far below what I needed to make our projects work. The way syndicators/investors make money is to pay less than a dollar for each dollar's worth of tax credits that a project generates. The tax credits last for 10 years, but the projects must commit to being affordable for not less than 15 years. (The credits are what is known as accelerated tax credits because they are earned over a 15-year period, but they are paid out over a 10-year period.) It's a very good deal for the investor and a very good deal for the developer. In return, the developer must agree to keep the rents affordable to the tenants and rent to low income families. Everybody wins, in theory. But ESIC only wanted to give us $0.44 for every tax credit dollar we had to offer. I had hoped to get at least $0.72 for every tax credit. I was stunned and more than a little worried. If ESIC was only offering this much, and I had an inside track with them, what would I get from other syndicators? I was afraid we were sunk before we even got in the water.

I made calls to six or eight other syndicators and I got prices ranging from $0.42 to $0.44 per credit. To put this in perspective, the investors I talked to were willing to buy something worth $1, but they were only willing to pay, at most, about 44 cents for it. The realization of this struck me as incredibly unfair. I hardly slept that night worrying about what we were going to do. I had based my assumptions on this program working and providing financing for our projects and revenue for our operations. I was sick that I had let everyone down, had raised expectations and given hope to some people only to see that hope dashed once again against hard reality.

But when I sat down the very next day with my own financial projections and calculated how much money ESIC and the other syndicators would have made by investing in our projects, assuming $0.44 per credit dollar, their actual yield would have been an obscene 38%, based on what is known as an internal rate of return or IRR. That means that the banks and other corporations were going to realize returns, over a 15-year period, of 38%, every year, for investing in a project intended to provide housing for low income families. To be fair to Enterprise, this was the market price at the time. But I was nonetheless outraged. When I had made my projections and calculations and come up with an assumption that $0.72 would make our project work, I had assumed an IRR of 18%, and I thought that was too rich. I wanted to compensate the investors for taking on a little extra risk with an unknown and inexperienced developer and undertaking relatively small projects. But a 38% annual rate of return was more than obscene, it was robbery; it was indecent, it was intolerable and incomprehensible. The marketplace, it seems, can all too often be indifferent to such considerations. I was mad, actually I was infuriated, and in the end that motivated me and made all the difference.

I called the president of the First National Bank of Strasburg, a small bank in an even smaller town, who turned out to be one of our strongest supporters, and set up a meeting. I then called a prominent local CPA and set up a meeting with him as well. I put together a nifty packet of materials, as close as I could come to a legal prospectus of sorts, that told the story of City Light, such as it was, what we intended to do, and the story of our first project. My intent was to show how an investor in our project could make an annual return of 18% and how you could drive by it every day and take pride in making the lives of some very poor families immeasurably better. I made my pitch to the bank and to doctors, dentists, lawyers, and other high earners who might be interested in our projects. Within less than a month the bank and other investors, mostly doctors and dentists, signed on to be investors for our first projects, at $0.72 per credit dollar. I had learned that these small banks, unfamiliar with the LIHTC equity marketplace, did not know the going price for tax credits. I learned something about myself also. I learned that I was good at meeting with potential investors, patiently explaining the complexity of the LIHTC program without overwhelming anybody and making my case without a hard sell. By making a passionate case for the need to redress a great wrong in Winchester, I was creating a new narrative. And I learned that I liked doing it.

Red Lining

To introduce the work of City Light to the broadest cross section of the business elite in Winchester as possible, I spoke to Rotary Club luncheons and Chamber of Commerce meetings at every possible chance. I met with groups of doctors, realtors, lawyers, and even car dealers. I had the best luck with bankers, mainly because I had some carrots to offer along with the guilt trip I was laying on everyone about the terrible conditions in the North Kent neighborhood that they ought to know about and were willfully ignoring.

As the LIHTC program was maturing and becoming the industry standard for the production of affordable housing, another law was finally getting some well-deserved attention from federal regulators. The Community Reinvestment Act, known generally as CRA, was first enacted in 1977, but few banks took it seriously back then. Over the last forty years it has been blamed by bankers for any number of ill effects and most recently it was used as one of the scapegoats for the great recession of 2008-2009. The law arose from the practice by nearly all banks, savings and loans, and insurance companies to "red line" minority areas.

Red lining is, as its name implies, the act of drawing a literal (on maps) and metaphorical (on attitudes) red line around low-income minority neighborhoods, and simply refusing to do business within the area falling inside the red lines. Banks and savings and loan institutions would take deposits from these areas, but they would be ever so reluctant to make a consumer loan, a car loan, or a mortgage loan to anyone living in those areas. It was a pretty sweet deal for the banks and S & Ls, but not so much for the depositors. The Community Reinvestment Act sought to punish lenders who could not prove that they had made a reasonable effort to make loans and to invest in the same minority areas from which they were drawing deposits. If they did not, there were penalties, but these penalties were rarely enforced and not much of a deterrent.

By the late 1980s, however, CRA had been strengthened and banks were seeing it as the hammer that it was originally intended to be. City Light offered a way for banks, especially smaller community banks like the First National Bank of Strasburg, to meet their obligations under the law and make a nice return on investment, too. I became a hot commodity on the community banker circuit throughout the Shenandoah Valley.

I would come home from these banker meetings, at times meeting with some of the wealthiest and most powerful people in the Shenandoah Valley, and I would be mystified by their lack of empathy for those who had so little. Mostly, I was struck by the near ubiquity of the notion that poverty is a choice, that poor people are poor because they have made a cascade of bad decisions and now they can't break out. Sure it's a shame, they would say, but society has limited responsibility when the poor created their own condition. One person would make such a comment and everyone else's head would nod in agreement. It is a story that made it easier for them to justify the higher rate of loan denials and the higher rate of interest, if indeed a loan is even made to a "high risk" customer.

Interestingly, one of the bankers offhandedly told me that the single greatest source of profits for his bank, as it was for many of his banking colleagues, was not interest from loans, as you would expect. It was from the overdraft fees I described earlier. I am sure the bankers saw no irony in their reluctance to lend to poor families, but still derive a disproportionate profit from such poor families.

I was saddened by the behavior I witnessed and the attitudes

I confronted. This was not the way I was brought up. I am often reminded of an incident when I was about 10 years old. An inexplicable blood clot had developed in the back of my right eye and I had essentially gone blind in that eye. An eye doctor agreed to see me and my mother dropped me off. She deeply regretted that she had to return to work as a grade school teacher and had to leave me alone with the eye doctor. (There was no such thing as discretionary leave in the Norfolk School System, where my mother taught.) So, I was a young kid left alone in downtown Norfolk, virtually blind in one eye, waiting to hear what in the world they were going to do to restore my eyesight, if anything. The doctor administered eye drops to dilate the pupils so that he could see well into my eyes, but it took a little time for it to work. He suggested I go down to the little coffee shop in the office building and get something to eat while I waited for the drops to work.

So, there I was sitting at the counter drinking a Coke and eating a burger. The friendly waitress asked if I wanted some fries to go along with the burger and I reached into my pocket and pulled out the remainder of the meager lunch money my mother had left me. But the drops had taken affect and I could not make out the quarter from the nickel from the dime to determine if I had enough money to afford an order of fries. A businessman sitting in the stool beside me asked if I had enough and I said that I couldn't tell. "I can't make out the coins," I said, as I fingered each coin trying to determine its denomination. "How much do I have here," I asked, holding out my hand to show the man the coins in my hand. "Don't you worry about it. I will buy you some French fries," he said. How nice, I thought to myself.

After he paid the waitress I thanked him. It did not dawn on me until afterward that he must have thought I was a nearly blind young boy who was destined to struggle his whole life. It was a moment of real kindness and I wish I could have explained to him that I was only temporarily disabled, but it was too late. I hope he felt good about the small gesture and I certainly appreciated it, even if I was a little embarrassed at the time.

That small gesture by a stranger left a big impact on me as a child. It told me that this gentleman assumed that I had a disability and that he could do a little something to make a difference in my day. It told me that he did not want to embarrass me by asking me about my eyesight, he just took note of it and decided to buy me a little more lunch. He didn't need my gratitude and praise, he simply did it because he could and he wanted to. I took all this in only after he left and after I enjoyed the fries.

The Community Reinvestment Act is one of those laws we ought not to require. Banks and insurance companies should not need the incentives built into CRA to do what they should be doing as a matter of course. They would argue that they don't need CRA; that they would do the right thing even without it, but the evidence is that they won't. Not everyone behaves like that businessman buying some fries for a little blind white boy, much less the Black single mom who needs a loan.

Encouraging Homeowners

A peculiar aspect of the LIHTC program, one not particularly cared for by most developers but cherished by the Congressional originators of the law, is a provision that allowed for the occupants of the rental units to become homeowners after the 15th year of service. The states did not really embrace this aspect of the law either, preferring the provision that allowed them to extend what is known as the "mandatory compliance period" for 30 years. Some states have taken this to absurd lengths. California, for example, extends the mandatory compliance period to 55 years. But none of it mattered under the law. If you chose to convert to homeownership after the first 15-year period was up, you could do that, and we intended to do just that for our projects in Winchester. That would accomplish two things: we would break the cycle of disinvestment in the North Kent Street neighborhood in a much more dramatic and visible way, and we would be creating housing that even our harshest critics could not dispute as a giveaway.

The tenants were indeed tenants. These would be rental units for fifteen years, but at the end of fifteen years each of the carefully screened and preselected candidates for the new houses would have the option of buying the units for greatly reduced prices. We would be creating homeowners. How could anyone object to that?

We would be building new houses in a neighborhood where a new house had not been built in decades, aside from a new replacement house we had built in coordination with the local AME Church. This was going to be a dramatic new project and it could change the way people thought about North Kent Street, at least that was our hope.

More importantly, though, this would be a way to break the cycle, at least in a small way in this one neighborhood, of families having no way to build wealth. Even though the tenant/owners would have to wait fifteen years before they could own the units, the mechanism we intended to use to convey the properties would provide a very steep discount on the price of the units, providing immediate equity for the families. We would employ this same mechanism in Indian Country in the years ahead, but with some dramatic differences.

We hit a snag right away. In the heart of the neighborhood near an infamous alley with a row of derelict buildings owned by a real slum landlord, near what was perhaps the most important institution in the neighborhood, the International Benevolent and Protective Order of the Elks, was the property we needed. This was the only piece of land that we could reasonably acquire that had any size or suitability for a project. We had to buy this land. There was a family living in a rundown house on one corner and that house also had to go. The derelict buildings on Haddox Alley had to go. The Elks Lodge had to agree to sell us just a part of their land. It was a little like putting together a jigsaw puzzle, where people not playing the game had some of the pieces.

We made a good deal with the family whose house occupied the corner lot. Their house was old and would not withstand a move. Instead we simply agreed that we would build them a new house and they would deed us the balance of the land they owned. Good trade, something I would learn more about when I began working with Indian tribes. We bought out the slumlord after some nasty negotiations and only paid a little more than we would have liked, but well within the budget. But before negotiations began with the Elks Lodge, we were confronted with the reality of a zoning problem that seemed right out of Joseph Heller's *Catch 22*.

According to the zoning rules in place, the minimum size for a residential lot was 50 feet of frontage on a city street with a minimum depth of 50 feet. This is a fairly standard level of density for single-family, urban development. It was perfect for our plans and would allow us to build ten new houses on the land we could afford to acquire. We would also create a new city street bisecting the property, paid for through the City's federal funding known as the Community Development Block Grant Program. What failed to catch my attention was the Helleresque further requirement that such lots have side setbacks of at least 20 feet on both sides, meaning no buildings could be closer than 20 feet from the lots on either side of it. Further, each building on these 50-foot lots must also have a front and rear setback of 20 feet, meaning that the building could not be closer than 20 feet from the street nor closer than 20 feet from the rear of the back-property line.

It amounted to this: if we wanted to build an affordable house on a lot that met the minimum size allowable under the law, according to that law, this house would be exactly ten feet long by ten feet wide.

Camelot It Was Not

At first, I tried to imagine what a string of ten-foot by ten-foot houses might look like. We would have to make them very tall, say four or five stories tall, to fit a family. They would look like Rapunzel towers all in a nice little row, parapets for each house, maybe a moat around the whole subdivision. We could call it North Kent Camelot. Or not.

There must be some mistake. I called the city planning director and said this could not have been intended. Why would the city have a rule in place that allowed for a city lot of one size then restrict the building that could be built on that lot such that it was infeasible to build on that lot? Then it dawned on me. That must have been their intention all along. They did not want lots of that size after all, but bigger lots. Then why did they have a rule allowing for small lots? Why not simply require larger lots to begin with? Well, that would be blatantly exclusionary, of course.

Also, virtually all of the lots in the neighborhood were conforming lots with respect to lot length and depth, although not so much regarding the side and rear set-backs. Most of the houses were no more than a few feet apart from one another, as you would expect in a dense urban neighborhood. Small lot sizes allow for greater density, which is good in urban areas if it is planned properly and has appropriate amenities such as vest pocket parks, sidewalks and such. But if the intention was to allow, if not encourage, affordable single-family development, these setback requirements were clearly not the way to do it.

We had hit on the issue. Affordability was not a concern. As land costs go up, the relative cost of the dwelling units must rise as well. In order to meet the setback rules, you would have to acquire at a minimum two lots and combine them to build a single unit. This was our Catch 22. Our project would be cut in half, we would serve half as many families at twice the cost. It would not be affordable. This zoning ordinance was framed so that it appeared to be reasonable, but it disguised the actual intent. "You see the problem here, right?", I said to the city planning director. "Well, it's a problem for you I guess," he said. "You can ask the Board of Zoning Appeals for a variance, but I can't promise anything."

We were not deterred. The site was perfect and the board wanted me to press on with the project. I prepared an appeal to the City's Board of Zoning Appeals (BZA), which met monthly. I had to formulate a detailed account of why we wanted the BZA to grant us the variances and submit it to the city's planning department and then they would review it and make a recommendation to the BZA. We set about making our case to the planning director and his staff.

With the help of the city planning staff we boiled our request down to fourteen variances and thirteen special exceptions when we made our appeal to the BZA. We showed the preliminary plans that had been prepared at no cost by a local architectural firm, Reader & Swartz, founded by two eager, young and passionate architects, Beth Reader and Chuck Swartz. They created a design of a single basic house plan that we could use for all the houses. By putting a different front porch or by changing the roof angle, each house would look dramatically different. Also, to help save costs, Beth and Chuck came up with a unique design for a basic house that was twenty-four feet by twenty-four feet. That would save time on saw cuts and save lumber by having very few angles and every wall would be a standard length. Contractors loved it.

We presented these preliminary plans and made our pitch, detailing the desperate need for housing, the positive economic impact on the community, the jobs it would create and the sense of hope it would instill in a neighborhood bereft of optimism. Even though the city planning staff had recommended our project for approval, the BZA denied our request.

I should not have been surprised given my earlier lunch-time reception from the city councilman, but I was nonetheless taken aback. The chairman of the Board of Zoning Appeals was a local building contractor. (Notice how concerned Winchester was about conflicts of interest.) In explaining the board's decision, he imaginatively combined both condescension and buck-passing by offering that I had a "good idea" but that he did not think that the Board of Zoning Appeals was the proper place to appeal this zoning issue.

Showing statesmanlike restraint, I did not immediately stand up and shout "You mean to tell me that the Board of Zoning Appeals does not think it is the proper place to hear a ZONING APPEAL?" But I held my tongue until he finished. He went on to state, in good bureaucratese, that four or five members of the BZA should not be the ones to consider whether or not this is good for the City. "This should be studied a little bit more by the guys we are paying to study these things."

Logically, I countered that the board, by virtue of its very title, was empowered, indeed was created, to make these sorts of decisions, to make exceptions to the inherent inequities inadvertently built into complex codes and ordinances.[26] Then he used the "Slippery Slope Argument," which is impossible to counter and nearly always nonsensical. I said as much in my reply and that was rather impolitic, I'll admit. I did myself and our cause no good at that meeting. The slippery slope argument sidesteps the question of whether not the proposal has merit in and of itself. It is a lazy argument. Indeed, as Hugo Mercier and Dan Sperber explain in their influential book *The Enigma of Reason*, "Human reason is both biased and lazy. Biased because it overwhelmingly finds justifications and arguments that support the reasoner's point of view, lazy because reason makes little effort to assess the quality of the justifications and arguments it produces."[27] And this was yet another example of what Dan Kahan calls motivated reasoning. The chairman of the Board of Zoning Appeals had made up his mind.

In fact, the BZA chairman looked aghast, positively thunderstruck that we were so strongly opposing his decision. Winston Churchill is said to have once described Charles de Gaulle's offended look as "resembling a female llama surprised in her bath." That was the look on his face when I dared to question him. Admittedly, I should have known better and played the game, but we had so much at stake with this project that my judgment was perhaps a bit cloudy, in the way that *War and Peace* is a tad long. I had already pointed out to the Board that virtually none of the dwellings in the North Kent Street neighborhood had the luxury of being greater than 20 feet from their neighbor's property line, and that virtually all of the houses in the neighborhood were situated on lots that were far smaller than the minimum called for under the current zoning restrictions, and that our proposed new project would meet this lot size requirement, if not the setback requirements.

I don't think the members of the board of zoning appeals were used to people pushing back. I not only questioned their decisions but their entire decision-making process. Their response was to label me a hothead, obstinate and arrogant. What broke my heart was the realization that men and women who sit in the seats of power, men and women just like the city councilman and the BZA chairman, believed that African Americans had had ample time to improve their lives since the "bad old days" of slavery and Jim Crow. They often cited successful Black men or women from modest or even tragic circumstances who overcame those circumstances to become doctors, lawyers, CEOs, or some other successful professional. The stories they tell one another hold more power than the evidence of how rare and difficult such success is.[28]

They believe that at least since the 1964 Civil Rights Act leveled the playing field once and for all (in their eyes), affirmative action, food stamps, housing vouchers, and of course, welfare, have collectively created a generation, indeed, multiple generations, of people unwilling to shoulder the responsibility for creating their own success stories, unable to wean themselves from government handouts. Today, Dr. Ben Carson, the African American former presidential candidate and current HUD secretary, uses his own example to aver that Black men and women can climb out of poverty on their own, without turning to government assistance, which he claims only perpetuates poverty. Dr. Carson's personal story, being raised by a single mom and living in public housing to eventually become a world-renowned pediatric brain surgeon, would be inspirational irrespective of his race. Overcoming the hardships of poverty and growing up in "the projects" is hard enough. But the very rarity of his success as a Black man proves the point. Why was Ben Carson uniquely immune to the supposed "culture of poverty" that seemingly surrounded him? Why are there so few such success stores, even ones less dramatic than his? If the culture of poverty is the culprit, why were there so few such successes prior to the Great Society that is supposed to have ushered in this culture of poverty? In the absence of this nefarious cultural affinity for government handouts shouldn't there have been more evidence of greater success, at least as defined through household wealth, before the expansion of welfare benefits, before the food stamp program, before Affirmative Action? But such evidence does not exist. Indeed, evidence has consistently debunked the notion of a "Culture of Poverty," especially the persistent notion that affirmative action is particularly insidious.[29]

The narrative that describes the pathology of the purposefully unemployed has become so ingrained in the minds of so many that it is gospel, it is comforting. It absolves the majority population of benefiting from subtle forms of discrimination. When the regulatory system props up the myths, or ignores the realities of inequity, it can be even harder to make the changes necessary to hasten more equitable treatment. When something as seemingly innocuous as a city's zoning and setback rules betray discriminatory impact, if not discriminatory intent, changing the rules is necessitated by the unmistakable realization that the system is flawed and in need of thoughtful redesign.

Neo-conservative James Q. Wilson, who for decades before his death in 2012 was one of the nation's most prominent political scientists, subscribed to the idea of a culture of poverty. In a 1967 letter to Joseph Califano, then Secretary of the Department of Health, Education and Welfare, barely two or three years into the Great

Society's programs blamed for this culture, Wilson wrote, "It is now quite apparent that a modern economy, however affluent, has great difficulty in doing much for anybody who finds life on the street corner more attractive than life in the factory" believing as well that "a substantial fraction of Negro men operate big-city hustles—pimping, petty gambling, pushing dope, defrauding tourists (and each other)."[30]

Excusing for the moment the nasty tone of his words, Wilson is ever so willing to overlook the abundance of evidence for structural and systemic racism that severely circumscribed job opportunities for Black Americans then and to this day. It was almost like after President Johnson succeeded in passing the Civil Rights Act of 1964 and the Voting Rights Act of 1965 that everything should get better overnight.

Among the other ubiquitous explanations for persistent poverty is the prevalence of single motherhood among Black and Native American households. Because it is perceived to be a choice, single motherhood has taken on the mantle of cause and effect of persistent poverty. But evidence does not support the idea that eliminating single motherhood would significantly change the overall poverty rate. Instead, it would have a negligible impact on the rate of poverty. Three social scientists, David Brady, Ryan Finnigan, and Sabine Hubgen, published an exhaustive study in the American Journal of Sociology that debunked this long-held explanation for poverty. And while it is true that single motherhood does indeed lower the potential earnings of such households and indeed contributes to the risk factors inherent in poverty, the study showed that being unemployed and having lower educational attainment were far greater determinants of poverty than is single motherhood.[31] It is yet another example of the certainty of so many that poverty is a function of personal and moral failings.

Chapter 5

Moving On

TOO MANY CIVIC leaders throughout the country tacitly and sometimes even explicitly reject the idea of white privilege[32] and declaim the insidious influence of reverse discrimination. But white privilege, real or imaginary, is immaterial—its presence or absence does not negate the reality of Black *disadvantage*. They ignore the realities of Fair Housing testers who, day in and day out, continue to find that Black and Native American applicants with the same or higher incomes, better credit ratings, and other favorable indices compared to white applicants are still denied rental apartments. This is true throughout the country, not just in the south. They deny the reality that boys and girls who go to segregated schools have lower test scores and eventually lower incomes than boys and girls from fully integrated schools. They deny the evidence that better qualified candidates with identifiably "Black" or "Indian" names on their resume, are nonetheless ignored in favor of identifiably white candidates, even if the white candidates have fewer sought-after attributes.[33]

Why are so many people unwilling to accept the fact that building wealth and success in the workplace, in school, in life, is dependent on a complex interaction of forces beyond one person's control? Generous-minded and thoughtful people will acknowledge that success in life often includes some assistance on the path toward success. Of course, it naturally follows that if you had help along the way, then the **absence** of such help might explain the failures of so many Black and American Indian families to share in the success.

And as any generous-minded and thoughtful person will attest, the creation of wealth and the absence of wealth crosses generations and geographies. It has long been known that the single greatest source of wealth in this country, at least prior to the Great Recession of 2008-2009, was home equity. In fact, recent surveys have shown that white families on average had seven times the wealth of African American families, due in large measure to home equity.[34] It would follow then, that zoning policies that restrict the creative use or reuse of land in predominantly Black neighborhoods, in contrast with public improvement dollars spent in the very neighborhoods that are already favored, contribute to the failure to build wealth in the disfavored neighborhoods.

When cities like Winchester fail to administer sensitive code enforcement, they're reinforcing the status quo in struggling neighborhoods. Code enforcement must recognize the differences between homeowners and landlords with differing financial means, while providing a mechanism to address obsolescence and deterioration in an affordable and systematic manner.

The argument that severely deteriorated minority neighborhoods do not deserve special low interest loans or other special improvement programs ignores the fact that before the Fair Housing Act became the law of the land, before the Civil Rights Act, before the Community Reinvestment Act, and before red-lining was outlawed, minority families had no housing choice other than the neighborhoods that were "set aside" for them. The North Kent Street neighborhood is one such place. To then say special incentives for North Kent Street would be unfair is to deny that discriminatory practices left those places vulnerable and under-nourished to begin with.

When neighborhoods deteriorate, values decline and homes build little or no equity and far less wealth is created. When no wealth is inherited or when too little home equity is available to support loans for all sorts of purposes that might build future wealth, this deficiency crosses generations. My father and mother did not have to live in a minority restricted neighborhood. The value of their home was not limited by the condition of its neighbors' homes. They did nothing to deserve that advantage. I did nothing to "earn" the modest inheritance that my brothers and I shared. Likewise, the children of homeowners in the North Kent Street neighborhood did nothing to deserve the disadvantage of living in a disfavored community.

The Wealth Gap

A 2017 study from the Institute on Assets and Social Policy at Brandeis University exhaustively analyzed the data from the Federal Reserve Board of Governors' Survey of Consumer Finances. The study shows that ". . . many popular explanations for racial economic inequality overlook these deep roots, asserting that wealth disparities must be solely the result of individual life choices and personal achievements. The misconceptions that personal responsibility accounts for the racial wealth gap is an obstacle to the policies that could effectively address racial disparities."[35]

The study goes on to show that attending college does not close the racial wealth gap. Indeed, it shows that the median white high school **dropout** achieves similar levels of wealth to a Black adult who graduated high school and went to at least some college. Their analysis indicates that being in a two-parent household does not erase the racial wealth gap: a median single white parent has more than double the asset base of a median Black household with two parents present.

> Even working full-time does not close the racial wealth gap. What closes the racial wealth gap is inheritance. The authors of the study show that "In effect, . . . the educational and wealth-building opportunities directly denied to people of color in past generations continue to reverberate in the lives of their children..." Furthermore, "Because white families accumulated more wealth over a history in which Black and Latino families were excluded from many wealth-building opportunities through discriminatory policies in housing, banking, education, and other areas, white families today have, in general, greater resources to pass on to their offspring. As a result, white families are five times more likely than Black or Latino families to receive large gifts, inheritances, and the amounts they receive are far greater.[36]

Of course, I did not have any of this data when I appealed to the Winchester planning board for a small loan fund for homeowners in the North Kent Street neighborhood, nor for the sensitive code enforcement efforts we sought. We appealed as a simple matter of fairness. We were denied, despite the availability of ample grant funds from HUD and other resources. And this plays out in neighborhood after neighborhood in city after city, all across the country. When there is such minimal means to borrow against the value of a house, businesses are not started, college costs are not met, inheritances are not bequeathed, and the next generation starts off behind the rest of the pack.

None of this is to say that poor African American households are blameless for their poverty. Bad decisions are bad decisions, bad behavior is bad behavior. As William Julius Wilson writes in *The Truly Disadvantaged: The Inner City, the Underclass, and Public Policy,* "There are two ways to dehumanize people: the first is to strip people of all virtue; the second is to cleanse them of all sin."[37] He is asking for some sense of balance. Understand that poverty is complicated, made worse by a pervasive willingness to overlook mitigating circumstances, to perpetuate stereotypes, and to deny the unrelenting reality that overcoming deep poverty is extraordinarily difficult.

Consider the little-known consequences of one of the most effective government programs ever created. The Federal Housing Administration (FHA) was created in 1934 and almost single-handedly created the suburban middle-class. In a research paper written by Jonathan Kaplan and Andrew Valls for *Public Affairs Quarterly* in 2007, the authors wrote, "Home equity, for many Americans, is a very important source of wealth, and the decades after World War II were ones of rapid home equity growth. They were the decades that saw the creation of a large, mostly suburban, middle class. But the middle class that was created was also mostly white, and this was due largely to government policies that (in many cases intentionally) excluded Blacks from the opportunities to get into the home market and benefit from home equity growth."[38]

The FHA Underwriting Manual, replete with only marginal changes over the period 1934 through 1968, established the FHA's mortgage lending requirements via its mortgage insurance standards. According to a study detailed in an article in *The Atlantic* magazine in 2014, "The FHA *explicitly* (emphasis theirs) refused to back loans to Black people or even other people who lived near

Black people ... Redlining destroyed the possibility of investment wherever Black people lived."[39] The manual used by the underwriters to determine where and to whom federally-backed mortgage insurance would be granted used a four-stage, color-coded ranking--green for the highest grade, blue for second highest, yellow for marginal and declining areas, and, of course, red for areas in which mortgages would be routinely denied.

The North Kent Street neighborhood in Winchester is the exemplar of the discriminatory policies of the Federal Housing Administration. Indeed, the official FHA manual included the instructions to its appraisers to favor areas with barriers between Black and white neighborhoods. The manual stated that:

> natural or artificially established barriers will prove effective in protecting a neighborhood and the locations within it from adverse influences...including prevention of the infiltration of ...lower class occupancy, and inharmonious racial groups.[40]

The railroad tracks that defined the North Kent Street neighborhood were not just a physical and psychological barrier, they were a sure-fire remedy against the "infiltration" of Black homeowners, who would be systematically prevented from borrowing against the value of their homes. City Light was determined to at least try to overcome the lingering effects of redlining that predominated for decades in North Kent. We were adamant that something had to be done to redress the disinvestment demanded by the old FHA policies. We succeeded to only a degree.

After a month of further study during which the Board of Zoning Appeals asked us no questions and asked for no testimony from anyone that we know of, they heard our appeal one more time. After extracting even more concessions from us on the size of the park we were installing for the project, which is not a requirement in any of the zoning rules but mysteriously became a bargaining chip in the negotiations, we won approval of the project. I don't think it was my powerfully persuasive arguments that won the day. I think it was embarrassment. I take credit for pointing out the lunacy of a regulation that could result in nothing more than a ten-foot by ten-foot house, but my arguments pointing out the discriminatory intent fell flat. I didn't care at that point.

We had our project approved.

Yet Another Smart-Assed White Boy

There was one more step to the North Kent project, and it led to one of the most mortifying moments of my life. We still had not convinced the Elks Lodge to part with the corner of their land needed to complete the entire parcel. I had met with the full Elks Lodge on two occasions and they were eager to see something happen in the neighborhood, but they had owned this land for decades. It was practically their only real asset. We had compromised pretty dramatically and reduced the size of our request from 13,000 square feet of land to now only needing about 3,000 square feet, leaving them the bulk of their original land. They were happy and gave their elected leader the authority to sign the sales contract.

Another of our original board members, Bill Buckner, arranged for me to meet privately with the president of the Elks Lodge at his home. It looked like the deal was about to happen. I was lucky to have Bill on my board and even luckier that he took me to see the leader of the Elks Lodge. Bill was a leader in the African American community in Winchester, a distinguished and elegant man with a voice only a half octave above that of James Earl Jones, and every bit as magisterial.

Bill picked me up in his car and we drove over to the president's home, a tidy house on the eastern edge of the North Kent Street neighborhood. We exchanged pleasantries and sat briefly at his kitchen table. I laid out the legal papers for him to sign and went over each page with Bill looking on. The president of the lodge seemed oddly disinterested and distracted but Bill kept assuring me to proceed, so I kept on going.

When I finished reading the fine print and finished going over the terms of the sale, I signed the papers on behalf of City Light and I handed the pen to the president. He stood up and asked me if I wanted some coffee. He was tall and erect with grey hair and wore a cardigan sweater and looked every bit the Black Mr. Rogers. I said no thanks and waited while he fixed himself a cup. He sat down and looked at the papers and fidgeted a bit and then looked a bit perplexed and asked me to go over the terms one more time, which I did. He then fixed himself another cup of coffee. This went on for some time, with more questions and the president asking Bill about his family. I was getting a little bit worried that perhaps he was getting cold feet about signing the sales agreement.

After another round of coffee and yet another explanation of the terms, I was worried these were more *his* concerns about the terms of the deal and were not the concerns of the rest of the Elks members. I then reminded him that the Elks Lodge governing board had voted to sell the land and had empowered him to sign the contract; I pointed out that we had had the land surveyed and platted just to fit their requirements, at considerable expense. I did not understand why he was now delaying signing the contract. I was terse and abrupt. Bill Buckner turned and looked at me with withering disdain. Up to that point, Bill had never shown me the slightest hint of anger. Even in the brief discussions we had had about life before the Civil Rights Act, he was restrained and stoic, displaying an equanimity that was inspiring. His look now was not so much a look of anger as one of bitter disappointment and dejection. It was like he thought better of me and I had let him down. He looked at me like a father whose son has just run the car into the ditch, after stealing the car. He put his hand on my shoulder and asked me to walk with him out onto the front porch. Damn, I was in for it now.

I think it took all of Bill's considerable self-control to very quietly suggest to me that I needed to be mindful of this older gentleman's dignity. I bloody-well needed to give him as much time as he needed and if he wanted to talk about Bill's family, then, through clinched teeth, he very slowly and quietly said that I **will** listen to him ask about Bill's family. Then Bill said to me that I would be staying out on the porch and that he would make sure that he got the papers signed. Sitting quietly on the front porch it finally dawned on me that the president of the Elks Lodge, who was in his late 60s or early 70s, might have difficulty reading and perhaps he was not about to sign something that he could not thoroughly understand, unless someone he trusted could vouch for it. Bill, obviously, could not do that in my presence.

I sat on the porch for another 30 minutes or so while Bill and the president talked quietly. Sometimes I could hear some genteel laughter, and eventually Bill emerged with the signed sales contract and I handed the president the check for the agreed upon amount. We drove away in silence and I felt like melting into the seat cushion on the way home. I was sure I had betrayed a dear friend and could never win back his trust. I was a young white man of the Old South, a man of privilege, pushing an older black man who had without doubt worked his entire life to achieve middle class standing, who was now being asked to do something that made him understandably nervous. And I could not wait a mere 30 minutes. I did not have the decency to see that maybe, just maybe, he had been exposed for the first time to the language of real estate law that I had become accustomed to over the last 10 years. I have no doubt that earlier in his life, this man had had to be deferential to nitwit entitled white boys and had had his fill of it and here I was, trying to do the right thing and doing just the wrong thing in the process.

I cannot undo that episode and I cannot purge it from brain and I remain ashamed of myself to this day. Every time I see a grey-haired Black man of a certain age, wearing a cardigan sweater, I practically break out in hives. I just cannot believe I was so stupid, thoughtless, and pushy.

Bank Examiners are Mostly Nice Guys

Now we had to put the financing package together so that construction could begin on North Kent Court. Once again, I reached out to the small community banks in the Shenandoah Valley and found several that ultimately became our investors. This led to the fortuitous meeting that eventually led us to Indian Country.

The Federal Reserve Bank of Richmond was getting interested in what these small community banks were doing and asked me to come to Richmond to explain. That was a fascinating trip. The Federal Reserve Bank of Richmond is one of the more conservative banks of the twelve-member Federal Reserve System. I got the call out of the blue from their banking supervision department asking if

I would come speak to some of the Reserve Bank's examiners who look at the safety and soundness of a bank's operations, and that includes a bank's investments. I readily agreed and drove down to Richmond and spent a couple of hours with a handful of the Richmond Fed's very buttoned-up bank examiners. They were not what I expected. I had feared a roomful of cheerless accountants who cared only about a bank's Tier 1 capital, its liquidity, and all the stuff that I knew so little about. Instead they wanted to know how City Light operated, how we made certain that our projects would cash flow and remain solvent and, surprisingly, they wanted to know what impact we were having in the community.

I was pleased to know they were interested in the depth of the housing need in Winchester and whether it was likely to be as great or greater elsewhere in the Commonwealth. They wanted to know how we could offer housing to such low-income families when it seemed that nobody else had been able to successfully do that. Of course, City Light's long-term financial health was of interest to them and would be felt ultimately by our investors, the banks they supervised. If City Light failed, our investors' money would be at risk. But we had taken steps to mitigate those risks and had waiting lists for each of the units we built. The fact that we had relatively small projects with relatively little exposure for the banks in the Fed's charge gave them considerable comfort. I left reassured that the banks supervised by the Richmond Federal Reserve Bank would not be told to stay away from tax credit investments. Indeed, I felt confident that they might even encourage some to investigate the opportunities further.

Good Jails Make Good Neighbors

When I returned to Winchester, work had begun on North Kent Court but my relationship with the city took another nose dive. A contentious issue was being debated between the City of Winchester and Frederick County. The city has its city council and the county has its board of supervisors. Decisions made by each are not binding upon the other, though they certainly have an impact on each other. There are separate school systems and separate planning and community development departments. The issue that was roiling the city and the county was where to put a much-needed new jail that both would share.

The city manager, an appointed professional administrator for the City of Winchester, was a diminutive former Marine. He was publicly lobbying for a large tract of land near the railroad tracks in, of all places, the North Kent Street neighborhood. The county had a spot outside of town on county land it preferred. I tried on several occasions to call the city manager to discuss his preference for the North Kent Street site, but he would never take my call. I never got a return call after leaving numerous messages. I tried the same with the mayor and had the same result. So, I wrote a letter to the editor of the Winchester *Star*. The point I made was that I doubted very much that the city manager would think that having a jail in his nice, middle class neighborhood would be a good addition to his community, yet somehow he thought it was dandy for the North Kent Street neighborhood.

The city manager had publicly stated that the jail would be good for the North Kent Street neighborhood because it would add hundreds of new jobs and would add a new building in a part of town that had not seen any new construction in decades. I countered that, while far more modest in scope, that North Kent Court was a new construction project that would have a more positive influence on the neighborhood than would a damn prison. I encouraged him and anyone else who thought that a jail in a residential neighborhood was a good fit to instead, imagine a little girl or boy walking out the front door on their way to school and the first thing they see is a van, disgorging prisoners, handcuffed and shackled, frog walking into the jail. Is that the inspiring, ennobling vision we'd want for that child to start the day?

The city manager took offense to the inference that he was only suggesting the North Kent Street neighborhood for the new jail because it was a poor Black neighborhood. He emphasized that this was the only logical spot available that was large enough. Notwithstanding, there was ample available vacant land within the city's newly developed industrial park, but a jail would be an unwelcome addition to a park actively seeking new office and industrial tenants. A jail just would not do there. But in the Black neighborhood, well, why not?

What struck me with this incident was the indifference to the already tarnished hopes and dreams of the people who live in the North Kent Street neighborhood. It is the same disregard that results in more minority neighborhoods being in closer proximity to toxic waste dumps than non-minority communities, and by a wide margin.[41] As if the railroad tracks were not barrier enough to limit values in the neighborhood, a new jail, a toxic waste dump of another sort, would surely be the last straw. Ultimately, owing nothing to our efforts, the decision was made to locate the jail elsewhere. A welcome victory.

Somehow, despite our good intentions, Marianne and I seemed to step into controversies like this everywhere we went, Marianne at the library and me at City Light. City Light continued to buy and rehabilitate homes in the North Kent Street neighborhood and add to its portfolio. We were increasingly successful in raising capital for development, and low-interest loans from the state's Housing Partnership Fund, whose use was restricted to project development. We were also raising funds from a variety of foundations. We were a finalist for the prestigious Maxwell Award for Excellence in Housing, awarded by the Fannie Mae Foundation, but the struggle to cover our operating expenses remained perplexing.

We had one of those "water, water everywhere, but not a drop to drink" sort of dilemmas. There was plenty of money to pay for our projects, but next to nothing to pay to keep the lights on. I was also having a recurring dream I first started having when I went to work at the Rouse Company in which a bear or a tiger is stalking me relentlessly and nobody seems to notice or care. But now I had a new and easy-to-explain dream.

In this dream, I was standing on a part of the Berlin Wall with a big sledge hammer, hammering away at the barrier between East and West Germany, except it was not East and West Germany at all. It was between east and west Winchester, between downtown Winchester and the North Kent Street neighborhood. I only had this Berlin Wall dream one time, but it was unforgettable and unmistakable in its meaning. I finally thought that we were making a difference, even if the good people at City Hall did not agree.

Marianne had transformed the Handley Library into a modern

and well-functioning library. She successfully lobbied both the city and the county for increases in funding and even wrote a grant to pay for a new book mobile that was a huge hit. She began planning for what eventually became the first new branch library the Handley Library had ever had. But the constant battle for dollars was wearing on her. She was making do with a budget based on about $5 per capita from both the citizens of Winchester and Frederick County. By comparison nearby Loudoun County funded their libraries with budgets of about $30 per capita, admittedly a more affluent county, but not *that* much more affluent.

Marianne dutifully pointed this out to the city council of Winchester and the board of supervisors of Frederick County, but they raised her budgets only by a pittance each year. Notably, the library got higher budget increases than almost any other of the city or county departments year after year while Marianne was at the helm, but the increases were still not what she wanted nor close to what she believed were adequate for the needs of the community. She was weary of fighting for every dollar for even the most basic improvements for the library. When friends in Minneapolis-St. Paul urged her to apply for the position of library director at the suburban St. Paul Ramsey County Library, a much larger and much better funded library system, Marianne was ready.

Alan Greenspan was No Einstein

About the same time Marianne was hearing from St. Paul, the folks at the Richmond Federal Reserve Bank had again asked me to speak at a meeting of Fed officials, this time at a small conference at the Board of Governors of the Federal Reserve System in Washington, DC.

The Fed building in Washington is on Constitution Avenue and is not nearly as impressive as you would think. The building in which the great and mysterious Alan Greenspan held court ought to be grand and imposing. It isn't. It is forgettable and uninspiring. This meeting was a conclave of each of the community affairs officers of the 12 Federal Reserve Banks throughout the country, and the Richmond Fed asked me to speak about my outreach to community banks and the need for affordable housing in small rural communities.

During the meeting, the Minneapolis Federal Reserve Bank expressed their interest in what I was doing with City Light. This led to a correspondence with Kathy Erickson with whom I would eventually make the "trip from hell" into Indian Country. Kathy was one of the Vice Presidents of the Minneapolis Federal Reserve Bank and was especially interested in my work with small rural banks.

There was a lunch break during the meeting and since I was not allowed to wander the halls of the building, I went out for a walk on the Washington Mall. One of my favorite places in DC is the National Academy of Sciences, by happenstance right next door to the Fed Board of Governors. At the corner of 22nd Street and Constitution Avenue, in the front yard of this building, is the Albert Einstein Memorial. One part of the memorial includes a marvelous, larger than life statue of Albert Einstein. It is oddly out of proportion, with its head maybe (appropriately) a bit too big for its body, but I love this sculpture. Robert Berks was the sculptor, the same man whose bust of John F. Kennedy is at the Kennedy Center for the Performing Arts and is of a similar style.

The memorial depicts Einstein lounging in a lighthearted posture. It is in a pretty, wooded setting and you can look up into his eyes and see what a humane and approachable genius he was. I bought a hotdog from one of the vendors near the Washington Monument and then sat with Albert and thought about his 1905 paper, "On the Electrodynamics of Moving Bodies" and his theory of the cosmological constant. Not really. I sat with him and thought about how upset everyone (maybe not everyone) would be if Marianne and I were offered jobs in St. Paul or Minneapolis. What if we decided to leave Winchester? Albert, inexplicably, had no answers for me.

We had succeeded in building considerable public good will in Winchester and throughout the state for City Light, but that good will was inexplicably not shared by the city's political leaders. They viewed us with suspicion or outright contempt and continued to harbor the view that the city had a starkly limited role in making life better in places like the North Kent Street neighborhood. Their old narrative was stronger than the new one I was trying to tell. They felt that we were, at best, a bit naïve if not entirely misguided.

Other cities were embarking on far more aggressive community development initiatives, including low-interest and even no-interest loans to homeowners to fix up their homes in deteriorated neighborhoods, undertaking sensitive and targeted health and building code enforcement initiatives to get problem buildings fixed or removed. I, on the other hand, was having no luck in getting the City Council to consider such things. We had nonetheless settled into a comfortable routine. Even our daughter, Elizabeth, had embraced what City Light was all about. One evening, Marianne and I were talking at the dinner table about marketing strategies and ways to both raise money and increase awareness of our mission when Elizabeth, listening quietly, asked what our "tag line" was. I had no idea that she even knew what a tag line was. I told her that we did not have a tag line. She was pensive for a few moments then she volunteered her suggestion: "City Light Houses. We Build 'em. You live in 'em."

I thought that was a pretty good tag line, but it never caught on with my board.

Marianne, too, found herself in a comfortable routine, neither challenged nor bored. We were both in a sort of stasis that probably could have been maintained for many years but would inevitably lead to our winters of discontent. We were worried how Elizabeth and her younger brother, Greg, would handle a move. Elizabeth was president of her elementary school's student council. At a party one fall day, a few dozen friends gathered with their children for an afternoon of fun and good food. At one point, there was a traditional bobbing for apples contest for the kids around Elizabeth's age—ten years old or so. Each of the kids, one by one, were weaving around the galvanized tub full of apples trying to get a grasp on one and come out with a prized apple. No kid had yet to succeed in sinking their teeth into an apple and coming up with a juicy McIntosh. It was becoming a real challenge to see which child would figure out how to do it. Finally, it was Elizabeth's turn. She sat at the tub and stared at the apples for a moment, then she put her hands firmly on either side of the tub, took a deep breath and zeroed in on one especially large and juicy apple. She put her little face directly over that apple and drove that apple to the bottom of the tub. First her face, then her head, followed by her shoulders, went entirely underwater until she had firmly wedged her chosen apple between her teeth and the bottom of the tub. Once she had a solid bite into the apple, she rose from the tub like Poseidon rising from the Aegean Sea, water cascading from her head and shoulders in torrents, soaked to the skin, with a huge little-girl grin on her face, triumphant.

Marianne and I knew then that she would do just fine if we had a move in our near future.

When we finally put Winchester in our rearview mirror, I was left without a framework for understanding why Black families were hamstrung with smaller inheritances than the average white family. I left without knowing much about the lingering effects of segregated and poorly performing schools, the misperceptions of Affirmative Action, the subtle discrimination in job applications or the generational effects of Black families holding fewer dollars in home equity and therefore having less family wealth than average white families. I had yet to put together that nearly all of this could be laid at the feet of government policies like the not-so-old federal FHA underwriting manual, local zoning restrictions, "re-sequencing" by banks large and small, and, of course, the toxic stories told and repeated every day about the culture of Black poverty.

I was about to find out how insidious these same forces are in Indian Country.

Part II
Building the Foundation

Chapter 6

Shivs and Arrows

AFTER JOINING THE Federal Reserve Bank of Minneapolis and a year or so after my arduous Trip from Hell, my staff and I made another visit to the home of the Oglala Sioux Tribe. On the reservation we had made a point of meeting Richard Sherman, the director of the tribe's parks and recreation authority. Richard is the quintessential game warden cum recreation director, with a little bit of Humphrey Bogart or Spencer Tracy thrown in to boot. He wore a rumpled khaki uniform that would not have looked out of place in the Serengeti, but instead his domain was the pine-topped hills and open prairie of the appropriately named Pine Ridge Indian reservation. We drove out to see the tribe's growing buffalo herd roaming free over several thousand acres of grasslands and badlands. Richard told us a tale that was almost too strange to believe. According to Richard, the tribe carefully manages their buffalo herd, tracking the well-being of the bulls, cows and calves that comprise one of the lasting remnants of the Lakota way of life. For the overall health of the herd it was necessary to occasionally cull one or two big bulls or old cows. In response to the need to raise revenue and the need to humanely protect the size of the herd, the Oglala Sioux tribe held an auction of sorts, selling to the highest bidder the rights to hunt and kill the designated bull or cow buffalo.

Surprisingly, a man who would travel all the way from Germany bought the rights to this "hunt," which would be carefully staged by Richard Sherman and his well-trained staff, all enrolled members of the Oglala Sioux Tribe. They met the heavily-accented German national the evening before and all agreed to convene the following morning to begin to stalk and shoot the buffalo. They explained how he should be well-prepared for a difficult day of walking through prairie and Badlands in search of the old bull and admonished him to show up early.

On the next day at the appointed time, the erstwhile big game hunter showed up in faux loincloth, barefooted and his only weapon was a bow and a quiver full of arrows.

Richard was horrorstruck, if also slightly bemused. This unshod German proto-Indian was determined to hunt the largest land animal in the western hemisphere with only a bow and arrow because he wanted to have an authentic Indian experience. Richard reminded him that the bull buffalo in question was still strong and healthy. It weighed in at a robust 2,000 pounds of surly muscle, hair, and horn, and could make 40 mph, outrunning both horse and, most certainly, the fastest man.

Despite his deep misgivings, Richard began the hunt and finally, over a slight ridge, they came upon the poor condemned beast. The German, without so much as a nod to Richard, let loose a weak missile from his bow and struck the buffalo in its ass, barely penetrating the deep fur and hide. The buffalo noticed, but apparently was not too concerned. The German once again shot an arrow, this time into the loins of the hairy creature. That got noticed. It was not a mortal wound, but clearly caused great pain and distress. Richard was more worried about causing unnecessary suffering to one of the sacred animals of the Oglala Sioux, but also concerned about the possibility of the buffalo turning on the stalking group, charging and goring the German, or immeasurably worse, one of Richard's staff.

After yet another arrow was loosed into the hide of the now enraged buffalo, Richard felt that he had no choice but to put the poor creature out of its misery. Richard joked that since there would be witnesses he was forced to shoot the buffalo rather than the German. One well-aimed bullet through the lungs and heart put him down and out of his agony.

The episode with the German big game *bwana* exemplifies the myths that surround Indian Country. He wanted to be an Indian, if only for a day. And he needed the experience to be a caricature of an Indian hunt to feed his ego-trip. Rather than seeing Indian Country as it is today, composed of separate nation-states, each with its own heritage, history, and culture living in a modern world, this nincompoop believed that Indians still wore buckskins, hunted with bows and arrows and could somehow enable him to reenact a primitive hunt. He was probably shocked to see that most members of the tribe did not live in teepees. His lack of understanding—his ignorance of what life is really like on the Pine Ridge Indian Reservation—led him to what could have been a disaster had Richard Sherman not intervened.

I sympathize a bit with the hunter from Germany. But as much as I admire the great Indian heroes of the past, as he did, and as much as I lament the tragic treatment of Native Americans, we run the risk of mythologizing all of Indian Country, past and present, by focusing solely on the buffalo hunt, or by remembering only Chief Joseph, Sitting Bull, or Geronimo. If we ignore the prosaic and quotidian, if we fail to see the daily lives of Indians, we fail to see them as people.

Not all Indians can track animals or criminals like Richard Sherman or even like Graham Greene (see *Dances with Wolves* and *Thunderheart*). Far more Indians work at the parks and recreation departments, at public schools and medical clinics, stores and shops, garages and law firms than are employed discerning the subtle paw-prints of cougars or the hoof prints of buffalo, although there are a few with those scarce jobs. The objectification of Indians relegates them to the realms of myth and make-believe—their problems aren't real or relevant in the world we live in. When we fail to see Indians as being just like us, it is easier for us to ignore them, to think of Indians as only remnants of the past rather than equal citizens, deserving of the same considerations, liberties and rights. This explains, at least a little, how states with large Indian populations made no mention of Indians in statewide planning documents for housing, economic and community development, or social services, as I was to find out in the years to come.

Go West, Young Man

Marianne got the call before I did. She was offered the directorship of the Ramsey County Library system in suburban St. Paul. This was a major library in Minnesota, a progressive state that truly values libraries and was willing to pay for the services. Her budget would be five times that of the Handley Library and her staff would be that many times larger. She was thrilled and was set to begin work at her dream job in the spring of 1993. Fortuitously, I was recruited about the same time to work at the Federal Reserve Bank in Minnesota. Our pending departures were front page, above the fold news in the Winchester *Star*. We were nothing if not newsworthy.[42]

In retrospect, the most important accomplishments of City Light were mostly invisible. We had built new houses, most notably the North Kent Court sub-division, and had rehabilitated about 100 other homes, including the conversion of the Johnson-Williams School in Berryville. Removing the cloak of invisibility that shrouded the North Kent Street neighborhood was our most long-lasting and important contribution to Winchester. I was a thorn in the side of the City Council and the Planning Commission, to say nothing of the Board of Zoning Appeals, and that meant that neighborhoods in deep decline could no longer simply be ignored. But ingrained attitudes are hard to change, and the City of Winchester still had a difficult time coming to grips with the twentieth century, much less the twenty-first century. As recently as 2016, the Winchester City Council defeated a motion to remove the Confederate flag from the city's official seal.

I became the manager of community affairs for the Minneapolis Federal Reserve Bank in August 1993. That meant that I would work with banks that belonged to the Federal Reserve System, as well as the Reserve Bank itself, to find innovative ways to bring capital to poor and minority communities in the Ninth Federal Reserve District. The Ninth is a sprawling, largely rural area encompassing western Wisconsin, the Upper Peninsula of Michigan, Minnesota, North and South Dakota, and Montana. At that time the largest minority in the Ninth District were Native Americans and I was greatly intrigued by the prospect of learning about and working with the tribes of the District.

Along with her colleagues at federal reserve banks in San Francisco and Kansas City, my new boss Kathy Erickson, whom I had first met at the Fed meeting in Washington in 1993, had begun an initiative to better understand the impediments to lending in Indian Country. One of the things Kathy wanted me to do was to expand that initiative. I could not ignore the issues in the other minority communities in the Ninth District, but the primary focus of my job was Indian Country and that suited me just fine. At the same time, I was asked to write the occasional article for the Minneapolis Reserve Bank's research-oriented magazine and meet with member banks to see what they needed in order to better satisfy their obligations under the Community Reinvestment Act (CRA). I'd also be doing some speechwriting for Gary Stern, the president of the Minneapolis Federal Reserve Bank, if the topic was related to CRA, Indian Country, or something else of which I had special knowledge.

I was not overwhelmed, but it was a challenge to juggle these things while also learning how to behave in a federal bureaucracy. The prestige of this new job was impressive. At City Light, it was a constant struggle to get people simply to return my phone calls. Of course, back then most of the calls involved me asking for money, so I can't really blame people for being reluctant to talk to me. But getting a return call in my new job as manager of community affairs at the Federal Reserve Bank of Minneapolis was ridiculously easy. Alan Greenspan had imbued the Fed with a reputation and an aura of power and competence. That aura trickled down even to a new guy at a regional Reserve Bank. It was amazing to see how often bank presidents either picked up the call right away or would call me back within minutes. If I wanted a meeting, that meeting was agreed to right away. If I needed information about a bank's CRA performance or their goals to meet their CRA obligations, I got that information in no time. I felt very important.

Community Affairs was a small division within the Banking Supervision Department. Banking supervision was the heart of the regulatory function of the Federal Reserve System, with bank examiners who would physically go to every bank holding company and Federal Reserve System member bank and 'examine' the banks' records and operations, very much like an audit. There are other banking regulators in addition to the Federal Reserve, including the Office of the Comptroller of the Currency, known as the OCC, and at that time the Office of Thrift Supervision (OTS), which has now merged with the OCC, as well as the Federal Deposit Insurance Corporation (FDIC), the agency of the government that insures everyone who has a checking or savings account, saving them from the risks of a bank default.

The primary purpose of the bank examinations is to make sure that the banks are operated in a safe and sound manner, that they have sufficient capital to withstand losses, and that they are not engaged in either outright fraud or just doing stupid things. These same regulators, the Federal Reserve Banks, the OCC, and the FDIC, also examine banks for their performance under the Community Reinvestment Act. This is where I came in. Banks have a variety of ways to satisfy the requirements under CRA and oddly enough, there was a significant level of both confusion and conflict between the examiners who look strictly at safety and soundness of a bank's operations and the examiners who wanted to see that the banks they were supervising were adhering to both the letter and the spirit of the Community Reinvestment Act. Safety and soundness examiners sometimes looked askance at a bank's decision to lend to what might appear to be a shaky non-profit, one like City Light, for example. At the same time, the CRA examiners would likely encourage just such lending. This sort of tension within the ranks of the various bank regulators was not intentional, but it resulted in a better overall process.

Over the next few years, I refined the strategies I learned on the job to overcome the roadblocks the tribes faced. But first I had a lot to learn about the Federal Reserve Bank, and a lot more to learn about Indian Country.

A SIV is Not a Shiv, or is it?

The early to late 90s was a period of sustained economic growth and Alan Greenspan, the chairman of the Federal Reserve Board of Governors, was considered a demi-god by far too many people. He kept interest rates low over the period, which many economists credit with ushering in the housing bubble that brought the economy to its knees in 2008. Chairman Greenspan believed that banks could self-regulate their own actions generally, and he did little to strengthen the regulatory functions of the Federal Reserve Banks.[43] That attitude crossed over to the other regulators as well. This was also a period in which the largest banks and bank holding companies were creating and trading exotic financial instruments called derivatives. They were eager to be involved in collateralized debt obligations (CDOs), credit default swaps (CDSs), and simple interest rate swaps.

Derivatives derive their value entirely from the value of some underlying asset, which sounds simple enough. But they were morphing into ever more complex and opaque vehicles and, unfortunately, some of these new trading vehicles were barely understood by the examiners at the regulatory agencies, the Federal Reserve Banks included. As would come into play in a far more important way later, the banks that traded in these exotic financial instruments, and Alan Greenspan's ability to assess their risks, were endowed with particularly dangerous illusions of validity.

Alan Greenspan's cavalier attitude toward bank behavior, as compared to most of his predecessors, was suffused with an irrational confidence in his ability to discern risks and avert catastrophe. Daniel Kahneman believes that the illusion of skill is not just exhibited by individuals, but is entrenched in the culture of most industries, whether financial, industrial, manufacturing, education, or others. Evidence suggesting that their success is far more a matter of luck than skill is threatening and is essentially disregarded.[44] As a result, we have periodic upheavals in industries built upon an assumption of impregnability. The banking system was and remains full of people who are convinced of their own special skills and special abilities to avoid calamities like the Savings and Loan crisis of the late 80s and, of course, the Great Recession of 2008-09.

As a case in point, at our weekly top managers' meetings at the Minneapolis Reserve Bank we would discuss how much exposure certain large banks, such as Norwest Bank, which was later absorbed by Wells Fargo, had to derivatives and other bizarre financial instruments. The question was if trouble arose unexpectedly could this exposure represent an unwarranted risk to the overall banking system? Or could it be confined to just a single bank or holding company? With a high degree of confidence, the Federal Reserve Board determined that these derivatives and CDOs posed no special risk to the system. But as Kahneman states, "Subjective confidence in a judgment is not a reasoned evaluation of the probability that this judgment is correct. Confidence is a feeling, which reflects the coherence of the information and the cognitive ease of processing it. It is wise to take admissions of uncertainty seriously, but declarations of high confidence mainly tell you that an individual has constructed a coherent story in his mind, not necessarily that the story is true."[45] The near economic collapse in 2008 might have been averted if the Board of Governors had employed a bit more scrutiny and skepticism than they were practicing back in the mid-90s.

I vividly remember one meeting, early in my tenure at the Fed. We were discussing an especially colorful form of derivative that seemed to me to be unnecessarily complex and indecipherable. I readily admitted my uncertainty and made the comment that even after hearing the explanation of how these Structured Investment Vehicles (SIVs) worked, if someone put a gun to my head I could still not adequately explain how they functioned. Everyone laughed and looked at me like *You poor dumb bastard. How can you not get this?* Then I made the mistake of saying to the group, "I bet not more than two or three of you in this room have any better grasp of this than I do." That went over rather poorly. Yet not one of them volunteered an attempt to set me straight. It was awkward as hell, and I felt like the little boy who pointed out the emperor had no clothes. I spoke the truth, I suspect they had no better understanding of SIVs that I did, but they could not bring themselves to admit it. Every federal reserve bank I would work with in those days from Minneapolis to Kansas City to Richmond could have been equally naked, and these were the same folks overseeing the safety and soundness of our nation's banks. To be fair, Fed chairman Alan Greenspan was soon to expound on the "irrational exuberance" driving the stock market (he first used the expression in 1996) and the same could be said of derivatives, interest rate swaps and the like. The Federal Reserve banks were not immune to this exuberance.

As it turns out, many of these off-balance sheet financial instruments—the SIVs—were about to sink, leaving few lifeboats for the innocent. Shortly after my unwelcome challenge to the other managers at the Minneapolis Fed in 1994, unanticipated interest rate increases nationwide led to major losses for banks and corporations holding interest rate and currency derivatives.[46] But no alarm bells were set off. These losses could be explained away as poor timing and bad luck; they certainly did not represent any sort of systemic risk, or so the thinking went at the Reserve Bank in Minneapolis, as well as at the Board of Governors of the Federal Reserve System back in Washington. Frankly, even though a SIV in banking parlance should not be confused with a shiv in prison parlance, there is nonetheless a striking similarity. Both a SIV and a shiv can be a painful, even deadly weapon. One is stuck in the ribs or run raggedly across your throat, while the other is just as deadly, administered by someone who is better dressed but every bit as pitiless as a prison thug. A SIV can be in many respects a hidden shiv to the nation's ribs as we all found out in 2008, one that stuck especially deep into Indian Country.

Character Loans and Checkerboards

Early on at the Reserve Bank, Kathy Erickson introduced me to Jim West, an enrolled member of the Cheyenne and Arapahoe tribes. He was a former banker who then had his own financial services and consulting business. Jim was a handsome and elegant man, with prominent cheekbones and long black braided hair making him unmistakably Native American. He was soft-spoken, charming and endlessly patient. He had the habit of turning his entire torso toward whomever he was speaking with, giving the distinct impression that what you were saying was ever so important to him and that you had his entire attention. Jim was one of the most physically and intellectually impressive men I had ever met. He came from what could be cast an elite Indian family. His father, Richard, Sr., was a highly-regarded artist with works in the National Gallery of Art and the Denver Museum of Art. The patriarch's namesake and Jim's brother, Richard, Jr., a Stanford-trained lawyer, was the first director of the National Museum of the American Indian and is currently the director of the Autry National Center in Los Angeles. Jim is no less accomplished if perhaps less well known.

With the reputation of the Federal Reserve Bank bolstering us, we began a series of training meetings in strategic locations throughout the Ninth District designed to help tribes, tribal people, and bankers learn how to do business together. Along with Jim, Mark Jarboe, a lawyer from the largest Minneapolis law firm, Dorsey & Whitney, also joined the training meetings. Mark was a tall, barrel-chested, red-haired and physically rather imposing man, but essentially a very gentle man, an expert in Indian Country law. A Harvard Law School graduate who had done some of the groundbreaking legal work on Indian gaming and casinos, he also understood the intricacies of banking law and the steps that needed to be taken to accommodate the conflicts that sometimes arose between standard banking procedures, tribal sovereignty, and tribal legal procedures.

I had little to do in these training sessions other than to introduce Jim and Mark to the bankers and tribal leaders who came to learn about why banks should be able to do far more business than they currently were doing with tribes and reservations. Through these meetings I learned nearly everything I needed to know about not only the legal differences between tribes and states—they are not analogous—and the cultural imperatives that led to so many unnecessary impediments to economic growth and prosperity on reservations.

At the meetings Jim West often used an anecdote to illustrate the way people can talk past each other without ever really connecting, regardless of their best intentions. In his story, a young Indian man goes to the bank for a loan. He has sufficient collateral, a good credit history, and is gainfully employed. By all measures, he should have been a candidate for what bankers call a "character" loan, if not a fully collateralized loan. It was to be a relatively small loan and well within his financial ability to pay back. True to the culture of his tribe, this young man was respectful and deferential to older men, especially men of higher social status. So he kept his eyes lowered during the meeting with the banker who had much higher perceived social status, and was also much older than the young Native American. So deferential was his manner that the young man avoided a firm and hardy handshake that might come off as too aggressive. Instead, his was a modest, respectful, barely discernable squeeze to the banker's grasping hand.

The banker on the other hand interpreted the young man's lack of eye contact and his "feeble" handshake as a lack of backbone and personal integrity. Therefore, the banker recommended against giving this well-qualified candidate a loan.

That story was one of many in which misunderstandings of Indian culture resulted in the potential borrower and the potential lender both losing. Of course, the borrower bore the brunt of the damage while the lender, a bank with more financial resources, could recover quite nicely, thank you very much. I am convinced that these types of misunderstandings contribute to the huge economic disparity between the non-Indian community and the Indian. Jim was trying to change banking practices by sharing a tale of a young Indian man, but I could see in the eyes of too many bankers that the overarching narrative they had heard before, that Indians could not be trusted, was the controlling narrative.

Former Speaker of the House of Representatives Tip O'Neil is reported to have believed that "All politics is local." Joe Biden put a finer point on it when he said "All politics is *personal*."[47] My corollary is that "All *business* is personal." Building personal relationships is crucial in moving public policy along, in creating coalitions of like-minded people with whom you have developed a level of trust and, in some cases, lasting friendships. This is just as crucial in building strong business relationships. Yet, trust and friendship in business are often as ephemeral as the seeds of a thistledown. Too often, people who don't walk in the same circles or are unwilling to cross literal or perceived distances, stay in their comfort zones by tacitly or overtly promulgating the dark rumors, stories, and jokes that put even more distance between them and the "others."

We're Not Playing Pinochle Here

I was soon to learn that another impediment to lending in Indian Country and, I believe, a significant cause of persistent poverty on Indian reservations, is the status of land. Nearly every reservation in the country is "checkerboarded." Within the boundaries of the reservation, some of the land is owned by non-Indians and some of the land is owned by the tribe, and some is owned by individual

Indians. When viewed on a map, ownership can resemble a checkerboard, with the non-Indian parcels colored white and the Indian parcels colored black or red. Much, indeed most, of Indian land is held in trust by the federal government for the tribes or individual Indians who own it. This so-called "Trust" land cannot be sold without the express written permission of the Secretary of the Interior, and that permission is almost never asked for and even less often granted.

By law, trust land cannot be taxed by the county or the state and that has led to considerable hostility between the states and tribal nations. The other, and undoubtedly the most painful aspect of the trust status of land, is that it cannot have a lien placed against it, cannot be alienated, without, again, the express written permission of the Secretary of the Interior, which, of course is not given. That means that the tribe or the individual Indian that owns land cannot use that land as collateral for a loan. That is a very big problem.

Trust land cannot be sold or mortgaged. That means that if an Indian has a nice parcel of ground and wants to build a house on it he must have enough cash to build that house outright because lenders are exceedingly reluctant to lend money for a house that sits on land that cannot be foreclosed upon and then resold in the event of a default on the loan. The prohibition on foreclosing on trust land and reselling it to recoup a loss extends beyond home mortgages. It means that if a tribe has trust land and wants to build a warehouse, an office building, or even wants to use the land as collateral for a loan to buy agricultural equipment like tractors and combines, it cannot do so. It must have enough cash to do it without using the land as collateral. That means the tribe or individual Indian must borrow using something else as collateral.

In contrast, non-trust land has what is known as fee simple title. Fee simple land, perhaps right next door to tribal or Indian-owned trust land, can indeed be used as collateral for a loan, and can be used to help a farmer buy equipment or seed, to allow a rancher to buy cattle, or to enable a homeowner to leverage a loan for a house. It can be used to start a business or to send kids to college or for any reason at all. Not so for tribes or individual Indians.

There are now a smattering of special loan programs like the HUD Section 184 loan guarantee program that provides a mechanism for banks to lend to Indian homeowners to buy or build a house on trust land. Yet the land remains off limits and cannot be sold or mortgaged.[48] So even if a tribe or an individual Indian could get a mortgage on the house itself, and presumably that land and its inherent value could be included in the mix, it rarely works out that way. We have seen even long-term Bureau of Indian Affairs (BIA) realty specialists refuse to value underlying trust land with anything close to its inherent value, the value it would have were it not constricted by trust status.

The net result is that every tribe and every individual Indian who has a piece of trust land has a big portion of its bank account frozen forever. Or a very significant share of their net worth is stricken from their balance sheet and a big fat zero is inserted instead. Because of the trust status of land, there are no Indian realtors actively buying and selling houses on Indian reservations. Even though it is theoretically possible to borrow against the value of the house alone, without the lender having a security interest in the underlying land, it is not routinely done, with the exception of chattel loans for manufactured homes (too often single-wide or double-wide trailer homes.) I suspect that if the authors of the report, *The Asset Value of Whiteness* (see Chapter 5) published by the Institute on Assets and Social Policy at Brandeis, had included Native Americans in their study, as they did African American and Latino households, they would have been astounded by the lack of wealth creation in Indian Country. Indeed, inasmuch as equity in a home is the source of over 80% of all family wealth nationally, the absence of this vital source of capital for Indians is staggering. The result is that Indian homeowners, owners of houses and sometimes trailers on reservations, share only in the ephemeral satisfaction of owning their home, leaving the capital accumulation for others.

Chapter 7

Have I Got a Deal for You

IF YOU THINK about Indians or know a little bit about current life on reservations, you probably have a vague notion that Indian reservations were at one time much bigger than they are now. You might have an ill-defined sense that some skullduggery perpetrated on Indians long ago moved tribes and tribal people onto lesser lands. Let me fill in the picture.

Henry L. Dawes, US senator from Massachusetts, was the primary author of the General Allotment Act of 1887. This act reapportioned the tribal lands that had already been greatly diminished, divvying up what was left into small parcels so that Indians could become something they were not: farmers. Dawes believed that it would be in the best interests of Native Americans if they all became farmers so they could be assimilated into the great American culture and no longer be savages, or so his thinking went. But the Dawes Act, as it became known, did more than just allot Indian lands to tribes and individual Indians so that they could grow crops and livestock, it also resulted in over 100 million acres of Indian land being taken from tribes and Indians, sometimes through fraud and thievery.[49]

It's important to remember that by 1887, Indian lands had already been drastically reduced through dozens of treaties between the US and the various Indian nations. Under the terms of these treaties, tribes had been promised this remaining land while the US government, in return for many more millions of acres being ceded by the tribes to the government, would provide health, education, and housing for tribes and Indians so long as "the grass grows and the water runs".[50]

These treaties, most still in force, have simply been ignored by the US government when it has been convenient to ignore them, which is pretty much all the time. So basically, the Dawes Act reapportioned to individual Indians small parcels of what was previously their own land (160 acres for the head of the household, 80 acres for adults that were not head of a household, and 40 acres for children under 18) that in far too many cases were insufficient for farming and ranching. Much of the land was in the Great Plains and many hundreds of acres would be needed to make ranching economically viable and farming was mostly out of the question due to soil conditions, weather, and just plain common sense. But common sense was in short supply when the US Congress was dealing with Indian Country. Under the Dawes Act, the land that the tribes thought they were keeping from the grubby paws of the federal government was declared surplus and offered for sale, at fire sale prices, to non-Indians. That is why so much of the very best land on many reservations, bottom land near rivers and creeks, land with arable soil, land that is good for farming and ranching, is today owned by white men and women rather than the previous rightful owners, the tribes themselves.

The nefarious "reallocation" of tribal lands did not end with the Dawes Act at the end of the 19th century. Despite the pleas of tribal officials and even white landowners, in 1948 the US Congress approved a plan from the Army Corps of Engineers to build a dam on the "prime river bottomland"[51] of the Mandan, Hidatsa, and Arikara, the Three Affiliated Tribes of the Ft. Berthold Reservation in North Dakota. The tribes were compensated, it worked out to about $33 per acre, and 153,000 acres of the very best land on the reservation was flooded. In a photograph commemorating the signing of the contract for the transfer of the land, George Gillette, tribal chairman, is seen wiping tears from his face. He is quoted, "You will excuse me if I say that the members of the tribal council will sign this contract with a heavy heart. With a few scratches of the pen, we will sell the best part of our reservation. Right now, the future doesn't look too good to us."[52]

And indeed, the future did not turn out well for the tribes after the dam was built. The tribal people of the Ft. Berthold reservation had spent decades struggling to adopt agriculture as their means of livelihood and had finally become successful farmers and healthy, productive people. After the dam, after the loss of their most productive lands, diabetes, heretofore unheard of among the members of the Three Affiliated Tribes, struck the reservation with a vengeance. By 2009 13% of the tribal people had diabetes, as compared to the North Dakota average of 6.5%. The percentage rises to over 41% for tribal members over age 35. They had become dependent upon the high carbohydrate food commodities that replaced their previous self-sufficient way of life.[53] This is one legacy of the disregard for the interests of tribal people that is exemplified by the Dawes Act.

But the Dawes Act had other long-lasting unintended effects. Once a family had been apportioned its acres under the General Allotment Act, the heirs to the original family received a pro rata ownership in that allotted land. It could not be apportioned to a favored son or daughter via a last will and testament and it could not be sold outright, and as a result, over generations the land has become what is known as "fractionated." It means that individual trust land once owned by a single Indian family or even a single Indian person, is now, in some cases owned in undivided common ownership by hundreds of descendants of the original owner. And these hundreds of fractional owners cannot do anything with the land unless they can get agreement amongst all or nearly all of the owners, a very high bar indeed.

In most cases the federal government manages those lands on behalf of all of the heirs. The U.S. Department of the Interior has grossly mishandled this responsibility, which includes any mineral rights as well as the grazing fees that might have been earned, for years and years. And none of this is what tribal nations wanted or ever asked for. It was imposed on them by the US Congress and has been diminishing the economic vitality of Indian people and tribal nations since at least 1887. Is it any wonder that Indian reservations are some of the poorest places in the US?

Elouise Cobell, a member of the Blackfeet Tribe in Montana, filed a lawsuit in 1996 after learning of the gross mismanagement of the billions in dollars of grazing fees, oil and gas royalties, and other income that should have been coming to the owners, the tribes and individual Indians, but instead was lost or otherwise utterly unaccounted for. The lawsuit languished for years and was mired in legal maneuvering but finally, in 2009, the Obama administration settled the suit and the US Congress agreed to create a fund to compensate, at least in part, the thousands of Indians who had been shortchanged for decades.

There is hope that at least some of the fractionated land can be re-structured and thus can become a more utilitarian resource for the tribes and Indian people. As a result of the settlement of the class action lawsuit, the US government set aside $3.4 billion to partially satisfy the claims of over 500,000 Indians whose interests in fractionated land were mismanaged for decades by the US Department of the Interior. The settlement also requires the US government to spend not less than $1.9 billion to buy back fractionated land interests and allow the tribes to once again own and control some of the land that they lost.

In 2016, the Blackfeet Tribe in northwest Montana saw $270 million from the settlement go to some 7,000 owners of fractionated land on the Blackfeet Reservation. After the owners receive their payment and relinquish their interests in the land, the land will be returned to the Tribe. The Blackfeet reservation is not unique; it has over 6,700 fractionated tracts held by over 8,100 individuals, covering over 812,000 acres.[54]

The Cobell lawsuit settlement was a rare triumph for Indian Country, yet it represents just a fraction of the money lost over the years. It amounts to less than $5,000 per Indian and is a pittance considering that by some estimates the Indians on average had been shortchanged by 10, 20, or even 100 times that amount.

Good Trades and Thirsty Horses

The US Government's theft and mismanagement of tribal lands and assets caused structural disparities and legal incongruities that have resulted in persistent poverty in Indian Country. Cultural factors also mitigate against the ability of capitalist enterprises to defeat poverty.

To illustrate, I was asked by the Reserve Bank to write an article for its magazine, *The Region*, that goes out to all the member banks and bank holding companies throughout the Ninth Federal Reserve District.[55] In this article I repeated a story I heard from Jim West. Jim related how "Joe," a young tribal member, had saved his money diligently and successfully arranged a small business loan from the Bureau of Indian Affairs (BIA) to open a small convenience store on his Reservation. Using his savings and the small loan, he built a store that sold gasoline, cigarettes, and groceries, primarily to Indians who lived on the reservation, but also to anyone who came into the store, Indian or non-Indian. But his business was failing. Joe could not seem to make a profit and was falling behind on his loan payments to the BIA. The store had a good location on a relatively busy street on the reservation. Neither the BIA nor some of the special consultants the BIA engaged to look at the store could figure out why this seemingly well-located and well-managed store could not make enough profit to stay afloat. Joe worked at the store almost every hour the store was open, sold out its inventory of small grocery items regularly and was doing enough volume in business that it should have been profitable. It was finally revealed, after several intense interviews with the owner, that he was a victim of his own culture.

It seemed that when a non-Indian came into the store, Joe sold that customer whatever the customer wanted, be it milk, soft drinks, cigarettes, gasoline, or any other of the hundreds of items on the store's shelves, at the price marked on the item, as you would expect. That price was intended to provide a reasonable profit margin. Joe also followed this reasonable business practice when a fellow Indian he did not know came into the store. The price paid was the price marked on the item. But when a fellow Native American came into the store whom Joe knew, there would very often be a different price for whatever the customer wanted, depending on the circumstances of that person's life at the time. If an elder came into the store, the price for the item became the price Joe had paid for the milk, or cigarettes, or whatever it was that the elder wanted. No mark-up, no profit, nothing even to recover the costs for keeping the milk cold.

Sometimes, if Joe knew that the customer was in dire financial condition with young children at home who were hungry and cold, he would sell the item at a price below what even he had paid.

What governed these disparate decisions was the long-inculcated concept of a "good trade."

In the culture of the Plains Indians, a good trade did not include the concept of a profit. A good trade was a trade in which I had something you wanted and you had something of *equal value* that I wanted, so we would trade each other for those things. There was no provision for profit in a culturally appropriate transaction. And it was impossible for this young entrepreneur to charge someone even the price he had paid for something if he knew that person needed the item and could only pay a lower price. He simply could not bring himself to charge some of his customers a price that gave him his margin for profit and overhead, even at the cost of staying in business. This would probably have worked out if most of his customers were tourists or visitors he did not know, but that was not the case.

Jim West told this story at the training sessions we were conducting throughout the Ninth Federal Reserve District, and it elicited a starkly different reaction from the bankers in the audience than it did from the Native Americans in the audience. The bankers were mystified. The Native Americans nodded in understanding. It is not a particularly widespread practice among Indian entrepreneurs, but it illustrated that there were cultural differences and a different outlook on life that the bankers needed to hear and understand. Likewise, the Native Americans in the audience needed to understand that what they viewed as cultural imperatives could very well be viewed by non-Indians as quaint, naïve, and foolhardy.

These training sessions made some progress, but also elicited some strange and inexplicable responses from some people who attended. In one of the more bizarre episodes a Montana banker insisted that his small bank had had very bad experiences lending to Indians. He told the story of a young Indian successfully awarded a car loan only to drive the new car onto the reservation and set it afire. The banker said that because of the tribe's insistence on exercising its sovereignty and immunity from lawsuits and the bank's resulting inability to retrieve the charred remains of the car, the bank had decided it could not do business with Indians.

I remember Jim West patiently asking the banker why the Indian borrower would have gone to the trouble of getting a car loan, which no doubt necessitated at least some cash as a down payment, and then unaccountably torch this new car? It made no sense. The banker suggested it was out of spite and agreed that it was inexplicable, hence his bank's seemingly reasonable decision not to do business with tribes or Indian people. And this was not the only time I heard this, or a strikingly similar, story. As Robert Shiller describes in his paper on *Narrative Economics*, this story was contagious and there is no telling how many bankers had heard it, taken it to heart, and decided not to do business in Indian Country.

At its heart, this story is a way to illustrate something the bankers simply did not understand. This story and others like it are intended, consciously or unconsciously, to justify the decision to avoid doing business with tribes and tribal people. What it really does is illustrate the power of narratives. The fact is, tribes, like federal and state governments, are indeed immune from civil lawsuits—unless they consent, in advance, to be in such jeopardy. This is what is known as *sovereign immunity*. It is grossly misunderstood by too many people, including too many bankers. They believe that their knowledge of Indian law is sufficient. It gives them just enough information to justify staying out of what could be and should be a good lending market.

They assume, wrongly, that a bank cannot enter into an agreement to lend money to a tribe or tribal person and then, if necessary, sue them if they fail to make payments on the loan. That is nonsense. Tribes can and do waive their immunity from lawsuit in order to borrow or engage in partnerships. The terms have to be explicit and entered into freely, but a waiver of sovereign immunity gives the parties to a contract or loan agreement or any other transaction the right to seek damages from the tribe. It is not a big deal.

Individual Indians have no such immunity from lawsuits. But rather than spend the little bit of time it would take to learn about the rights of tribes and tribal people, too many bankers and other businesses assume they already know enough from the stories they have heard to conclude that it is just too risky to do business with tribes or Indian people.

Another of these tall tales we heard from a banker left me nearly dumbfounded. At that same training session, the president of a small bank in South Dakota was particularly resistant to our message. We were making the case that an increase in lending in Indian Country would lead to an overall increase in business. This could be facilitated by simply reaching out to tribal people with an open mind and willingness to learn more about the legal and cultural differences between the Indian and non-Indian worlds, hence the rationale for the training session they were all attending. He was having none of it and was insistent that there was no bridging the gap between Indian Country and mainstream business practices. He then told this story:

> I know this Indian fellow who was given a new HUD house. Brand new mind you. First thing he did was to take a chainsaw and cut a hole in the outside wall of his brand spanking new house so that his horse could drink from the bath tub.

This banker went to great pains to assure us that he liked Indian people and certainly was not racist, not by any means, "No-sir-ee." But his "Old Man and the Saw" tale was the gospel truth and it had to be told. The reservation in question was the Pine Ridge Reservation in South Dakota. There is, of course, no evidence that anyone on any reservation has ever received a new house, or any house for that matter, new or old, from the Federal Department of Housing and Urban Development (HUD) and then promptly cut a hole in the bathroom wall to facilitate the stress-free hydration of his equine companion. (Horses, as prey animals, are loathe to stick their heads inside a hole in a building, leaving them vulnerable to predators.) But it was clear that the banker wanted to believe it and he told it with such enthusiasm that there is no doubt that he had told it many times before and likely would again.

There were a few eyes rolling among the other bankers in the crowd, and universal disbelief from the Indians in the audience, but he was not deterred in his belief that it simply was not possible to have a profitable line of business with tribal people because you could not trust them to manage their most important assets. I got into trouble with my boss back at the Reserve Bank because this same banker wrote me a letter some days after the training session volunteering his bank as the co-sponsor for the next planned training session to be held in Chamberlain, South Dakota, along with the Minneapolis Federal Reserve Bank. I promptly wrote him back and told him that while we appreciated the offer, the Reserve Bank could not in good conscience have a co-sponsor of our "Lending in Indian Country" training sessions with a bank that had expressed an unwillingness to see Indian Country as a viable business opportunity. Furthermore, his hostility to the very idea was well known and by having this bank as a co-sponsor we would be sending a decidedly mixed message to the other banks and Indian people we hoped to attract to the training sessions. It seemed that I had punched a bit above my weight class. That letter should have come from someone above me in the hierarchy at the Minneapolis Fed. I was reprimanded, but not too sternly.

Ironically, both while I worked at the Reserve Bank and later with my work independently of the Fed, I heard this same story six more times about an Indian cutting a hole in their house so that a horse could drink from the bathtub. The second time I heard the story, while on a plane from Minneapolis to San Francisco, the reservation in question was, of all places, the Red Lake Reservation in Minnesota, home of the Red Lake Band of Ojibway. This tribe is not known as an especially avid equestrian society. What disturbed me the first time I heard this story was not that someone would be so foolish as to cut through the bathroom wall of a nice new house. What disturbed me was that people *want* to believe such recklessness and are eager to repeat it. It is heartbreaking the way people will go to such lengths to diminish communities and societies they really do not know and do not understand. It is one of those urban myths, in a rural setting, that people hear once and it fulfills a need to justify the disparities in life on and off Indian reservations. And they love to tell the story so much that after they hear it for the first time, thereafter it becomes their story.

In his paper, Robert Shiller says that "The narratives have the ability to produce *social norms* that partially govern our activities, including our economic actions."[56] The bankers who tell such stories recite these tales and make no loans, or fewer loans, to Indians while the merchants and travelers who hear and tell these stories are less inclined to grant credit or patronize what few businesses there are on reservations. The stories, the narratives we tell, corrupt the perception we have of Native Americans and drive away economic activity, hardening the conditions and lessening the opportunities of people already struggling with remote locations, poor infrastructure, and other disparities.

Shiller believes that "Popular narratives may have a spirit of 'us versus them,' a Manichean tone of revealed evil described of others in the story. Jokes are quite often at somebody else's expense—members of some other group." He goes on to state that "We need to understand the narrative basis for macroeconomic fluctuations, and to think about how narrative economics ought to be more informing of policy actions now and in the future."[57] Banks make fewer loans, something we were trying to combat at the Minneapolis Federal Reserve Bank, and businesses suffer as a result. Businesses fail, supporting the self-fulfilling prophecy of the story-tellers who lamely lament the scarcity of thriving businesses on reservations.

Richard Thaler and Cass Sunstein write in *Nudge: Improving Decisions About Health, Wealth, and Happiness* that "Biased assessments of risk can perversely influence how we prepare for and respond to crises, *business choices* (emphasis mine), and the political process."[58] If you hear time and again stories about how Indian borrowers default on their consumer loans (and maybe even burn the collateral or cut a hole in it), you will be much less likely to do business with an Indian. This is especially true if you are a banker or investor. And the stories you hear might be vague and ambiguous. You might only remember hearing something about the mysterious "sovereign immunity" and that is enough to confirm your bias that Indian Country is too complicated to mess with.

Bangladesh and Grocery Stores

The Federal Reserve Bank gave me the greenlight to increase my community affairs staff. I was committed to adding a Native American to help us better understand Indian Country and to help me effectively advocate for tribes and tribal people. At our next "Lending in Indian Country" training session with Jim West and Mark Jarboe in Chamberlain, South Dakota, I met yet another elegant and soft-spoken Native American, Gerald Sherman, brother of Richard

Sherman, the parks and recreation director for Pine Ridge. Gerald was a branch manager for a bank serving the Lower Brule Sioux Tribe (one of only a handful of banks doing so nationally). Previously, he had been the founder and first executive director of the Lakota Fund. The Lakota Fund was and remains one of the most influential non-profit micro-lending organizations in the country. Gerald had been the recipient of a Ford Foundation grant that funded his trip to Bangladesh to meet Muhammad Yunus, the founder of the Grameen Bank. Gerald took what he learned from him and came back to the Pine Ridge Indian Reservation and began his own version of micro-lending to very poor members of the tribe in Pine Ridge.

The Grameen Bank is the largest and most successful lender to the very poor, almost always women, who borrow as little as a few dollars to buy fabric to sew and resell or make baskets for sale. The bank instituted a lender and borrower relationship known as solidarity lending or peer lending. Under the bank's process, a group of very poor borrowers, generally five or six women, would form a sort of collective in which each member of the group would assist the others. While they did not guarantee the loans of the other members of the group, there was considerable peer pressure to make payments on time and in full. Under the rules, if a group member borrower fell behind on her payments the other members of the group could not borrow. That natural peer pressure helped increase the loan payment record of the bank and ultimately led to over $7 billion in tiny loans being made to people who had been utterly destitute before coming to the bank.

The peer lending success was and is astounding and the Grameen Bank and Muhammad Yunus were jointly awarded the Nobel Peace Prize in 2006 in recognition of the work they had done not just in Bangladesh, but also through inspiring other groups. The Lakota Fund copied their methods and lent to people who sit on the lowest rungs on the economic ladder. After hearing what Gerald had accomplished at the Lakota Fund and how much he still wanted to accomplish in Indian Country, I persuaded him to come to the Fed. Gerald had such an illustrious background that frankly, he should have had my job and I should have been working for him.

Gerald became my third employee and helped me to hire the rest of the staff. In reviewing some of the dozens of resumes we received for the open positions, I noticed an oddity found in virtually all of the resumes we received from Indian people seeking one of our jobs. In addition to a listing of skills and experience and education as you find in any resume, the Indian applicants would invariably have a short notice, "Sober 5 years," or "Sober 18 months," or something along those lines. I mentioned to Gerald that this seemed highly unusual and he explained that without such information highlighted in the resume, the default assumption, at least by other Indians, was that the applicant was still drinking. This was one more example of the differences between Indian Country and the non-Indian world, that indicated both the tragic circumstances of so many people, but also displayed a ready willingness and courage to confront that sad reality.

With the new job, Gerald had to relocate to Minneapolis and uproot his family from their rural life. That proved to be far more of a challenge than we anticipated. Gerald and I would have long talks about the root causes and possible solutions to gut-wrenching poverty in Indian Country. Gerald had been born and raised on the Pine Ridge Indian Reservation and knew firsthand what living in extreme poverty does to families and individuals. A Vietnam veteran, Gerald had himself struggled early in his life and had an enormous empathy for people with alcohol and substance abuse problems and who barely got by day to day. He is a big man, with enormous hands that belie his gentle nature. He was not brooding or morose, but behind his dark eyes you could see that he had borne more pain himself and had seen more pain than most men could withstand.

At each of the meetings we held Gerald would start out speaking Lakota and then seamlessly switch to English. It was a dramatic and touching illustration of the differentness of Indian Country. It is a testament to his character that he became a practical and resourceful leader at the Lakota Fund and had an enduring need to do more to help Indian people. I was fortunate to have him work with us at the Reserve Bank. We immediately set upon a plan to target specific reservations in the Ninth Federal Reserve District and to do something with national implications.

Jim West and Mark Jarboe were teaching me about the impediments to lending and investing in Indian Country. From Gerald Sherman, I was learning about life on Indian reservations. It was time to come up with a strategic plan for the Fed's Indian Country Initiative that might prove replicable to other reservations and might have far-reaching implications. The question now became, *could we get the Reserve Bank to step out of its pinnacle-sitting perch and do something that would be a bit uncomfortable and maybe even a bit risky?* I leaned heavily on Gerald and Liz Wahlstrand, my young assistant who had also endured the Trip from Hell.

In the meantime, we formalized our relationship with Jim West and Mark Jarboe and created a video series to be called, aptly enough, "Lending in Indian Country." Over the next 12 to 16 months, we began videotaping each of the training sessions and editing the resulting mix of Jim and Mark teaching their course and interacting with the audience. The participants sometimes offered the best learning opportunities simply by asking the questions that we had not considered, and sometimes by offering heartfelt anecdotes about the times lenders and borrowers have failed as well as succeeded in Indian Country. The result was a six-hour video series that was geared to both bankers and investors, but also to tribal people who were eager to see more capital in Indian Country. In large measure, the video series was a collection of stories; a new narrative for Indian Country that we hoped would encourage bankers and lenders and investors to do more business on reservations.

The "Lending in Indian Country" series was a step in the right direction, but we wanted to do something that had immediate, practical results. So, we began visiting even more reservations to see what they needed and what the Reserve Bank might be able to do. It was on our visit to Pine Ridge where we heard about the aforementioned, unlikely German buffalo hunter. Gerald arranged for his brother Richard to meet us and impart his understanding of the needs of the Pine Ridge Indian Reservation.

After Richard told us his story, we set out to meet with the tribal leaders on Pine Ridge and the other reservations on our itinerary. At every meeting the tribal leaders told us that capital formation and banking services were very important, but that their reservation was in the midst of a housing crisis. I was growing frustrated because I suspected that I personally could do something to help with the housing crisis, but we could not find a way for the Reserve Bank to do anything about housing. Instead, we began to focus on the economic development needs of the Pine Ridge Indian Reservation.

Pine Ridge was statistically the poorest reservation in the Ninth Federal Reserve District, with the highest rate of persons and families living below the poverty line, the highest rate of teen pregnancy, the highest rate of high school drop outs, the highest rate of overcrowding in housing, and most distressingly of all, the highest rate of teen suicides. And because Gerald had such extensive knowledge of the reservation it seemed like a natural choice to target Pine Ridge for our strategic plan, whatever that turned out to be.

After conducting interviews with tribal officials in Pine Ridge and meeting with Gerald's successor at the Lakota Fund in the little village of Kyle, South Dakota, it became clear that access to good quality food on the reservation was a big problem. While there was a tribally-owned grocery store, after meeting with its manager and talking to residents and the staff at the Lakota Fund, we learned that most residents of the reservation would make a grocery run all the way into Rapid City rather than buy the bulk of their groceries at the reservation store. The food at the reservation store was unimaginatively displayed, lacked the variety that you can find at the modern super markets in Rapid City or anywhere else in the country for that matter. More importantly, the fruits, vegetables, and meat were well below the standards you would find in most grocery stores off reservation. We began to focus on what the Minneapolis Federal Reserve Bank could do to increase the quality and availability of food bought for consumption at home on the reservation.

Kyle is nearly the geographic center of the reservation. Driving from Kyle to Rapid City is at least an hour and a half one-way trip, yet many residents of the Pine Ridge Indian Reservation would regularly make the drive into Rapid City to buy groceries. This added a burden onto the backs of families who already faced enormous disadvantages. We thought that if the Reserve Bank could find a way to encourage the development of a new grocery store, or expand and improve the existing grocery story, we would make a very significant difference in the lives of the families living on the reservation. Furthermore, having visited nearly every reservation in the Ninth Federal Reserve District, the need for modern grocery stores was not confined to Pine Ridge. The term was not in use back then, but many Indian reservations are vast food deserts which contributes to poor health and likely contributes to poor performance in school for kids as well. We thought that this project had the potential to be something the Reserve Bank could put on the road and make a huge difference on reservations throughout the country. We began preparing for what we knew would be a tough sell to the senior staff at the Bank, but we were optimistic that the potential was so great that they might give us some room to make it happen.

Our optimism was misplaced.

Chapter 8

Great Falls and Great Ambitions

THE MINNEAPOLIS FEDERAL Reserve Bank, like every reserve bank, has a research department that is full of PhD economists who study and prepare reports and papers on issues in some way related to banking, monetary policy, and employment. These economists keep track of economic activity, industrial and manufacturing output, agricultural output, and other anecdotal evidence of how the economy is performing in each of the twelve Reserve Districts. The Board of Governors summarizes the findings of economic activity in all twelve districts eight times a year in what has become known as the Beige Book. Its official name is the Summary of Commentary on Current Economic Conditions by Federal Reserve District. It is called the Beige Book simply because its cover is always beige. I sought out and started lobbying the folks that prepared the Fed's Beige Book about our ideas to do something about food on Indian reservations. I got a surprisingly good reception, which gave us a false hope.

We thought that the first thing we should do is prepare a thorough market analysis, much like I used to do when I worked at the Rouse Company, to see what the demand looked like for the category known as "Food at Home," when, as the name implies, consumers buy food at grocery stores, take it home, and prepare meals for themselves. The Consumer Expenditure Survey, prepared by the Bureau of Labor Statistics, gives us very accurate information every year differentiated on a regional basis. Because people in New York City will behave differently than folks in Montgomery, Alabama, it is important to make distinctions between consumer behavior in the northeast as opposed to what people in the southwest or in other parts of the country are more likely to buy.

A few of the economists at the Minneapolis Reserve Bank were mildly enthusiastic about assisting us with the analysis of demand for a grocery store on the Pine Ridge Indian Reservation. Once I had their early support, even if somewhat tepid, I drafted a long and detailed memo to the senior staff that included as much detail as I could muster, having not yet done any of the research. This memo discussed how the Federal Reserve Bank could use its considerable reputation to give credibility to the research. We hoped that if the analysis demonstrated that demand was larger than the local sales at the grocery store in Pine Ridge would suggest, if it showed an "outflow" of grocery dollars from the reservation, that that credibility could lead to the creation of a new or expanded grocery store to serve the families on Pine Ridge.

I also included a section of my memo outlining how we might be helpful in structuring the new grocery store, suggesting ways to finance the new or expanded store that would involve local banks and perhaps some government guarantees to smooth the way. I was asked to send a copy of the memo to Sandy Braunstein at the Board of Governors in Washington and that is when the trouble began.

Sandy Braunstein was the longtime director of the Board of Governors' Division of Consumer and Community Affairs. She is a formidable woman. She lived the talk, had strong opinions, and had an encyclopedic knowledge of CRA and the Federal Reserve System. The community affairs officers of each of the Reserve Banks had frequent meetings with Sandy and her staff in Washington. I vividly remember my first meeting in Washington after my appointment to the Minneapolis Reserve Bank. A dinner had been scheduled at the Board of Governors offices on Constitution Avenue and after the dinner, at a rooftop reception, Sandy blithely strode up to Chairman Greenspan and pulling me along introduced me to the wizard himself. Chairman Greenspan seemed utterly indifferent to who I was or where I was from. I distinctly remember that his handshake was cold, clammy, and weak. And he did not look me in the eye either. He had a look on his face that betrayed a complete lack of curiosity about me and what my Reserve Bank colleagues were doing. (Somehow, I doubt that Alan Greenspan would have had a hard time getting a loan from that banker in South Dakota who was so concerned about getting a firm handshake and a deep and meaningful look in the eye.)

I did not expect Alan Greenspan to remember me or care who I was, but I was chagrined to see how transparent his disinterest was and how little he tried to hide his indifference. I have always believed that true leaders, men and women who have real power and use it wisely, are often capable of warmth and genuine concern with the people who do not have great influence and are not leaders of formidable institutions or movements. Maybe I just caught Chairman Greenspan on a bad night. But I think that what I saw that night and what the country was victim to over the next decade was a man who had been deemed a genius, indeed a wizard, who had a level of influence on the national stage that was nearly unparalleled. As it turned out, he probably should have exhibited a little more humility.

Protocol called for our memo to go out to Sandy and a few days later I got a call from her. She expressed strong sympathy for our goal but said that what we proposed conflicted with the role of the Federal Reserve System and that it was not the job of the Reserve Banks to intervene in the marketplace, as well-meaning and helpful as we might want to be. She indicated that the Federal Reserve System simply could not risk the opprobrium if for some reason the grocery store failed and the Fed was held accountable. She then either called or sent a memo to my bosses in Minneapolis and the fate of our little project was sealed. I never knew how it was decided, but within days I had been told that the project was a non-starter and I should look at less interventionist ideas for our division's strategic plan. Inasmuch as we had spent nearly half a year vetting this project, without a sense that it would be squelched at the Board of Governor's level, this was a kick to the gut.

To make matters worse, Gerald Sherman was suffering in his job at the Reserve Bank. His family never settled into life in the Twin Cities and Gerald's job involved as much travel within the sprawling Ninth Reserve District as mine did, which meant a great deal of time away from home. At a meeting in Denver at the Kansas City Federal Reserve Bank's branch office, I had the occasion to witness Gerald's considerable charm and see that his job, while potentially influential, was not taking adequate advantage of his abilities.

His remarks were inspiring and moving at a meeting with other community affairs staff from several other Reserve Banks and with bankers and tribal people in attendance. He sprinkled his speech with phrases from his ancestral language. He told heartrending stories about life on Pine Ridge and the struggles of Indian people.

Afterwards, I had to give Gerald the bad news that the Board of Governors had deemed our nascent grocery store project too risky for the Federal Reserve System and he just smiled and shook his head. It was not a shock to Gerald to learn that our project was not enthusiastically endorsed and was destined for the shredder. It happened all too often in Indian Country and he was sort of used to the disappointment. He then told me that he had been talking to a large bank in Montana about working for them and he was inclined to leave the Reserve Bank. With everything falling apart in my little division, I could not blame him for looking to move on and it gave me the sense that it was likely time for me to move on, too.

Epiphanies and Tragedies

The undeniable fact was that I was never a good fit at the Minneapolis Federal Reserve Bank. Like Sandy Braunstein had said, it was not the job of the Federal Reserve System to intervene in the market, aside from its mandated role in raising and lowering the discount rate, which indirectly results in higher or lower interest rates. It has a mandated purpose of seeking stable employment and stable rates of inflation, all through monetary policy rather than fiscal policy. It is also a regulatory institution and could never be entrepreneurial in its outlook or its actions. The Federal Reserve System is filled with brilliant people who had a much firmer grasp of what the Reserve Banks could and ought to be doing than I did.

Being manager of community affairs was sort of like being an ambassador without portfolio. I was not a regulator, though I had some limited influence with the regulators in the office. I had very limited influence with the president of the Minneapolis Reserve Bank, Gary Stern, aside from writing the occasional speech for him when the topics were on areas outside his experience, particularly Indian Country. Even in that regard my influence was minimal. In each of the speeches I wrote for him, he edited out the most heartfelt and emotional passages I'd crafted, preferring to be far more detached and academic in his words. The issues that arose through enforcement of the Community Reinvestment Act seemed of less than secondary interest to him. But those were areas of real passion for me and it hurt to see my words discarded so casually. But of course, the president of a Federal Reserve Bank has a different role to play, and while his words were not parsed, studied, and scrutinized like Alan Greenspan's, he had to be far more careful in what he said than I did.

I came to the Federal Reserve Bank with the hope and expectation that I would have more influence and do greater things than I had been able to do as the director of a small non-profit. Ironically, what I found out was that I had more opportunities to change people's lives at City Light than I had at the Federal Reserve Bank. The realization of that stung. Being an ambassador without portfolio, a sinecure, was not what I wanted to be, even as the prestige of working at the Fed was considerable.

About the time that Gerald announced that he was resigning from the Reserve Bank I was on another of my trips visiting reservations. Yet again at every reservation I was met with the reality of a housing crisis that seemed stubborn and mysterious. At every reservation, I asked why the tribe was not using the Low Income Housing Tax Credit program to build new affordable housing and to redeem and replenish the deplorable existing housing on the reservations. Each time I was met with a blank stare. "What is the Low Income Housing Tax Credit program?"

We had another "Lending in Indian Country" seminar scheduled for the Helena Branch of the Minneapolis Reserve Bank, so I added a trip up to the Blackfeet and Rocky Boy's Reservations in Northern Montana. Both reservations suffer from intractable poverty and hopelessness. I was earnest in my job and tried to direct our discussions toward banking and capital formation, but in an unbroken pattern, the tribal leaders I met implored me to assist them with housing for their tribal members. I could do nothing to help them.

I spent the last day of my trip at the Rocky Boy's Reservation, learning that Rocky Boy is a mistranslation of the Chippewa words for Stone Child, among other interesting and captivating bits of arcana. After touring the few economic development opportunities they hoped to get going, I had a late dinner with the tribal chairman and a few tribal council members, then started my drive back to Helena.

During the drive I found myself fixated on the reception I received at both Blackfeet and Rocky Boy's and the desperate need for housing throughout Indian Country. Somewhere between Great Falls and Helena, on Interstate 15 at about midnight on a clear and cold evening, I got off the highway and pulled over to the side of the road. The mountains loomed majestic. The sky was clear, there were no other cars or trucks, no competing light to diminish the brightness of the billions of stars overhead. Martin Luther King, Jr. is believed to have once said, "Only during times of darkness can you see the stars."[59]

Standing there beside the rental car, looking up at the stars and the surrounding mountains, I felt that in this place, on this night, I had a commitment to fulfill. The majestic night sky demanded that it be grand and maybe even poetic. In a dramatic, slap to the forehead moment, I realized I knew how to do something important. Building affordable housing for the poorest families in the country was not banal or mundane, and I had a special skill. I could do something to make life better for hundreds, maybe someday even thousands of Indian families, and the stars and the mountains inspired me to do it now.

The Federal Reserve Bank in Helena was on Neill Avenue, near Last Chance Gulch. When I drove up there the next morning I thought that it was indeed poetic that I had made up my mind to go back to my first passion while driving on Last Chance Gulch. I had to take this chance and I had to do it right. I was so excited I could barely pay attention to the seminar. I tried to act interested in the questions from the bankers in the audience. Afterwards, I made straight for home to ask Marianne if she thought I was crazy or inspired or maybe just stupid.

By now Marianne was familiar with my yearnings and job peregrinations. She knew that I was not thrilled at the Reserve Bank and that I was searching for work that would have greater impact. When we talked it out, she was convinced that it was not a bad idea, that I needed something else and whatever it was, it would likely be better than being unhappy at my current job. We were lucky that our mortgage payment, and for now anyway, our expenses, could be covered from just her salary as the director of the Ramsey Country Library system. We would have to watch our pennies and be very careful, but we would have enough time for me to get established in some income-earning way.

It helped that Marianne was making quite a mark on the library world by successfully adding a coffee shop to the Roseville branch library. This was one of the first, if not the first public library to add a full-service coffee shop entirely within the confines of the building. The Roseville branch had become the busiest library in Minnesota and one of the busiest libraries in the nation, considering books checked out on a per capita basis. Marianne successfully negotiated a groundbreaking deal with a local coffee shop, Dunn Brothers.

Marianne's success at the Ramsey County Library System gave me great comfort in taking the plunge into starting a new business. Now I just had to figure out how to go about working with Indian tribes to help solve their housing crisis. I knew I had the technical skills to bring the Low Income Housing Tax Credit (LIHTC) program to Indian Country, the question was, did they want the product I proposed to offer? I had made up my mind to leave the Federal Reserve Bank, I just had to figure out when.

On the morning of April 19, 1995, I remember coming to the office in an annex directly across the street from the iconic Federal Reserve building in downtown Minneapolis. It was around 7:00 am, my usual arrival time, and I was trying desperately to remain engaged in the work I had been hired to do. Shortly after 9:00 am on that fateful morning, I heard an alarm go off below at the entrance to the Reserve Bank building. Then the barriers at the entrance to the parking garage suddenly started to rise out of the pavement. I saw several armed guards running to each of the corners of the building, something I had never seen before. The guards looked nervous and were running with one hand on their holstered side arms. Something untoward was happening. Was the Reserve Bank being robbed?

Within minutes, around 9:30 am, we began to hear that something horrifying had happened, but not in Minneapolis. Word began to spread that a bomb had detonated at an office building in Oklahoma City housing dozens of federal agencies and there were likely to be many victims. Word then began spreading on the Reserve Bank's internal email system that the main bank building was closed and there was to be nobody allowed in or out for the time being. In the annex, we were not considered to be at risk so weren't restricted from leaving the building. Within the hour there were more armed guards visible at the entrance to the Reserve Bank, at the corners of the building and at the main intersection at Washington Street. We began to hear reports that the building in Oklahoma City was the regional federal office building and that similar office buildings throughout the country were being locked down in case there was a conspiracy to bomb other federal agencies, including the twelve Federal Reserve Banks.

Eventually, the connection was made that the bombing in Oklahoma City was timed to coincide with April 19th, the second anniversary of that botched and disastrous raid at the Branch Davidian compound in Waco, Texas. By about noon we had all relaxed a bit and felt confident that the attack was confined to Oklahoma City. The bomb that destroyed the Murrah Building was equivalent to over 5,000 pounds of TNT and injured over 600 people in addition to the 168 who were killed, including 19 children. The truck had been parked in front of the building directly below the building's day care center. Within days Timothy McVeigh had been determined as the likely perpetrator, in custody in nearby Perry, Oklahoma, by pure chance, mainly because he drove away in a car missing a license plate.

For several days things were uneasy at the Reserve Bank and everyone felt a bit vulnerable. As the extent of the damage and the enormity of the tragedy became known, I was once again proud to be an employee at an institution that had such a noble mission, but my resolve to leave the institution where I was proud to work did not weaken. If anything, it made me more intent on the need to do whatever I could to lessen the inequality and the disparity of hope between Indian Country and the rest of the country.

A Good Way to Move On

Over the next couple of weeks, I determined that there were no good reasons why tribes had not been able to take advantage of the very financing mechanism that was being used to produce over 90% of the nation's affordable housing. There were no legal restrictions. There were no real cultural impediments other than a general lack of experience with the world outside of HUD rules and regulations that tribes had long ago learned to live with, if grudgingly. Of course, states had no real interest in expanding the pool of applicants for tax credits since they were oversubscribed anyway. While some states actively sought to expand the base of participants in the tax credit program, especially Minnesota and Washington, most states saw the intense competition for credits as an excuse to let the marketplace dictate who sought the precious credits. Going out to the Indian reservations to talk about the LIHTC program had little appeal for most states and the housing crisis in Indian Country was not well known, or even known at all, in the very states that had the largest Indian populations, including Montana, North and South Dakota, Oklahoma, and even California. While California was known for its generally progressive attitudes, that was not the case when it came to Indian Country. That official indifference to the needs of Indian tribes in California would become a major concern of mine in the years to come.

Once I had confidence that there were no insurmountable barriers to using the tax credit program in Indian Country, there was no reason to delay my reckoning at the Minneapolis Federal Reserve Bank. My tenure as manager of community affairs needed to come to an end. The Minneapolis Reserve Bank had taken the lead nationally in better understanding lending and borrowing in Indian Country. It partnered with the Kansas City and San Francisco Reserve Banks, but the real progress was made by the Minneapolis Bank. I had a small part in that progress and I am very proud of that. But the real plaudits should go to my predecessors at the Minneapolis bank and my successors, too.

The Minneapolis Bank would go on to create The Center for Indian Country Development, an institute focused on the study of economic development on Indian reservations. That was no doubt a direct result of the work that started before I joined the Reserve Bank, but also the result, in part, to my brief experiment as a federal employee. What I learned while with the Minneapolis Federal Reserve Bank allowed me to create something of far greater value than I could ever have imagined. It afforded me a window into life on Indian reservations, or at least a perspective on the challenges ahead in Indian Country.

Chapter 9

Wounded Knee and Cannon Ball

IT WAS THE SPRING of 1995, a good time to start something big. The go-go nineties encouraged grand plans and high confidence in entrepreneurial efforts. Right away, I formed a new company that had completely unrealistic expectations, a trait I shared with every entrepreneur who has ever created their own start-up. Politicians who proclaim that what entrepreneurs need to start new businesses are more tax breaks amuse me. What hogwash. Nobody starts a new business thinking, "Wow, I will have a lower tax rate and get all kinds of tax incentives! I better start my new business here and now." No, entrepreneurs start new businesses because they think they have a better product, a better service, and a better way to deliver that product or service. They all think that they are going to get rich because they will be smarter and better than everyone else.

Taxes are the least concern of entrepreneurs when they are starting a new business. Someday, after they have made a big splash with their new business and they are making the big bucks, then they might be concerned about taxes. But not at the beginning. My expectations were unrealistic because I simply underestimated the difficulty of landing my first tribal client and the resistance to the whole idea of investors entering into partnerships with tribes. I simply had to be smarter, had to have a better mousetrap than the guy who had tried to do this before me. Then it occurred to me—had anyone already tried to do this?

Apparently not. There was a project in the works with the Umatilla Tribe of Oregon, but it was not part of a concerted, dedicated effort by a company whose sole purpose was to do such projects with tribes. I kept an eye on that project, but concluded that I would otherwise be alone, throughout Indian Country, in trying to bring tax credit financing to Indian reservations.

The first thing I did was contact Gerald Sherman at his new job in Montana and ask him for some advice. I wanted to know which tribes Gerald thought might be interested in the LIHTC program and who he could recommend. He did not hesitate to suggest that the Lower Brule Sioux Tribe near Chamberlain, South Dakota, with a progressive housing director, Deb Isburg, would be a good candidate. Dropping Gerald's name when I called got me in the door.

Deb Isburg was a smart, middle-aged woman who had had her fill of political in-fighting and interference at the Lower Brule Housing Authority. She simply wanted to get things done and had no time for grandiose plans that might take years, if ever, to come about. As her name implied, there was far more below the surface than above. She was a powerful force and I did not want to be a Titanic to her disappointed iceberg. She wanted to meet right away, so I scheduled a trip out to see her. I also began looking at other tribal opportunities in South Dakota.

Gerald and I talked often about the Lakota Fund and he mentioned that the Yankton Sioux Tribe was also interested in expanding their services to include real estate development, with affordable housing as a possibility. I called Dani Not Help Him, the executive director at the Lakota Fund and someone with one of the most intriguing names I ever came across in Indian Country, and set up a meeting. I now had three tribal prospects for my long drive west. Fortuitously, some months earlier I had learned about a small but growing non-profit in Eagle Butte, South Dakota, on the Cheyenne River Sioux Reservation. This small non-profit, Oti Kaga, Inc., was eager to find a new way to finance housing and so a fourth tribal prospect for my first clients emerged. Landing them as paying customers, however, took longer than I imagined.

The Lower Brule, Pine Ridge, and Cheyenne River reservations are in the softly rolling hills of the South Dakota prairie. You can see the wind as it blows across the grasses and it is easy to imagine what life must have been like when Lewis and Clark paddled up from St. Louis. The first tribe that expedition encountered was the Yanktonai Sioux, the ancestors of the current Yankton Sioux. Lewis and Clark were warned by the friendly Yanktonai to avoid the more obstreperous Oglala Sioux, if they could. They did.

The Missouri River and its many small tributaries and creeks nourish a landscape that is mesmerizing in its vastness. You can see storms roll in from the west. Sometimes the sky turns a ghastly green and that means a tornado might be in the offing. Winter blizzards have been known to freeze cows solid, dead as they stand in the fields. But before the cows there were buffalo, in numbers too many to comprehend. In 1871 Colonel R. I. Dodge of the US Cavalry claims to have witnessed a herd of buffalo that was 25 miles wide and 50 miles long. At a very low range of only 15 head per acre that would have the herd at about 12 million.[60] The sight must have been awe inspiring.

Today, the mule deer and the pronghorn antelope are the only wild herds on the South Dakota prairie. There are buffalo herds managed by the tribes, though their numbers are in the hundreds, not the millions. As you drive through this seemingly endless expanse of grasslands, your thoughts and concerns can't help but slow down, seem less momentous, less urgent, at least for the next hundred miles. This defined how my first marketing trip to Lower Brule would shake out. The prairie infused me with patience and perseverance.

My goal for the first meeting was to explain how valuable the LIHTC program could be for tribal housing authorities. I thought I could just step right into the *hows* and *whys* of tax credits. But the prairie and the folks who call it home had other ideas. They wanted to know me first, to understand who I was and why I was making this pitch. Of course, this makes great sense. Tribes and Indian people have been harassed and coerced, lied to and cheated, for over 200 years. They have grown to be mistrustful of anyone, especially white people, selling them something that purportedly will make their lives better.

The Dawes Act ("Have I got a deal for you!") was still fresh in their minds, and the tribal leaders were understandably wary. The US government has abysmally failed to live up to the treaty obligations outlined in other such binding documents including the Fort Laramie Treaties. In fact, there were two major Ft. Laramie treaties that first granted and then took back much of the lands of the Great Sioux Nations, including the Black Hills of South Dakota, which the Sioux Tribes still claim. Understandably, my first meetings with all four of the tribes were more about *who* than what. I settled into an awareness that this might take a while and could not be rushed. I scheduled another meeting for a few weeks later to dig deeper into both the who and the what of my little company. Clearly, I had to make a commitment to them that demonstrated my willingness to see it through and make good on my promises. I intended to do just that. I was going to break the mold of white people taking advantage of tribal nations, at least as far as I could do so.

My new enterprise is what is now commonly referred to as a *socially-motivated* business. Although not a non-profit, my company had an altruistic mission: to help Indian tribes develop affordable housing. The business had to be sustainable for their sake and mine. So it had to be a hybrid between the non-profit world and the profit-driven corporate model via a business that nobody else had tried to do before me.

What's In a Name

I named my new company Housing & Community Development, Inc. The descriptive nature of that name would help it stick in people's minds, but I honestly hated it. Names mean a lot, especially in Indian Country, I would learn. Sometimes they don't mean what you think they mean.

When I first met Dani Not Help Him, the director at the Lakota Fund, I asked about her surname, Not Help Him. I assumed that it was a name depicting someone who had somehow been shamed and not deserving of help. She told me that the surname is derived from members of one of the warrior societies among the Lakota comprised of men who were destined to be the first line of defense against invaders or other tribes who might raid or battle the Lakota. A warrior designated as *Not Help Him* was said to be so brave and so dedicated to the safety of the village that he would lay down his life for the tribe or village and nobody was supposed to help him as he performed his sacred duties to protect the village. She said that some Not Help Him warriors would go so far as to sink a stake into the ground and have another warrior lash their leg to it so that they could not retreat in the face of certain death. *You were not to help him*, Dani explained, because his death was in furtherance of the protection of his people. Just thinking of this, the dignity, the courage, and the generosity of these warriors brings a lump to my throat, to this day.

There are similar Indian names that some people might find a bit odd, or to the uninformed might have a pejorative connotation. One of the most prominent names of the Crow Tribe in Montana is White Man Runs Him. The first White Man Runs Him was a scout for General Custer at the Battle of the Little Bighorn who survived the battle, living until 1929. The Sioux and Cheyenne were enemies of the Crow and White Man Runs Him served his tribe honorably, but don't mention that to someone from the Northern Cheyenne or Sioux Tribes. I was once in a meeting with the executive director of the Northern Cheyenne Housing Authority, Dr. Annabelle Rowland, who leaned over to me, *sotto voce*, and asked, "Do you know what the most common name is on the Crow Reservation?" I did not. She got a look on her face like she'd taken a hearty bite of a persimmon and said, "*White Man Runs Him.* That is the most common surname on the Crow Reservation. I would not have such a name. I would be disgusted to have such a name."

The Northern Cheyenne and Crow Reservations sit side by side, but they are miles apart in history and tradition. The Northern Cheyenne fought with the Arapaho and the Lakota against the US Cavalry, notably at the Battle of the Little Big Horn. The Crow were scouts for the US Cavalry and were the long-time enemies of the Cheyenne, Lakota, and Arapaho Tribes. The disdain in her voice over a name that implies obedience to the US government told me that old wounds remain fresh for some Indians.

Another, highly esteemed name is *Young Man Afraid of His Horse*, who was a great Lakota leader. These colorful and historical names defy assumptions. Afraid of His Horse is a mistranslation of *Men Are Even* Afraid of His Horse. Quite a different meaning. Think about it—instead of thinking, "what a wimp, he's afraid of his own horse," it actually means this guy is so tough that people are not only afraid of him, but they are scared of his horse, too. Damn, I better give that guy a pretty wide berth.

Indian Wars Past and Present

My introduction to the romantic names of Indians and the painful history of Indian Country came as a young man in college in 1973. As a freshman I picked up the best-selling, *Bury My Heart at Wounded Knee*, by Dee Brown. By coincidence, the actual modern-day Wounded Knee uprising began on the Pine Ridge Reservation in South Dakota in February of that year, and lasted about three heartbreaking months. The book, however, chronicles the brutal treatment of Native Americans by the early colonists, then by settlers moving west, and of course, through the pitiless policies of the US government as it waged war against the Indians, then decreed and abrogated treaty after treaty with dozens and eventually hundreds of Indian nations.

When I read Dee Brown's seminal work, I distinctly remember thinking *Why in the world are we not taught this in elementary school, or at least in high school?* To have so thoroughly whitewashed the tragic hand we had in the diminishment of the great Indian nations, indeed in the near genocide of whole populations, weakens us as a people. I was mystified by the reluctance to teach the truth. I remain mystified to this day by that unwillingness to own up to our collective guilt. Instead of a factual narrative of the violent subjugation of Indian nations, we have contagious personal narratives of lazy Indians, drunken Indians, Indians who carve a hole in the bathroom wall to water their horses. In the very least, a thorough and honest interpretation of events would help to blunt the power of the stories told by unthinking bankers, thoughtless travelers, and anyone who repeats the destructive tales of Indian life.

What was taking place in South Dakota in 1973, just 83 years after the massacre of Lakota men, women and children by the US Cavalry, was a stark reminder that we have a nasty habit in this country of marginalizing people who get in our way and a propensity to forget the tragic results. It has not been official government policy for decades to disregard Indian nations and reservations, but tribes have been ostracized and Americans know next-to-nothing about the tragedies unfolding on Indian reservations to this day. Nonetheless, in 1973 the village of Wounded Knee on the Pine Ridge Indian Reservation was making the evening news only because armed men on horseback with long braided hair were threatening to take over the government of the reservation. Members of the American Indian Movement, known as AIM, had come to Wounded Knee, including Russell Means and Dennis Banks, with the hope of ousting the tribal chairman, Richard Wilson, who was considered corrupt by a large majority of the tribal population. In a grisly apropos acronym, Wilson's followers were known as Goons: Guardians of the Oglala Nation. The Goons apparently used methods appropriate to their name to rough up anyone who did not follow Wilson's orders.

Members of AIM were generally known as *traditionals*. They wore their hair long and spoke Lakota, or as much of the language as they knew, and believed in preserving the traditions of the great Sioux Nations. The 1934 Indian Reorganization Act, among other things, encouraged standard governance on tribal nations, including elected tribal councils with council presidents or chairmen and chairwomen, and election districts that oftentimes crossed clan boundaries. Even though tribes had the right to ignore this "encouragement," most tribes adopted constitutions with governmental structures including elected tribal councils and tribal presidents or chair people. I was later to learn how this culturally out-of-sync governing has in many cases turned out to be more of a hindrance than a help as tribes govern themselves.

For hundreds, indeed thousands of years, tribes had gotten along just fine governing themselves, largely through consensus. Now, with two-year election cycles ensuring continuous politicking and constant chaos, the Oglala Sioux Reservation was mired in poverty, fraud, and corruption. Wilson was seen as being at the heart of it. The US government came to his aid when he resisted an impeachment effort. The Bureau of Indian Affairs set up a cordon of armed men around the government offices to protect him. This set the stage for the uprising that did not end before at least one white man and two Indians were killed, and another one was missing and presumed murdered.

The men and women of AIM, the traditionals, specifically chose Wounded Knee to stage their protests and occupation because of its great historical importance to the Lakota people. Wounded Knee was the site of perhaps the most egregiously wanton murder of Indians by the Cavalry under the guise of a "battle" since the Massacre of Sand Creek in Colorado in 1864. The Indian Wars had come to an end by the late 19th century; most of the treaties had been signed, under duress in nearly all cases. In the fall of 1890, rumors began circulating across the West of the Messiah who could teach a Ghost Dance that would return dead men to life. If you danced the Ghost Dance and wore the Ghost Shirts, sacred shirts painted with magic markings to ensure that no harm could come to the dancers who wore them, new powers would come to the Lakota. It was thought that these shirts could repel the bullets fired from the guns of the US Cavalry. Even Sitting Bull, the most admired and revered Lakota leader, believed in the Ghost Dance. This worried the US Army as the Ghost Dance spread from reservation to reservation.

Ironically, the Ghost Dance was more Christian than pagan. According to Dee Brown, the Indian Messiah commanded, "You must not hurt anybody or do harm to anyone. You must not fight. Do right always. Preaching nonviolence and brotherly love, the doctrine called for no action by the Indians except to dance and sing. The Messiah would bring the resurrection."[61] The Indian "Messiah" was a 34-year old Paiute Indian named Wovoka who had a dream, a vision, that Jesus returned to earth to usher in the time for Indians to take back their lands, but not by violence. He urged his followers to dance the Ghost Dance and to make peace with the white man.[62]

By November of 1890, the Ghost Dance had spread to so many reservations that schools reported pupils skipping classes, trading posts were empty, and farm work was going undone. On December 15, 1890, a Cavalry detachment was sent to the Standing Rock reservation to place Sitting Bull under arrest to allay worries that the Ghost Dance phenomenon might cause a general uprising. The capture of Sitting Bull was intended to force him to denounce the Ghost Dance. One of his compatriots, Catch-the-Bear, shouted "You shall not do it!" and tried to shoot one of the soldiers to free Sitting Bull. In the melee, Sitting Bull was killed.

Grief overtook the reservation and hundreds of Lakota left the Standing Rock and Cheyenne River Reservations and sought refuge in several Ghost Dance camps. Big Foot, a Cheyenne River Miniconjou leader, was on the run, if you could call it that, and the War Department wanted him arrested. Sick with pneumonia and coughing up blood, Big Foot was traveling in a slow-moving wagon, miserable and destitute, when the Cavalry caught him and his followers. There were 120 men and 230 Indian women and children. The Seventh Regiment, under the command of Major Samuel Whitside, surrounded Big Foot and his followers. Colonel James W. Forsyth, now commanding what was George S. Custer's former regiment, took control from Whitside, who otherwise seemed to have things well in hand. Forsyth botched things.

Whitside had decided to let well enough alone and did not insist on disarming the Indians. Forsyth, perhaps remembering Custer's fate, thought the better of that and decided to take away the warriors' blankets in order to better search for guns, knives, and axes, leaving the Indians fully disarmed. It was December 29, 1890, and the Lakota had no warm clothing and now no blankets either. The Cavalry soldiers went about the encampment demanding that the warriors give up their guns. A young warrior named Black Coyote had paid a high price for his rifle and did not want to part with it. And he was deaf. When they tried to take it from him, in the confusion, a shot rang out.[63] The slaughter that followed left 153 men, women and children dead, but many more crawled away to die later. Big Foot died and there is an iconic photograph of him, gruesomely posed in the snow frozen in pain and death.

It has been estimated that over 300 Lakota, largely women and children, died in the Wounded Knee Massacre. Twenty-five soldiers also died, many apparently from friendly fire since the Indians had been virtually disarmed. Astonishingly, twenty Medals of Honor were awarded at the "Battle" of Wounded Knee.

As a young man, reading *Bury My Heart at Wounded Knee*, I would come back to a dreary dorm room in dreary Winston-Salem, North Carolina, and listen to Judy Collins on the record player. Her mellifluous singing voice, pure and lilting, but ultimately sad and lonely, is linked in my mind to the news of the uprising in Wounded Knee, South Dakota. I was glued to the evening news and went every day to the Z. Smith Reynolds Library on the Wake Forest campus to read every newspaper I could get. The Christian Science *Monitor* had especially thorough coverage. There was no cable, no CNN, no 24-hour news coverage, back then.

Of course, in 1973 I had no inkling that I would someday work so hard to bring a little bit of justice and equity to Indian Country. I had always been acutely attuned to anyone who might be an underdog. What was happening in Wounded Knee, South Dakota drove home for me the fact that injustice and intolerance were as present in Indian Country as they were in the Jim Crow south. Unfortunately, the lessons learned in the hills northeast of the village of Pine Ridge in 1973 are still being taught in the Dakotas.

Water Protectors and Deadlines

In the summer of 2016, the months long "occupation" of Cannon Ball, North Dakota, on the Standing Rock Sioux Reservation to protest the construction of an oil pipeline slated to run underneath the Missouri River, is sadly reminiscent of the Wounded Knee resistance, without the deadly violence. This time, thousands of non-Indians joined the cause of the *Water Protectors,* as the Indian demonstrators called themselves. Paying little heed to the history of pipeline breaks and massive spills that despoil the environment, Energy Transfer Partners (ETP), the company that owns the Dakota Access Pipeline, discounted the danger to the Missouri River, the only source of water on the reservation.

While there is some justification to ETP's claim that they sought and received permission for the pipeline from the state and federal regulators, the failure to recognize that the Standing Rock Sioux Tribe had a different permitting process and a different public hearing process, exemplifies the on-going subordination of Native people and their governance of their own land. The inflexibility in the face of tribal opposition and ETP's bullying tactics illustrate the gross ignorance by billion-dollar corporations, the Corps of Engineers, and the state of North Dakota of the legitimate rights and needs of Native Americans. The construction of the pipeline exposes a gross misunderstanding of the sovereignty of the Standing Rock Sioux Nation. Energy Transfer Partners and the US government's actions blatantly disregard the rights of a people who have been ignored, mistreated, stolen from and lied to for generations.

The tribe bears some responsibility for the debacle. Apparently, it ignored many of the early public hearings held to provide information and get comments from the public for the impending pipeline. The tribe did not organize a comprehensive protest at a time when it would have been more propitious to do so. Neither did it offer objections publicly nor retain legal assistance at the outset of the proposal for the pipeline. Tribes rarely have the legal resources to fight state and corporate battles. There is also the long-standing refusal by states and non-Indian companies to take tribes seriously. They run roughshod over tribal people and tribal interests. Chronic underfunding of tribal government operations and administration played a part too. Whatever the explanation, it results all too often with tribes unprepared for grave challenges to their lands and resources. And all too often the tribes lose. But not always.

A 2013 court case illustrates both a tribe's negligence and a court's willingness to overlook that negligence in furtherance of a greater good. The Navajo Nation applied for a very large grant, over $17 million, from the Bureau of Indian Affairs, under a program known as the Indian Self-Determination and Education Assistance Act. It completed the grant application and submitted it on October 4, 2013, even though the federal government at the time had been shut down because the US Congress could not come to agreement on a budget. Does this sound familiar? There were some Interior Department employees still working—signing for things and doing other odd but apparently important jobs. The grant application was received by a bona fide Interior Department employee, signed for, and logged in, and that meant that a very important ticker started.

Under the rules for the grant, the federal government had 90 days to score the application and give the Navajo Nation an up or down vote. However, the Interior Department did not think that the ticker had indeed started on the 90-day window of approval. Instead, they believed it started after the federal government had been restarted, on October 17, 2013, after the Congress overcame their rancorous dispute. That 13-day difference of opinion became very important. The Interior Department sent a letter to the appropriate person at the Navajo Nation letting them know that the ticker did not start, in the eyes of the Interior Department, until October 17, 2013. They never received a reply from the Navajo Nation.

The Bureau of Indian Affairs was the department within Interior that was handling the grant application. On November 7, 2013, they sent another letter to the Navajo Nation informing the tribe that they had applied for too much money and that they had until November 29th to respond with some agreement on a smaller grant amount. The Tribe never responded to this letter either. The federal government sent yet another letter to the Navajo Nation, this time asking for more time to review the application, which was apparently allowable under the rules. But this letter came to the Navajo Nation on January 9, 2014, seven days after the tribe believed the 90-day window had already expired on January 2, 2014, as they understood the timeline.

The grant was denied by the Interior Department and the Navajo Nation sued the federal government, contending that the Interior Department had failed to follow its own rules and had not given the tribe an up or down decision within the 90-day approval period. The United States Court of Appeals for the District of Columbia Circuit agreed with the Navajo Nation and instructed the Interior Department to make good on the grant application, in the full amount.[64] Good deal for the Navajo Nation.

What is disconcerting about this is that nobody at the Navajo Nation responded to the letters from the Interior Department on three separate occasions, nor did they respond, apparently, to telephone calls from the Department. It worked out well, this time, for the Navajo Nation, but it exemplifies the difficulties tribes have in meeting the expectations of government agencies and businesses. Unfortunately, in my experience the failure to look at letters and respond in a timely manner, the failure to return phone calls, is all too often the norm and not the exception. To be fair, for tribes it must be like playing a game in which the rules are written down but are never followed. Or the rules apply to white people and state and local governments, but not to Indians or tribal governments. Why bother? And that is not to say that the grant the Navajo Nation sought was not needed and should not have been awarded to them. But it stands to reason that something this important required a more business-like and diligent pursuit of the grant. Perhaps, waiting out the Bureau of Indian Affairs was a canny strategy on the part of the Navajo Nation, gambling that the different interpretation of time would squeeze out an unlikely win. I doubt it. This has the hallmarks of carelessness and dumb luck, abetted by a weariness that rules and procedures never seem to work in a tribe's favor.

But there is yet another plausible explanation for the self-defeating behavior of so many tribal people. It has long been recognized that there is a correlation between poverty and counterproductive behavior. Poor people have less access to preventive health care and are less likely to follow complex drug protocols. They have parents who are overwhelmed and provide less attentive care. Predatory lenders prey upon the poor and create self-defeating cycles of bad decision followed by bad decision. According to Anandi Mani and Sendhil Mullainathan, in *Science*, "The poor must manage sporadic income, juggle expenses, make difficult tradeoffs. Even when not actually making a financial decision, these preoccupations can be present and distracting. The human cognitive system has limited capacity. Preoccupations with pressing budgetary concerns leave fewer cognitive resources available to guide choice and action."[65] Mullainathan calls this a "cognitive tax." The conditions listed in the *Science* article are present in Indian Country to a greater extent than they are anywhere else in the US. The poverty is deeper, the betrayals by pay-day lenders and other predators are more constant, and the things that make life easier for everyone else, like reliable public transportation, good quality food at reasonable prices, wholesome distractions like libraries, swimming pools and sporting venues, are mostly missing. Is it any wonder that meetings are missed, that letters aren't answered, that opportunities are squandered?

The folks at Standing Rock should have attended the public hearings and mustered a far more robust protest to the Dakota Access Pipeline far earlier than they did. Things worked out for the Navajo Nation, not so much for the Standing Rock Sioux Tribe. In my view, the Water Protectors would have been strengthened if they had vigorously protested the pipeline through the public hearing process; if they had demanded, as they apparently could have, additional environmental analyses much earlier than they did, if they had mustered a legal protest that was timely rather than rushed, perhaps the outcome would have been different. But they did not. Greater respect and deference could and should have been shown by Energy Transfer Partners, the state of North Dakota, and the Corps of Engineers. Instead, I am convinced that Energy Transfer Partners, and even the government of the State of North Dakota, were emboldened to continue the construction of the pipeline because they, too, had heard the stories, the dark narrative of Indian Country, and felt justified in their contempt. But it is also reasonable to conclude that the officials at Standing Rock and Navajo were collectively exhausted, that their cognitive well had run perilously dry. Facing daunting challenges with so few resources left a void in their response time, in their enthusiasm to take on yet another obstacle. The cognitive taxes were too high.

I came to understand and have sympathy for the people of the Standing Rock Sioux Tribe and the people of the Great Sioux Nations with whom I chose to work when I started my company even though I also struggled to overcome cavalier attitudes toward deadlines, and slow or no responses to letters and calls. But the government agencies and the businesses seeking to work on tribal lands also have a special obligation. Even though ETP may have sent letters and made numerous calls, when so much is at stake—when so many lives are in the balance—it should not be business as usual. Extra steps are warranted. When your call is not returned, make another call, then another. If your letter is not answered, send a fax, send an email. Drive to the tribal headquarters and find out what is going on. Build relationships, become culturally competent, and acknowledge that things happen differently in Indian Country. Energy Transfer Partners didn't do that, which is regrettable. The Interior Department didn't do it either, which is inexcusable.

Of course, extraordinary steps shouldn't be necessary, but they are. There should be mindful sensitivity to the unique challenges of Indian Country. As a matter of course, as a simple matter of business necessity, there should be more persistent and determined attention with respectful recognition of the hardships and losses endured by tribal people. Unfortunately, government agencies and businesses rarely meet even minimal expectations for justice and fair dealing.

All of this was on my mind as I fixed my intentions towards Indian Country. Marianne and I decided to be better.

Chapter 10

Not an Auspicious Beginning

MY FIRST FOUR tribal clients were Lower Brule, Yankton, the Lakota Fund, and Oti Kaga. All were in South Dakota, all shared the history of Wounded Knee, all required persistence and extra care, and all of them presented a bit of a dilemma. The tax credits are competitive, and I did not want to have one or two of my tribal clients competing against my other tribal clients. It was a problem solved mostly by circumstance.

Since none of these tribes had ever developed housing with the LIHTC program before, and since no state had yet to award credits to an Indian or tribal applicant, I decided to make each project very small and as similar as possible, given the particular needs of each tribal customer. That way, each customer would be on a similar competitive plane with the other and the state would not be confronted with four potential projects that would use up a significant chunk of the state's total tax credit pool. As it turned out, I was successful in persuading each of my new tribal customers to undertake very modest first projects, to help them learn about the tax credit program and not be overwhelmed by a new set of obligations. Even with my clients' willingness to undertake strikingly small and very similar projects, I was almost consumed with worry.

With the exception of the Lakota Fund that had some experience with non-tribal/non-governmental donors, this would be my clients' first experience with outside investors who had expectations that the tribal projects would perform just like non-tribal projects. Two of my new customers were Indian housing authorities, created as political instrumentalities of the tribe, and the other two were non-profit corporations. The housing authorities, just like housing authorities outside of Indian Country, were very comfortable with HUD rules and regulations and had been complying with them for decades. But neither had ever been in a partnership with a non-Indian organization and neither had ever been subject to the kind of scrutiny that accompanies an award of tax credits. This scrutiny would come from the state on behalf of the IRS and from their investor, who had the most to lose if the Indian housing authority failed to live up to the requirements of the tax credit program. As it turned out, this worry was misplaced.

While the Lakota Fund and Oti Kaga had no experience complying with HUD rules and regulations, these two non-profits did have experience dealing with donors who, like investors, have expectations for their contributions. The non-profits more readily grasped their obligations under the LIHTC program. With all four customers, I spent many hours going over the requirements and expectations the IRS, the state, and their as-yet unknown investors would have for the tribal developers. The stakes were high. If my very first tribal clients were ill-informed or improperly prepared, not only would it work against the goal of increasing affordable housing for tribes in crisis, it wouldn't look good for my company either.

I was determined to make sure my tribal customers fully understood what they were getting into. Working with investors who had limited knowledge of Indian Country had long-range implications for both investor and tribe. This was made more difficult because these investors mostly did not care about the plight of poor Indians. I was nonetheless diligent in pressing these points.

Some commentators have described the LIHTC program as the "National Lawyer and Accountant Full Employment Act." Indeed, it is an unnecessarily complex program and because of this complexity you must have advisers to assist you at nearly every stage of the process. I found the one person who would prove to be the best adviser Indian Country could ever hope to have. Angela Christy was known to be one of the top tax credit lawyers in Minnesota, but she also had clients in dozens of other states, all trying to make their tax credit projects succeed. After only a single meeting, Angela eagerly agreed to help me as I sought to bring tax credit financing to Indian Country. She was enthusiastic and committed from the first project.

As the years passed and a few projects turned into hundreds, Angela always made sure the projects complied with the law and were not burdened with unwanted special provisions. Angela's involvement assured that the tribes were protected against the many things that might go wrong. Angela had a mantra, "We will find a way." No matter how dreadful things looked, and this happened with virtually every early project, Angela would look at the problem and reassure me when I was frantically trying to find a solution. "We will find a way" to fix this, she'd say and then she would do just that. Over the next 20 years there were projects that seemed fated to fail, that investors and state allocating agencies had given up on, but Angela always found a solution. Every time.

Angela is yet another in a long line of strong women who have had an enormous impact on my life. She is also short of stature, like Judy Humbert in Winchester. While short, she is an intellectual and legal giant. With an under-graduate degree in chemistry, she expected to become a patent lawyer. But tax law and real estate law somehow won the day. She calls herself a simple "dirt lawyer." She was anything but simple. She helped my new company overcome the hesitancy of investors and the obstinacy of states and she became a mentor to me.

I certainly needed the help. From the very beginning, I knew I was building a business that could become life-changing for thousands of Indian families. My years at the Federal Reserve Bank of Minneapolis in which I was immersed in tribal history and culture taught me that Indian culture is an enduring part of America, but it is also enduringly apart from America. That is its blessing and its curse. Life on Indian reservations remains steadfastly separate and distinct from the rest of the U.S. That is likely the only way that Indian culture can survive, but its separateness means poverty persists and hardens, social ills deepen and fester, and life remains more difficult for the families born in places like Kyle, Eagle Butte, Red Lake, or Lame Deer.

The rules governing the tax credit program require that a market study document the need for the housing and the credits being sought. This was right up my alley. I had been a market analyst at the Rouse Company, and Marianne and I had operated a market analysis firm for five years. I knew how to do this and could make a compelling case, especially in light of the mandated federal preference for projects that intend to serve the lowest income people. For example, I could show that 63% of the total population on the Yankton Sioux Reservation lived below the poverty line, as compared to the statewide average of 11%. The per capita income on the Yankton Sioux Reservation was only $2,854 as compared to the statewide per capita income of $10,661—barely 26% of the statewide per capita income. The per capita incomes on the reservation were only 19% of the national per capita income of $14,420. The same was shown for each of the other reservations and the depth of poverty was astounding, nearly third world by comparison.

To illustrate the contrast, consider what Wallace Stegner, novelist and environmentalist, wrote about the distinctiveness of California:

> In a prosperous country, we are more prosperous than most; in an urban country, more urban than most; in a gadget-happy country, more addicted to gadgets; in a tasteless country, more tasteless; in a creative country, more energetically creative; in an optimistic society, more optimistic; in an anxious society, more anxious. Contribute regionally to the national culture? We are the national culture, at its most energetic end.[66]

Changing out California for Indian Country, I would rephrase it:

> In a prosperous country, we are less prosperous than most; in an urban country, more rural than most; in a gadget-happy country, have fewer gadgets; in a tasteless country, more defined by culture; in a creative country, more attuned to history and tradition; in an optimistic society, without hope; in an anxious country, more stoic and tenacious. Contribute regionally to the national culture? We are invisible.

This little company we were building had a grave and serious responsibility. We could not screw up. We could not mislead the tribes or fail them. They had been betrayed and lied to and stolen from for over 200 years. If we failed them they would never trust us again; they would lose the chance to help solve the housing crisis with one of the few tools available to them: the tax credit program. The window would close and probably never reopen. As if that were not hard enough, I knew that we would have hostile states and unknowing and skeptical investors who did not understand what we were trying to do, who did not share our mission, and who didn't care about Indian Country. I had set the course of my new business, my life in many ways, and I never reconsidered, not once, even when things looked the bleakest. We were determined to make my new company succeed and determined to make a difference in Indian Country. It has never been easy. I did not expect it to be, but I never thought that it would be quite as difficult as it turned out to be.

One Win and Three Losses

It got difficult right away. I spent months in South Dakota with my tribal clients, all worthy of an award of tax credits and all scoring nearly identical scores in the grading. We submitted them to the South Dakota Housing Development Authority on time. Now we just had to wait until the awards were announced. I had looked at the history of awards made by the SDHDA and I knew that our four projects would score high enough to win credits for each tribal customer. I had structured the projects such that no single project would use up so many of the credits that it would endanger the other tribal projects and indeed, would not leave too few credits for the rest of the non-Indian projects likewise seeking credits. I knew that I had created what I thought was a Goldilocks situation—not too big, not too many, not too ambitious. I was confident that the SDHDA would see the wisdom of awarding credits to each of my customers, indeed would have no choice but to award my tribal customers the credits the projects deserved and desperately needed. They had other ideas.

My mistake was taking for granted that the SDHDA would appreciate my logic, understand the importance of the first Indian

Country applications in the nation, and agree with my strategy of purposely limiting the four projects to small allocations so as to ensure that all would be approved. I did have many telephone calls with SDHDA to clarify certain parts of the application process and I had come to know several of the people who worked at the SDHDA quite well, if telephonically. But I never met with anyone at the SDHDA nor scheduled a time to come to see them and lobby for my customers. I was negligent in not seeking them out and explicitly telling them of our plans and about the steps we had taken to make sure SDHDA would recognize how important, exceptionally needed, and groundbreaking they were.

I had been very careful in how I described each application for each of my tribal customers. Each application was sufficiently different to warrant unique attention. Yet there were many similarities in need, with gross disparities between tribal incomes and housing conditions compared to both the nation as a whole and South Dakota in particular. Each applicant had similarly low incomes and very high rates of deteriorated housing present on all four reservations. I wrote narrative descriptions of each tribal project, showcasing, for example, how the Lakota Fund project would include management practices that drew upon their Grameen Bank-inspired peer lending experience. The Yankton Sioux project would reach out especially to single mothers with children. The Oti Kaga project on Cheyenne River would coordinate closely with the Cheyenne River Tribal Housing Authority to reduce its housing authority waiting list. The Lower Brule project would seek to include comprehensive homeownership training as a part of its long-term management goal. We had created a compelling case for each tribal project. The SDHDA didn't see it that way.

In early May 1996, I was on a marketing trip to the Menominee Tribe in Wisconsin, at the airport in Green Bay, when word came out that the SDHDA had made its awards. What I heard shocked me. Only one of our projects would be funded, the Lakota Fund on the Pine Ridge Indian Reservation. I was floored and I immediately called my customers to give them the bad news. But after delivering the dreadful news I called out to the SDHDA and asked how I could have miscalculated so badly. I needed to know how three of our projects could possibly have failed to score high enough.

The SDHDA acknowledged that all four applications had scored the same in the grading. "If that is true, then why didn't all four receive an allocation?" I asked through clenched teeth. I was told that even though the applications were basically identical, the SDHDA Board of Directors, following the advice of the staff, felt that only one tribal application could be approved. Since Pine Ridge was the poorest of the reservations, they approved only the Lakota Fund application.

As a general policy, the SDHDA does not share the rankings and scoring of tax credit applicants, but they did release them to me for all the projects that applied in the first round of 1996. I was gob smacked when I saw that our four applications were all ranked in the top ten. Specifically, our projects were ranked 3, 4, 6, and 7. Eight projects were awarded credits, including the first two applications and the application ranked number 5, another non-Indian application, but then skipping to our Lakota Fund project, ranked 7th. The SDHDA awarded credits to projects ranked 10, 14 and 15, all non-Indian projects, instead of our higher rated projects.[67]

There are rules; we followed the rules. The scoring process was supposed to weed out the applications that were not worthy, or at least not as worthy as some others; we had proven our case. This was just wrong. In hindsight, my failure to put in the time in Pierre (pronounced "peer" by anyone who has been to South Dakota), the state capital, may have cost us. I didn't cajole the SDHDA staff and Board about Indian Country, and that might have spelled doom for three of our four Indian customers. After a period of self-recrimination, I got mad. It was like the Winchester Board of Zoning Appeals all over again: illogical, subjective, uninformed, and entrenched.

Nobel laureate Daniel Kahneman provided another explanation, "We can be blind to the obvious, and we are also blind to our blindness."[68] The SDHDA had seen all four applications from Indian Country, but had they really seen all four? I think they were victims of the Müller-Lyer illusion.

In Müller-Lyer's famous psychological experiment, two parallel lines are shown, one with trailing fins and one with leading fins. (See below.) The parallel lines are identical in length, but to nearly everyone who sees the lines, the one with the leading fins appears longer than the line with the trailing fins. The broad implications of this experiment speak to the way human beings make determinations: even after measuring the two lines to prove that they are identical in length, even after we know with certainty that they are identical in length, we will still see one line as longer than the other. We can't help ourselves.

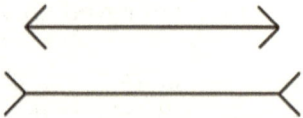

As this relates to the SDHDA scoring, I think they were blind to the obvious, and just as blind to their blindness. The SDHDA board saw all four of the applications, saw that they ranked higher than non-Indian applicants, yet still rationed out just one award to Indian Country. Whether it was their inability to see four unique opportunities or the gravity-like pull of the apathetic status quo—just a bunch of Indians fixed in a cycle of despair beyond any real public policy's obligation—or both, the net result was the same. A very real tragedy remained invisible to people who had the power but apparently not the ability to recognize it, or to recognize the bias that blinded them.

Winchester notwithstanding, I had never been confronted with such injustice and inequity, and I was at a loss to explain it to my tribal clients.

What's Fair Is Fair

Graciously, my three "losing" clients agreed that I had done my job and that the SDHDA had done what the tribes feared--shut out the Indians once again. But we decided not to let it go. We began by objecting to the awards at the next SDHDA board meeting. We made a lot of noise, to no avail and finally we filed a Fair Housing complaint with HUD alleging discrimination in the allocation of federal housing tax credits.[69] A fair housing complaint is about as close to a lawsuit as you can come without all the rigmarole and I had not anticipated having to take this step. Jarringly, I was confronted by a real-world manifestation of what I had heard Jim West and Mark Jarboe talk about during our "Lending in Indian Country" seminars.

Jim and Mark often described how some states with large Indian populations disliked the presence of Indian tribes within the state boundaries. They resented the fact that Indian people living and working on Indian lands were not subject to state income and excise taxes and that Indian land was not subject to county property taxes. These states begrudged the tribes the money the state and counties claimed to spend on police and fire protection, even though in nearly every case there was a tribal fire and police department or BIA police to provide tribal people the protections they needed. I presumed this attitude was only a passive animosity, not an active barrier. But I was wrong, it was active and demonstrative. The contagion of false and negative narratives about Indian Country had seemingly spread to the SDHDA and had infected the staff, as well as the Board.

It was abetted by a pervasive misunderstanding of what it meant to be Indian. On too many occasions to recount, I heard people say either that Indians don't pay state taxes or in some cases even federal taxes. There is no provision for Indians to be exempt from federal income tax. Likewise, if an Indian lives off of the reservation and works in a business that is not Indian-owned or tribally owned, there is no provision for an exemption from state taxes, assuming the state has an income tax. South Dakota has no state income tax.

The only Indians who are exempt from state income tax are people duly enrolled as a member of a federally recognized tribe who also work on an Indian reservation in an agency or business that is either tribally-owned or owned by an Indian who is also duly enrolled and a member of the tribe. I have to admit that there is more than a little ambiguity here; the Supreme Court has issued contradictory rulings over the years and Congress has not done anything to clear up the muddied opinions. Still, I had heard too many times to count the notion that Indians get a monthly check from the federal government just for being Indian. There is no such provision. But like the story of the Indian who cuts a hole in his house to water his horse from the bathtub, it is something people want to believe because it vindicates their sense of superiority and excuses their racism.

These pervasive myths about Indian Country infiltrate the attitudes of people who serve on boards like the SDHDA and staff the offices of government agencies. They have the power to grant or withhold hundreds of millions of dollars that could naturally flow to Indian Country, but too often do not because of the insidious hold these attitudes have on the people with the power. How else can it be explained why no state, including, of course, South Dakota until 1996, had ever awarded Low Income Housing Tax Credits to a tribal applicant? The state agency responsible for allocating precious federal tax credits to the lowest income communities in their state should have created outreach efforts to educate the tribes and help them gain access to the credits. Tribes did not get their fair share of the more than $10 billion that was annually generated for affordable housing.

This time at least one tribal applicant had been selected and I began working immediately with the Lakota Fund to secure an investor for their project. At the same time, we did not relent in our efforts to overturn the denial of credits for Oti Kaga, the Yankton Sioux Housing Authority, and the Lower Brule Housing Authority. I just could not let my tribal customers down with "Sorry, I did my best," and simply move on. So, I went to the SDHDA board meetings, I continued to write letters and have the tribal leaders do the same. The SDHDA made specious arguments about geographic distribution, even though they gave the bulk of the credits to urban projects. They argued that they wanted diversity in the awards made to developers even though four of the eight projects awarded credits were sponsored by only two for-profit developers.

The most egregious claim the SDHDA made, however, was that 12% of the state's total allocation was made to Indian applicants even though Indians only represent 11% of the state population. What the SDHDA failed to acknowledge was that even though Indians may only represent 11% of the state's total population, they account for over 80% of the state's poorest population and account for the vast majority of over-crowded and inadequate housing units.[70]

Finally, our efforts to force the state to grant credits to all of our projects paid off, but not as a response to our complaint. The SDHDA awarded credits to Yankton, Oti Kaga, and Lower Brule late in the year, explaining that several non-Indian projects that had been awarded credits earlier in the year had either returned the allocation or the projects had proven themselves infeasible. Now, it seemed, the SDHDA had "found" sufficient credits to make awards for all of our tribal projects. Halleluiah!

The SDHDA's explanation rang a bit hollow. It seemed far more likely that the Fair Housing complaint forced the SDHDA to conclude that awarding credits to these three additional Indian applications was the path of least resistance. It would be less complicated than marshalling a defense against strong evidence that they had violated the rules governing the tax credit program, and easier than withstanding the extremely bad press that would result from battling the tribes and HUD. I was not Pollyanna-ish in my view that the fear of bad press contributed to this decision. It was not likely that within South Dakota the state allocating agency would be viewed badly for their treatment of the tribal applications. It was outside of the state, at the national investor conclaves and among the other state allocating agencies that the SDHDA would likely be judged more harshly. That is where the pressure was more likely to come, and I believe that played the bigger role. By this time, late 1996, the LIHTC had become firmly established as the most effective housing initiative in the nation. Its administration by the state agencies was being closely monitored and scrutinized. This was, in my view, the most important factor in the SDHDA miraculously finding sufficient credits for each of the tribal projects.

However it happened, it was good to be moving forward at last.

Show Me the Money

But we still had big problems. While waiting and hoping for the award of credits, I had been working industriously to find an investor for the Lakota Fund project. No luck. Every syndicator, the aggregators of investment funds, had the same response: "We don't understand Indian law and we don't know how to go about closing a deal on an Indian reservation, so we will pass on this opportunity." To make it worse, these same investors were all advising me to give up on Indian Country. They were saying that it was unlikely I would ever find a syndicator to take the risk of being the first to do a deal with a tribe. It was discouraging and I found myself having to fight the urge to give up and find another way to finance housing on reservations.

This reluctance to even consider something that might be "exotic" partially explains why conditions in Indian Country have been so bad for so long. It is understandable in some respects. I heard time and again that "We have a fiduciary responsibility to place our money in safe investments, balancing that safety against the desire to maximize the profits we and our investors realize." Indian Country's separateness—its remoteness—made it exotic. This was going to be harder than I thought. We had no track record to point to that would prove how safe and secure our investments would be. We could only agree to lower pricing, which would generate higher yields. And of course, lower pricing hurt our projects. It was a price the tribes would have to pay.

Finally, after more than five months of near constant effort, after calling and meeting with dozens of potential investors, I got the first serious attention from a small syndicator from Boston, Michel Associates. They listened and miraculously did not seemed scared of Indian Country. I prepared memo after memo and letter after letter describing the nature of doing business in Indian Country and how we had taken steps to mitigate the risks that are inherent in any real estate deal. And of course, we agreed to lower pricing, much as it hurt. Michel Associates became our investor for the Lakota Fund and for the other three projects, too. This small syndicator was an outlier. It was eager to invest in our projects mostly because it had fewer non-Indian opportunities. Michel Associates was consistently edged out by larger investment funds as it sought deals; when we came along they saw us as a sort of last resort to deploy their money. I was happy to have them but remained worried that if they became more successful in their pursuit of non-Indian deals they would abandon us without remorse.

Notwithstanding my fears, and without any alternatives, we began what is known as the *due diligence* process for the Lakota Fund, our first project. For the uninitiated, the due diligence process is a form of torture inflicted on people of good will by people who are trained to believe that Murphy's Law (that is the law that says if something can go wrong, it will go wrong) is a governing principle of life. Due diligence is a way to age the young, to turn summer into winter, to make tsunami waves in a shallow puddle, to make the sane crazy, and to turn hope into despair. We had no choice, but we did have a secret weapon; we had Angela Christy.

Due diligence is, of course, quite necessary and prudent. As its name implies, the investor undertakes an investigation to determine if the project is what it says it is. Does the developer, in our case the Lakota Fund, have the deed to the land upon which the project will sit? Is there a cloud on the deed of any sort? This project was the only one of the four to be on fee simple land, land not held in trust and mortgageable in the case of a default. It could be seized if necessary. The due diligence process includes literally hundreds of other steps, each one designed to prove that the project can proceed and will not be challenged by someone or that access to the site will be restricted or that the building site is not dangerous. The process was everything it was supposed to be and my sanity was sorely tested.

Bombs Away

We had to prove, understandably, that the land had been properly surveyed by a licensed surveyor using standards known as the American Land Title Association (ALTA). But ALTA surveys were rarely used in this remote corner of the world and no local surveyors could provide the certification that the investors demanded. We also had to investigate the environmental condition of the land through what is known as a Phase I Environmental Assessment. Because HUD was issuing a grant for the project, which in turn was used as a loan for tax purposes, the explanation for which I will spare you, they wanted an environmental assessment, too. But the HUD environmental assessment is different from the investor-required Phase I assessment. Basically, the HUD environmental assessment was concerned mainly with the impact human beings were going to have on the land, particularly endangered species, both plant and animal, and important archaeological or cultural sites that might be hidden on the land and potentially disturbed.

Nobody wanted to build over a long-ago burial site or long forgotten sacred meeting place. By contrast, a Phase I environmental assessment is largely concerned with the impact the land might have on human beings. Does the land have underground petroleum distillates leaking into the soil that might do harm to people? Are there any other toxic substances on or near the site? Was the land ever used for some purpose that might have left dangerous chemicals or substances in the ground that might someday lead to harm?

Oddly enough, this became a trouble spot simply because the attorney for Michel Associates was apparently a World War II history buff. He had, it seemed, recently read about how some parts of the Badlands, a stunningly stark but beautiful part of the Pine Ridge Indian Reservation, had been used as a bomber training ground during World War II. Where else but Indian Country! Apparently, there were some fears that some unexploded ordnance was still lying in wait for an unlucky foot to trigger an explosion. The land for the project was miles away from the former bomber training ground and was not even a part of the Badlands, not by any conceivable notion in fact, yet the attorney wanted assurances that the land did not have unexploded ordnance and that nobody would step on a bomb dropped by a B-17 Flying Fortress in 1942. We had no way to give him that assurance without doing an incredibly expensive investigation of the ground, using ground penetrating radar, that in fact might itself trigger an explosion. It was all ridiculous since the land had never been within the bombing range and no suggestions from anyone had ever even so much as joked or hinted that the land had once been a bombing range, but the lawyer insisted. The whole thing brings the Lawyers and Accountants Full Employment Act to mind.

We also had to prove to the satisfaction of the lawyers and accountants for the investors that the project could pay its bills if tenants decided not to pay rent. We insisted that the Lakota Fund had years of experience dealing with very poor families, since they were a micro-lender, making loans and collecting on those loans from people they knew and trusted. We had a waiting list of potential tenants and back-up tenants in the event those tenants did not work out. And the proposed rent for these families was so low, only about $200 per month for a 3-bedroom or a 4-bedroom house, that these tenants would not be burdened by the proposed rent. But they were not satisfied. They wanted evidence that the Lakota Fund could cover all of the expenses in the event that every tenant failed to pay rent for a full year. We could not provide that assurance.

There were dozens of other impasses for this little project. It looked like we were never going to satisfy the demands of the lawyer or the accountant for Michel Associates. But Angela Christy chanted her magic words, "We will find a way." And she did.

Angela and I sat down with the HUD administrators and drafted a grant to loan agreement that satisfied their requirements and that Angela knew would satisfy the IRS and the investor. She convinced the lawyer that even if an errant young pilot for a B-17 Flying Fortress had dropped some bombs somewhere he was not supposed to drop them, it was not on our land. I don't know how she did this, but she did. I flew out to Boston and met with the investor and finally convinced them that there was no need to demand a guarantee against a full year of no tenants making payments, something no developer anywhere else would be asked to do. After months of back and forth, Angela and I had provided enough assurances to the investor's lawyer that we could finally close on this deal. We had supplied over 200 separate documents and a promise that I would deliver my next born male child to the lawyer. Our first project in Indian Country became a reality.

With apologies to Edward Bulwer-Lytton, "It was a dark and stormy closing."[71]

Photo Gallery

Figure 1: Lillian Somoza being crowned queen of the 1940 Shenandoah Apple Blossom Festival

Figure 2: Above the fold news!

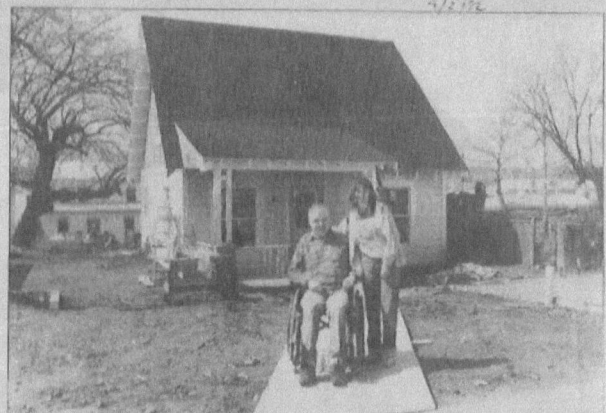

Figure 3: *Winchester Star* news article about the North Kent Court Project in Winchester.

Figure 4: Advertisement for Indian Lands

Figure 5: Gerald Sherman, left, and Mohammed Yunus in 1988.

Figure 6: George Gillette, second from left, Tribal Chairman of the Three Affiliated Tribes, weeps as A.J. Krug signs the land contract taking 155,000 acres from the Ft. Berthold Reservation for the Garrison Dam, May 20, 1948.

Figure 7: Chief Big Foot frozen in the snow after the Massacre of Wounded Knee, December 29, 1890.

Figure 8: Angela Christy is the attorney at Faegre, Baker, Daniels who never encountered a problem she could not overcome.

Figure 9: Chief Joseph

Figure 10: A typical travois, used to carry Plains Indians' belongings from place to place.

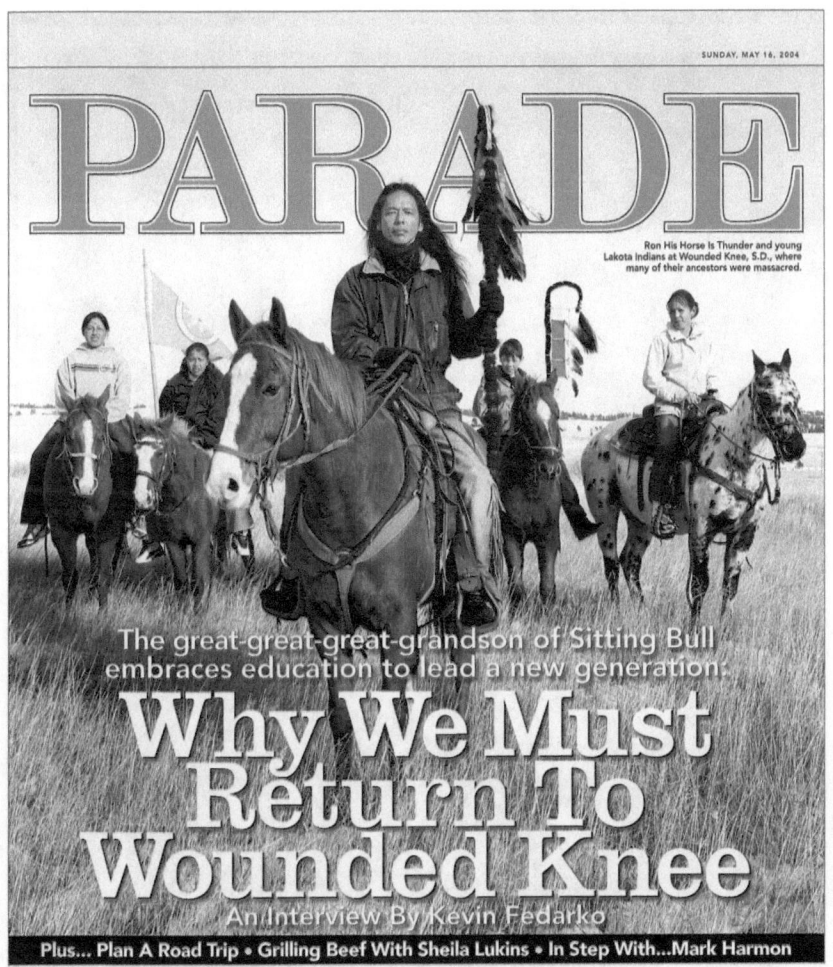

Figure 11: *Parade Magazine* cover story about the "Future Generations Ride" led annually by Ron His Horse is Thunder. This is the May 16, 2004 issue.

Figure 12: Chief Alchise (Alchesay)

Figure 13: The Burial Announcement for Maurice (Moose) Lambert.

Figure 14: Peter Rothermel painting of Patrick Henry addressing the Virginia House of Burgesses. Richard Bland is seated in the foreground left.

Figure 15: This new electric substation on the Navajo Reservation brought electricity to over 400 families that had never before had service.

Figure 16: The Colville Homes II project that was awarded the Charles Edson Award for Excellence in Affordable Housing in 2013.

Chapter 11

A Big White Ugly $#@%&

OVER THE NEXT 25 years or so we had difficult closings, but none were quite as hard or crucial as the Lakota Fund project closing. If this project had failed, my little company likely would have failed with it. On at least a dozen occasions over the years, one investor or another, on one project or another, said they were giving up and abandoning our Indian Country project. We would then make frantic calls and last-minute visits and pull them off the cliff. We always found a way, usually with Angela Christy's help, to save the day. But that was in our future. For now, the Lakota Fund project needed our help. It was a small project for this investor, but a crucial project for Indian Country. The LIHTC project for the Umatilla Tribe in Oregon had also been approved, and it looked like tribes might finally get access to their fair share of the billions of dollars in equity provided for affordable housing. Nonetheless, we knew that a failure here would squelch the hope and sap the good will we had worked so hard to create. This project was going to be our first, but I had three other tribal projects in South Dakota to get underway and another with the Red Lake Band of Ojibway in Minnesota. We had to make this first project work and we did, but not without multitudes of curse words and hundreds of hours of lost sleep.

It was looking like the business I had bet my future on would succeed. Perhaps we had indeed found a way to open the gates to millions of dollars for Indian Country. But it looked equally clear that every project had a tenuous grasp on success and that the misunderstandings about Indian law and culture could derail our efforts. It was time to take a more serious look at my business plan. The fact is, in the first year of my new business I did not take the time to reflect on the risks I faced and the threats to not only my business, but to tribal use of the LIHTC program. I was just too busy trying to land my first tribal customers and then get my first tribal projects approved, funded and underway. I never sat back and considered the nature of my relationship to the tribes I hoped to work with and the investors who would be providing the money for the projects. I never even thought deeply about the relationship I would be building with the states who had the power to determine the fate of my tribal projects and thus the fate of my new company. But I had to do all of that at once when the State of South Dakota finally decided to award credits to the four Indian applicants, followed by Minnesota awarding credits to the project on our new client, Red Lake Reservation, all in the same year—1996.

When someone starts a new business, they carry the risk that their product, whatever it is, might not be appreciated by the marketplace. Their product might be too expensive or might even be too cheap. Competition might drive down their margins. Tastes change. Most entrepreneurs understand these risks and have strategies to overcome them, at least the successful ones do. What most small businesses cannot cope with are risks that are unseen, that are unknown. We believed that we had a good price for our product, that our customers would want what we had to offer. There were no competitors. What we did not predict was resistance from the state agencies.

Our product really had three customers: the tribes themselves who had to believe in us and want our help; investors who wanted to buy the tax credits and who could be persuaded that Indian Country posed no greater real estate risk than any other market; and, the state allocating agencies who decided who would win the beauty contest and be awarded the credits. We had a strategy for all three of our customers. What we did not fully understand was that states might not behave in predictable ways. We did not calculate that the narrative of Indian Country, the stories heard and told, would be such a formidable barrier. In many ways, the struggle in South Dakota was a wake-up call. It gave us an inkling of things to come.

Tribes have many needs, but we believed that our company could be part of the solution to one of the most intractable problems. We thought we had the potential to make a real difference. But we were on a steep learning curve.

My first visit to the Red Lake Reservation taught me a bit more about being prepared. I had arrived at the Bemidji airport in far northern Minnesota early in the morning and Jane Barrett, the executive director of the Red Lake housing authority, had assured me that a car would be waiting to take me up to the reservation. It was a bitterly cold December day with temperatures well below zero, perhaps 10 degrees below or maybe even 15 degrees below zero. It was a typical northern Minnesota winter day, bright and sunny, cloudless because it was too cold for the air to hold moisture. It was so cold that being outside for more than a few minutes was life-threatening. One of the odd things I learned about living in Minnesota is the peculiar noise snow makes when it is 10 or 20 degrees below zero or colder. When it is that cold and you walk on snow it squeaks. I'm not sure why, perhaps because it is simply too cold for the snow to melt and become sort of slushy when you walk on it. No matter, but it does take away some of your dignity. When a young Indian man was there to greet me and lead me quickly to the waiting car, I sounded like a small dog with a chew toy as we walked to his car. I assumed, by the way, that the car would be well heated. Not so much. We got in the car and headed toward Red Lake, about a 30-minute drive from the airport. After about 10 minutes, I was shivering like that little lap dog with the chew toy. The driver made no motions to turn on the heater, so I asked him if he could turn the heat up "just a smidge." He turned to me, smiled and said, "Oh, this car doesn't have a heater. It broke several years ago. Don't worry, we'll be in Red Lake in about 15 minutes."

"Really, it's like 15 below out here," I said.

"Oh no, no," (pregnant pause and impish smile) "It's about 40 below. But we will be in Red Lake in about 25 minutes," he said.

"Wait, you just said we would be there in about 15 minutes, now it's 25 minutes?" I pleaded.

"Well, I didn't want to worry you," he said with a slight chuckle.

I had a winter coat and hat, but I was not outfitted for 40 degrees below zero. By the time we arrived at the housing authority office I could not feel my feet or hands and I could barely manage the door. When I got inside I sat by a little space heater and wondered if my toes would have to be amputated. I was such a wuss.

Soon Jane Barrett and her chief deputy, Linda McGraw-Adams, both enrolled members of the Red Lake Band of Ojibway, came out to greet me and asked me if the drive was okay. I told them that I would survive but asked that on the return trip to the airport to please have a car with a heater. They both laughed and said they would see what they could do. It seemed that this housing authority used everything, wasted nothing, and even though this car had no heater, it still ran and there was no sense in spending their scarce money on such a luxury as a heater.

Jane Barrett is a quiet and self-effacing woman who epitomizes the very best of Indian housing authority professionalism. She has had a long career on the reservation, notably working with the Land Recovery and Settlement Act, assisting Chippewa tribes recover land that had been wrongfully taken over the years in Minnesota. (Remember the Dawes Act.) Jane and her long-time friend and colleague, Linda McGraw-Adams, manage the Red Lake Reservation Housing Authority together and share the difficulties and the pleasures of providing housing for families and friends and very often, relatives on the reservation of their birth. Linda attended boarding schools on and off the reservation and, like Jane, went to college at nearby Bemidji State University. They are both quick to laugh and inspire a deep loyalty from their friends and co-workers at the Housing Authority. Jane is stoically reticent to talk about herself. In 2002, her oldest son, James, was killed in a hunting accident on the reservation and she unhesitatingly and lovingly assumed custody of his children. She raised them along with her remaining three children. In 2017, Jane's husband was killed in a car crash. She has had to endure far more than her share of tragedy. Such is life in Indian Country.

A calamity struck the Red Lake Reservation in March 2005 when a former student of the Red Lake High School shot and killed his grandfather and the grandfather's girlfriend, then went to the school and killed five students, a teacher and a security guard before killing himself. Like all reservations, every institution had relatives and dear friends among the dead and the Red Lake Reservation Housing Authority was no different. Jane and Linda had the responsibility of managing their own grief along with the anguish felt by their employees. The high school is just to the west of the housing authority, with school playing fields and modest pow wow grounds directly behind the housing authority. It was frightening and disheartening for Jane and her staff to be so close to such a dreadful tragedy, but having weathered her own personal tragedy, Jane was able to bring her staff back to some semblance of normality and they continued working amidst the grieving families and friends. Even though we would go on to do more projects on the Standing Rock Reservation (19 projects and over $40 million in capital), I am most proud of the 13 projects and more than $33 million in capital we brought to Red Lake over 25 years.

After I thawed out we got right down to business. The deadline for applying for tax credits in Minnesota was fast approaching and because of this Jane and Linda did not have the luxury of taking time to get to know me. They had no time to get a feel for my trustworthiness, to spend the time it would take to ensure that I was the right person to help them. They had to take a chance because, well, they had a housing crisis and very limited funds. They needed investor equity to bridge the gap between what little they had and how much they needed. I told them I was the guy for them and they believed me, they trusted me. I was all ready for a long slog of old world wooing, but instead we had an Indian Country version of speed dating.

Jane and Linda brought in Richard "Borgy" Borgstrom, the housing authority's in-house architect, and we started sketching out a first project. Borgy was a retired Chicago architect who tired of designing Gold Coast condominiums and wanted to do something he could really be proud of, so he offered his services to Red Lake. They snatched him up and were one of the only Indian housing authorities in the nation to have their very own staff architect. Borgy was a genuinely sweet man who knew what was needed in Red Lake, understood the costs to build on the reservation, and had absolutely no pretensions. We had settled on a 16-unit, single-family housing project on scattered sites throughout the reservation and I left with a signed contract. It was one of the best days of my business life, even if my toes ached for about a month afterward.

Indian Country had a true friend, if anomaly, in Richard Borgstrom. Very sadly, Borgy died of throat cancer in 2010, but not before he left a string of well-designed and efficient houses during his

19 years at the Housing Authority. He was 77 years old at the time of his death but was very fit and looked far younger. He received his architecture degree from the University of Minnesota, but completed advanced studies at the University of California, Berkley, and worked in California for years, mostly on very high-end buildings and houses. He was a sought-after architect but found his passion in Red Lake, living in a tiny, forlorn apartment next to the Indian Health Service Hospital on the reservation and commuting to a home in Lake Vermillion on the weekends. He designed utilitarian houses that could be built by local Indian craftsmen, not because he felt that utility was the sole determinant, but because he was acutely aware of the budget limitations of the tribe. You could not but love Borgy and I harangued him whenever I saw him to please stop smoking. Jane and Linda eventually forbade him from smoking in the basement of the housing authority, where he had his design studio, and he would go outside to enjoy the vice that eventually killed him. Jane Barrett went to be with Borgy when he died, at 3:00 am on August 15, 2010. Borgy's wife had died two years earlier and his children were on their way to see him when Jane took it upon herself to sit with him. So Borgy got to spend his last few hours with someone who cared deeply for him, loved him, and teased him good naturedly.

Big Fish and Big Problems

The Red Lake Reservation is named, appropriately, for the largest lake in Minnesota. It consists of more than 288,000 acres between the Upper and Lower Red Lakes. Lower Red Lake lies entirely within the boundaries of the reservation. For years, Red Lake supplied the Red Lake Band of Ojibway with ample fish, including large walleye and northern pike. It was overfished for a time, but the tribe's fisheries department instituted a ban on harvesting and the two most important species have made a remarkable comeback, providing jobs once again for tribal members. Red Lake is thought to be unique among Indian reservations for having all land within the now diminished boundaries of the reservation tribally owned with no private land holdings. This is known as *aboriginal title* and contributes to the Band's strong sense of history and culture.

Red Lake is the most remote reservation in Minnesota and has struggled for years with very high unemployment, exceeding 60% by most estimates. The reservation's isolated northern location coupled with its stubborn hold on Ojibway culture contribute mightily to its separateness, and not incidentally, to the pride members of the band hold in abundance. Consistent with a durable sense of their own unique character, the Red Lake Band of Ojibway chose not to join the six other Minnesota bands as they formed the federally recognized Minnesota Chippewa Tribe, fearing a loss of their own separate identity and cultural heritage. Red Lake is a fiercely independent place, but I always felt graciously welcomed when I visited the reservation.

It's Not Just Cancer Clusters That Are Deadly

By the time we had started work in Indian Country and for years afterward, sour predictions from state tax credit allocating agencies would prove again and again absurdly inaccurate. Most believed that Indian housing authorities already had adequate funding, were poorly managed, and were incapable of performing at a high standard, particularly the standards expected of tax credit developers. By contrast, I observed Indian housing authorities as likely the best managed housing authorities in the nation. What most non-Indians, especially those at the state agencies with the power of the purse, failed to recognize or appreciate is that Indian housing authorities have been grossly underfunded for decades. Yet they keep the houses they own and manage fully occupied even though the standard Indian HUD house was little more than a box doing a poor job of keeping the weather out.

Indian housing authorities were always a stepchild to the real priority for HUD, which was large urban housing authorities like Los Angeles, New York, and Chicago. Reflective of their cultural incompetence, HUD consistently mandated that housing on Indian reservations be developed in clusters, much like suburban cul de sacs, even though this went against the desires of Indian people who cherished privacy and open space. Remember, on most reservations land is not at a premium. There is on most reservations, at least in the northern Plains, Montana, and Arizona, more than sufficient room to accommodate this important cultural preference for open space. But HUD insisted on this more "efficient" configuration. This demand for efficiency resulted in bad feelings and a lack of respect for these cramped neighborhoods by the people who were supposed to make their homes there. This insistence on clusters of houses, bad as they were, would have been much more acceptable to tribal people if HUD had allowed the people living in the clusters to fill out the units in the clusters with relatives, cousins, aunts and uncles, brothers and sisters. Clans are very important in many tribal traditions but the cluster housing that HUD demanded did not allow for this kind of familial tie.

Historically, Congressional appropriations have been so paltry that Indian housing authorities could not replace outdated, poorly designed and inadequate housing. So they learned to make do. Our first project with the Ft. Peck Housing Authority in Montana, for example, was the rehabilitation of small, indeed comically small, three- and four-bedroom houses that had been built in the 1960s. For inexplicable reasons that made sense only to the designer at HUD, the bathroom in these units—the single bathroom mind you—had its only sink out in the hallway, not in the bathroom. With capital that we provided through tax credits, they were able to put the sink back in the bathroom and make other commonsense changes that the housing authority had never before had sufficient money to do on their own.

In Indian Country, the units owned and operated by tribal housing authorities are almost always overcrowded. State allocating agencies and others fail to appreciate the challenges faced by housing authorities that serve the very poorest families in the U.S., with some of the deepest social ills that accompany nearly all poverty communities. They serve these families in some of the most remote regions and in arguably the harshest climate conditions in the country. People like Jane and Linda pull that off every day, yet they are uniformly considered poor managers by bureaucratic institutions that have no direct experience informing their opinions.

Jane Barrett, Linda McGraw-Adams, and their devoted staff at the Red Lake Reservation in Minnesota, in far northern Minnesota, manage houses that had virtually no insulation when the units were first built in the 60s, 70s and even in the 80s. All this in a place where winter can literally kill you in minutes. And this is the norm for Indian housing authorities. I dare say that if the Los Angeles housing authority served a population with 50%, 60%, and even 80% unemployment like you find in Indian Country, with an average winter day having temperatures well below zero, in units that were poorly built and inadequately maintained because there was simply too little money to cover the costs for anything other than the most routine maintenance, something would have been done. More money would have been appropriated, better units would have been offered to replace the obsolete units and more aggressive social services would be readily brought to bear on the pathologies inherent in communities where hopelessness was the companion of nearly every child and every adult. But that is not what happens in Indian Country. Indian housing authority directors like Jane Barrett manage to keep the units full, to keep their families safe from the elements, and they do it miraculously with good cheer and a ready smile. They had more patience than I was able to summon when we struggled with state allocating agencies who showed so little regard for the difficult and burdensome conditions faced by Indian housing authorities.

Jane Barrett of Red Lake, Bob Gauthier at the Salish and Kootenai Housing Authority on the Flathead Reservation, and Maurice Lambert at the Ft. Peck Housing Authority, and so many of their peers were daily confronted with yet another impediment that their white colleagues in St. Paul, Pierre, Helena, and other state capitals did not experience or understand. Indian people remember the treaties that resulted in millions of acres of their traditional homelands being unhappily relinquished in return for promises of *housing*, education, and healthcare for all Indians on the reservations, *forever*. They know and believe that these were solemn promises, often consecrated with blood, and that the US government has not kept those solemn promises. Why, then, should they pay rent for a house that does not meet even the simplest demands of their culture, which would in the very least include an east facing entrance, or maybe have sufficient room for the large family gatherings that color the life of Indians? Why should they be compelled to pay rent for a house that should be recompense for the land they no longer have, for the life they were promised but has never been delivered?

In practical terms, this means that Indian housing authorities have a monumental problem collecting rents. HUD demands that rents collected must cover a very large share of the costs to run a modern, efficient, professional housing authority, therefore they limit the funds available to housing authorities. They assume, wrongly, that the rents will be collected and that the rental income will supplement the limited HUD funds they receive. But tribal housing authorities simply cannot collect all that rent, at least not in the amounts needed to keep the houses painted inside and out, keep the roofs from leaking and the windows from transferring the cold into the bleak interiors of the units. This is because tribal people know they have been wronged; they know it is not right. Even when tribal leaders point out to the families that without rent the housing authorities are hamstrung in their beleaguered efforts to maintain the houses and won't have money to build new housing to meet the needs of emerging families, the families nonetheless resist. Reasonably so, because they know it is just not right.

Indian Country is a mass of contradictions. The pragmatic side of the leadership on nearly every reservation I ever visited lamented the unwillingness of so many families to pay even a modest rent for the houses the tribe provided. But they were loath to confront the issue. Tribal leaders would pass eviction ordinances and then quietly urge the housing directors not to aggressively enforce that ordinance. The housing authority directors, the best ones anyway, would work hard to weed out the most egregious malefactors—the tenants who physically abused the units and who consistently paid no rent but made demands on the authority staff. Over time, most Indian housing authorities have come to the realization that the refusal to pay rent, even if grounded in a reasonable and justifiable disobedience, was harmful and self-defeating. The better housing authorities began to plead with their tenants, their housing board members, tribal council representatives, and even tribal court officers, that if the US Congress was not going to provide for them and HUD was no longer the provider of first and last resort, then they must be the source of their own salvation.

Over the 25 years or so we have been working in Indian Country we have seen tribal housing authorities come to grips with the financial realities of serving desperately poor tenants, with the parsimonious funding from the US government, and with operating costs that exceed their off-reservation colleagues' expenses. These are the housing authorities, like Red Lake, and the Salish and Kootenai, that have long-standing leaders like Jane Barrett and Bob Gauthier who built reputations for honest dealing, who made pragmatic decisions, and who governed their agencies with tender concerns for tenants in true hardship. State agencies with power over funding to tribes and non-tribal entities alike can and do learn about Indian Country. In some cases—too few, mind you—those agencies have changed their policies after gaining a better understanding of Indian Country. They learned that the base assumptions harbored for so many years were mostly false, terribly hurtful, and counter to the interests of Indians and non-Indians alike. If my company helped advance this cause, it was driven by mission and necessity. We had to confront the obstinate and obdurate resistance or we would have failed and tribes would continue to be consistently denied the funds that were their due.

Sweet Talking Will Get You Only So Far

With each project, we learned. I began to cajole the state allocating agencies by praising the steps that seemed to work and by addressing their misapprehensions about Indian housing. With the notable exceptions of Washington and Minnesota, the states' tribal housing policies in the 90s could be defined as pusillanimous at best and outright hostile at worst. I began to speak at every possible conference, meeting, or small gathering of housing professionals, especially investors, and worked to bring tribal people together with the people they needed on their side. My hope was that if the investors became sufficiently interested in these opportunities, the state allocating agencies would take note and be more willing to accommodate the special circumstances of Indian Country. Telling this story to powerful gatekeepers consumed at least half of my time, but my company and tribal access to billions of dollars depended on it.

Tribes are enduringly apart from everyday life in most states. This separateness can create misunderstandings no doubt, but it also breeds deliberate neglect. There was some outright hostility and racism on the part of some of the agencies' staff. Mostly, it was ignorance, sometimes willful; usually the lassitude was the result of too little guidance from top leadership, too little time to do the things that the majority demanded, and too little attention from the tribes themselves.

In contrast to Minnesota, the most difficult state was South Dakota. The South Dakota Housing and Development Authority carefully and skillfully disguised their hostility when it came to the interests of Indian Country. I believe this hostility emanated directly from then Governor Bill Janklow. There were few people in public office with a worse reputation than "Wild Bill," a nickname he liked and earned. During Janklow's last term in office, he was stopped 16 times for speeding by state troopers but never ticketed.[72] Perhaps they should have taught him a lesson, at least once. What ended his political career was his tragic recklessness. He raced through a stop sign on a country road and killed motorcyclist Randy Scott in 2003. The state finally sanctioned Janklow with imprisonment.

The governor had an abysmal reputation in Indian Country. Janklow had years earlier been accused of raping a 15-year Indian girl who was his family babysitter when he was a legal services lawyer on the Rosebud Reservation. An FBI investigation of that alleged rape determined that there was insufficient evidence to pursue a trial. He was, however, disbarred from the Rosebud Tribal Court. A year later, he became the attorney general for South Dakota. After his stint as attorney general, he was elected governor.[73] Happily, after Janklow left office, the attitude at the SDHDA seemed to change and they became far more willing to acknowledge there were unique considerations due Indian Country.

One could see garden-variety racism in South Dakota simply by observing the different treatment afforded people. Driving back to Minnesota from the Pine Ridge Reservation one warm spring day in 1997, I stopped for gas at a station on Interstate 90. I tried the pump but it was locked out. Looking up I saw a drive-up window type of arrangement where the gas station attendant sat. He saw me, waved his hand and remotely unlocked the pump so that I could fill my tank. While I was filling my gas tank, another car pulled up. This was a new car and well-maintained. The man got out of the car, wearing a colorfully beaded western vest and long braids; he was unmistakably Native American. When he did the same as me, the attendant motioned him over to the window and I saw that he was instructed to pay for the gas in advance of filling his tank. Soon thereafter, while still filling my tank, yet another man pulled up. This was a rattletrap pickup truck and the man who got out, to be generous, did not look prosperous. He was unmistakably NOT an Indian. He looked like a cross between Tom Petty and Ted Nugent. He was motioned to just fill up, no need to pay in advance. Only the Native American had to pay in advance. I was left wondering if the Indian man had noticed what I had just seen, and I presume that this is an everyday occurrence for him and many other Indians in the Great Plains and the Southwest. What does that do to your heart?

Overt racism in Indian Country is qualitatively different from the kind of racism you see in the South, in such places as Winchester. There is no Indian Country equivalent of the redneck driving his pickup truck with a Confederate flag billowing in the draft. It is a racism played out in more subtle ways, like failing to schedule predominantly Indian schools for the statewide basketball tournament, or even having few certified Indian basketball referees. Basketball is a big deal in Indian Country. Sometimes it is found in the willful neglect when drafting the rules that govern the Low Income Housing Tax Credit program.

This is Not a Joke (Well, Maybe Just a Little)

One of the most persistent characteristics of Indian Country is an almost morbid humor directed at its own condition. Perhaps that is how tribal people manage the soul deadening mugging of their dignity. Shortly after the incident at the gas station, I was asked to be a speaker at a large gathering of tribal housing officials and investors in Rapid City, South Dakota, under the watchful eyes of Mount Rushmore and the sacred Black Hills nearby. One of my antagonists, an investor representative for Enterprise Social Investment Corp., was asked to speak about how tribes might better position themselves to take advantage of investor dollars. In my view, this investor, who became a thorn in my side, grossly misunderstood the cultural and financial realities of Indian Country. He meant well, but he was a former minister, austere as an undertaker. To be fair, he was not among the investor and lender crowd that believed that Indians couldn't be trusted. Indeed, he was one of the few investors who saw the need for greater investments in Indian Country. However, he seemed not to understand the financial straits of tribes and had not spent the months and years I had coming to grips with those grim realities. He believed that no investor, including the one where he worked, the same syndicator that had given me such low pricing for my projects in Winchester, could invest in a project with an Indian tribe if that tribe did not enforce policies to fully collect the rents due. He believed tribes had to charge rents on the tax credit projects that approximated the rents charged by non-Indian projects. I knew that this was simply unrealistic, that tribes were not yet able to demand such high rents in the face of such daunting poverty. Even the best tribal housing authorities like Red Lake, Salish and Kootenai, and others were working in that direction but could not come close to such higher rents.

During his talk, the Enterprise investor rep was trying to describe the chasm between the expectations of investors and the realities of Indian Country. He chose a poor metaphor. He referred to a "big, wide, ugly ditch" that separated Indian housing authorities from non-Indian investors and lenders. Unfortunately, or fortunately, depending on your sense of humor, he did not enunciate well and what he said sounded much different to the Indian audience at the meeting. Every time he talked about this "big, wide, ugly ditch," which was quite often in his talk, it was heard by most of the people in the audience, including me, as a "big, *white*, ugly *bitch*." At first there were some uncomfortable looks in the audience, but soon everyone figured out that he did not intend to say what they were hearing. Folks began to smile and quietly laugh every time he used those four loaded words. After he finished his talk, he looked to me and I could not hold it in any longer. Laughing and shaking my head, I thanked him for his talk. He was completely unaware of the mistranslation by his audience and he thought I was merely being cruel. I hurriedly explained to him why I was laughing, and why there was so much laughter in the audience for something as awful as his big ditch and he finally understood. I did not see him laugh though. Several friends from tribal housing authorities came up to me later, demonstrating their famously sardonic sense of humor, "Man, we have to find that big, white, ugly bitch and get rid of her. She is really hurting Indian Country."

Indian people, in my experience, have an uncanny ability to laugh at themselves and their circumstances. On more than one occasion someone introduced himself to me facetiously as Luke Warm Water, followed by a hearty slap on the back. They somehow strike a balance between jocularity and anger. Humor is the shield they sometimes carry to help them cope with the pervasive sense of despair that some reservations may never overcome the intractable poverty and the persistent hopelessness.

A familiar refrain from non-Indians is, "If things are so bad on reservations, why don't Indians leave and find work or opportunity outside of Indian Country?" That question is the go-to response whenever a difficult issue arises. Jim West, Gerald Sherman, Jane Barrett and others would tell you that the loss of Indian identity is worse than the affliction of poverty. The terrible reality is that many of the smartest, most ambitious and most capable Indians do sometimes leave the reservations. Gerald Sherman wanted to stay on the Pine Ridge Reservation, but the harsh conditions, the failing schools, the lack of suitable opportunity for him and his children led him to leave, just as it did Jim West who left the Cheyenne and Arapaho Reservation in Oklahoma.

Many hundreds of thousands of Indian families choose to stay on their reservations among their families and their tribal kin. I understand why the land exerts such a hypnotic hold on Indian families. To some, the landscape may look bleak and unforgiving. It means something else to the Indian families, whose ancestors fought and died in those lands, who hunted and fed their villages with the wildlife with which the Creator endowed their lands. The creation stories vary among the tribes. The Creator in some tribal cultures takes on animal form, a raven, a bear, or for the Lakota, the Creator is Wakan Tanka, the buffalo.[74] I have driven over the Badlands of the Pine Ridge Reservation in South Dakota. I have driven through the vast, unpopulated landscape of the White Mountains on the Fort Apache Reservation where Geronimo befuddled the US Cavalry. I have driven up one side of Going to the Sun Road in Glacier National Park and down the other, to make my way onto the Blackfeet Reservation in Montana. These places are like no other, some bleak and some touched by a magnificent beauty that is spellbinding. What might enthrall me, what might make me look up in wonder, means far more to the people who call it home. It is part of the blood and the sinew of Indians; to ask Indians to leave their homeland is like asking them to cut off an arm or a leg. To expect them to leave is to demand from them a payment too great.

We lament the loss of family farms and we offer special incentives to keep those farms alive. We believe that the small family farm is the bedrock of America and we should do all that we can to restore farming and small-town life. We make no comparable effort for Indian communities. They are excluded from the American Dream despite their status as Native Americans—the first among us all. Our lives are richer because of the 500 languages spoken in Indian Country – indeed we are safer because of the Code Talkers of World War II; our lives are richer because of the music and art that emerges from their culture where it is most alive: on reservations. Their culture existed before North America was "discovered" by Europeans. We should honor and respect it.

Chapter 12

The Duke and Kareem

DEPENDING ON WHO you're talking to or which map you're looking at, the White Mountain Apache Reservation is also known as the Fort Apache Reservation. It is the home of the famous Fort Apache from the days of the old Indian Wars. The 1948 movie *Fort Apache*, starring John Wayne and Henry Fonda, was unique for its time in that it portrayed Indians not as violent savages, but as complex individuals in an established and multi-faceted society, equal to but separate from the white society they were battling.[75] The actual Fort Apache is now a national historic site under the control of the White Mountain Apache Tribe. It has the original officers' quarters, enlisted men's barracks, the original stables for the troopers' horses, and all the other buildings and parade grounds of an Army post from the late nineteenth century. The reservation also had one of the largest stands of white pine in the world until two devastating forest fires, one in 2002 and another in 2011, consumed millions of trees. It is nonetheless a stunningly beautiful place with magnificent pinon, juniper, and cedar trees in the lowlands, and heavily pine- and Douglas fir-forested highlands. It is also renowned for having a habitat that produces perhaps the nation's largest elk, with bull elk the size of horses with splendid antlers.

About four miles west of the old Fort Apache are the Kinishba Ruins. Kinishba is basically a 13th or 14th century pueblo-style "apartment" complex that may have housed as many as 1,500 people. After checking in at Nohwike' Bágowa, the White Mountain Apache Cultural Center and Museum next to Fort Apache, you can visit the ruins of this fascinating village made of locally quarried stone on a bluff above a creek that was fed by the White River.

Lore has it that the conquistadores visited the village over 500 years ago.[76]

The White Mountain Apache Reservation has an almost mystical attraction. Notably, it attracted Kareem Abdul Jabbar to become the assistant basketball coach for its high school. I think that testifies to its supernatural powers. What else would explain why Kareem would spend a year of his life with the Alchesay High School Falcons volunteering to teach young Indian boys something about becoming men?[77] Kareem got to know the people of the White Mountains three years earlier while doing research on the Buffalo Soldiers who had served at Fort Apache. He detailed the history of the Black cavalry soldiers in his book *Black Profiles in Courage: A Legacy of African American Achievement*. These soldiers, some former slaves or the sons of former slaves, served honorably and courageously with the US Army in the latter part of the nineteenth century. The high school where Kareem coached is named after Chief Alchesay, who served as a scout with the US Cavalry along with the Buffalo Soldiers and was the recipient of the Medal of Honor for his bravery. It was said that after he tried to convince Geronimo to surrender, he and Geronimo became lifelong friends.[78]

I did not uproot myself and my family and live on the White Mountain Apache Reservation like Kareem did, but it nonetheless had a hold on me like no other reservation. I met with the board of the Community Development Corporation and with the tribal council and was seduced by the beauty of the area, despite the apparent poverty in Whiteriver, the site of the tribal headquarters. The good humor of the Apache people was evident every time I visited. Many of the housing sites on the reservation have clever names that demonstrate their innate humor. One of the largest communities, in Whiteriver itself, is known as China Town. It is called China Town because most of the houses were, for inexplicable reasons, built on stilts that elevated the houses by five to eight feet and gave them the appearance, so they thought, of Chinese houses built along the shores of the Yangtze River. Another community is called Life Savers because the houses had been originally painted the colors of the rainbow and the houses, at least to some, resembled the hard candy of that name. But my favorite is Ben Gay, a community largely comprised of elders, who apparently needed something to ease their muscle pains.

Meeting with the tribal council was always a treat and sometimes intimidating. The council was at that time made up of tribal members whose first language was Apache and they would hold council meetings in a mix of English and Apache. Whenever they wanted to discuss something that they did not want a non-Indian guest or witness to understand, they would break into Apache. Once, after my son-in-law, Phil Glynn, had joined the company, we were testifying to the tribal council about the prospects for a project and they were discussing the merits of the project among themselves entirely in Apache. But on occasion I would see a smile creep out on nearly every face and the word "basketball" would be interspersed in their Apache dialog, usually followed by a few chuckles. Phil is 6'5" and apparently, they were discussing his potential on the court, there being no word in Apache for basketball. Hence the English word emerging incongruously in what we thought was a serious discussion of the merits of the proposed project. They never took themselves too seriously, nor us for that matter.

Damn, Not Again

After weeks of meeting with the staff of the Community Development Corporation, we settled on a project in the McNary district of the White Mountain Apache Reservation consisting of 20 detached single-family houses. It met all the criteria the Arizona Department of Housing imposed on all competing applications. We were well positioned because the income of the residents we intended to serve was lower than any other applicant, the location of our project was near necessary services and amenities, and we were suited to other similar criteria. The score we received should have been enough to win an award of credits. Indeed, our score placed us in the winning category, but we were once again denied credits. In this case, the rationale was that because the land for the project was held in trust, it had no value.

One of the competitive categories stated that in-kind services or donated land for a project would be included in the calculation of an award. Somehow the Arizona Department of Housing concluded that the land we were leasing from the White Mountain Apache

Tribe, for $1 per year, had no underlying value and thus the value of the avoided costs could not be considered in the competitive calculation. John Lopach was the manager of the LIHTC program in Arizona, and his deputy was Cindy Coen; both were reasonable and competent professionals. Unusual as it sounds, John had a doctorate in Renaissance literature, making him decidedly stand out in the tax credit world. Cindy was a hard-working, no nonsense sort of person who believed in the process and fought to maintain the legitimacy of the allocation procedure by ensuring that there were no foul-ups and no shenanigans in how projects were selected. When we complained that our project should by rights have been awarded credits, both John and Cindy were sympathetic, but they were apparently held hostage by one or more attorneys the state hired to look into our case.

The attorneys held fast to the notion that land held in trust had no inherent value. That was, of course, an idiotic position to take. Absent the trust status, which was something the tribe could not contest and did not impose on themselves, the land certainly had as much value as any other tract of ground, if not more. It had considerable attributes, with an abundance of pine trees, crystal clear air, and access to major recreation facilities. We sent the attorneys copies of similar transactions in which trust land was deemed to have inherent value. We had Angela Christy write an opinion that the avoided costs of a land transaction are routinely used in other states. We made no headway with the attorneys who eventually just stopped taking my calls and stopped returning email messages. Maybe we should have called Kareem.

The attorneys representing the Arizona Department of Housing were certain they were right. I am just as confident that they undertook no concerted effort to consider there might be some flaws in their thinking. They had all the information they needed, which of course, was limited to what they had seen, and that, apparently was enough for them. They were blind to their blindness. Effectively, what the lawyers were doing was creating a new and improved version of redlining for Indian Country. Just like the residents of the North Kent Street neighborhood in Winchester, if all lands held in trust were deemed valueless Indians would be consigned to the same perpetual cycle of poverty.

Luckily, in Arizona there was a robust organization that could help us out. The Arizona Inter-Tribal Council had an office in Phoenix and I went to them for help. Dave Castillo was the director of the Inter-Tribal Council and he shared an office with Susan White, a consultant who worked exclusively in Indian Country on health and welfare issues. Dave had an aura of dignity. Susan was quietly resolute and slight, but her appearance belied a gritty determination. She was also generous and willing to engage. Case in point, a few years after we first met, I took my son Greg to Phoenix for a visit and had a meeting that did not interest Greg. Susan volunteered to spend the day with Greg, 15 at the time, and he came back with a new haircut with blond highlights that delighted Greg and semi-shocked me. It was Susan's way of connecting and it worked.

Susan was as outraged as we were at the outcome of the LIHTC competition. She and Dave began making calls to the Arizona Department of Housing and met with the same results. The lawyers simply dug in their heels and refused to even consider the possibility that they could be wrong. I think they assumed we would give up and go away. John Lopach and Cindy Coen were still sympathetic, but the attorneys were immune to the protests from Dave and Susan.

Susan convinced us that our only likely solution was to file a Fair Housing complaint, just like we had done in South Dakota. I was resigned to this, if not enthusiastic, and wrote a long and detailed memo that became the basis for the complaint. Susan was on the HUD Fair Housing investigator like a chicken on a June bug. There was not a chance that this investigator, who at first expressed doubts that our case qualified, was going to do anything but become an ardent advocate for our project. He did not have a choice, but he may not have known it. Susan was relentless and passionate. Ultimately, the investigator agreed that the complaint had merit, the way a leaf agrees that following the air current in a tornado has merit. It was inevitable. Susan was a force of nature.

Advocating for our projects against the mind-numbing system was a Sisyphean process. Were we fated to a file-an-application/file-a-lawsuit uphill battle every time we had a tribal project? It seemed so. The complaint was filed with HUD in San Diego, at the Fair Housing and Equal Opportunity regional office, and they notified the Arizona Department of Housing. I do not know what happened next, whether they contacted the state's attorneys who had been so uncompromising, or if someone above them made the decision, but shortly after the complaint was filed, within days in fact, we were notified that, by golly, it seems that land held in trust does indeed have inherent value and this project did indeed deserve an award of tax credits. I had learned yet another lesson that would stay with me for the next twenty years--going to the mattresses[79] works. Over the ensuing years, we completed six more projects on the White Mountain Apache Reservation, all six with the housing authority.

The executive director of the White Mountain Apache Housing Authority at that time was Dallas Massey. He would go on to become the chairman of the tribal council. Dallas once told me that there were more than one thousand families on their waiting list for a decent house. This list included families living in their cars because there were no more affordable dwellings. They could be seen washing themselves and their children in the river. Is this what it had come down to? After all their sacrifices, destitute families were washing their children in the White River and living in their cars. Hearing these stories helped me justify the often-contentious relationships we had with people in positions of authority who denied these housing projects.

The Pattern is Broken

Shortly after the award of tax credits for our project on the White Mountain Apache Reservation, wonder upon wonder, we learned that our project with the Salish and Kootenai Housing Authority on the Flathead Reservation in Montana had also been awarded credits. This project, with the unlikely non-Indian name of Felsman Addition, lured me into a false sense of security. I had no misgivings about the application, knowing that the sponsor, the S & K Housing Authority, was well-managed and had a reputation for being innovative. The executive director, Bob Gauthier (inexplicably pronounced Goatchee), was one of the most respected directors in all of Indian Country. He was a sometime tribal judge in the S & K tribal court system and a formidable power on the reservation and in his dealings with HUD. He would eventually gain a seat on the Montana Board of Housing. Gauthier was well known and respected outside of Indian circles, too, serving on the Advisory Council of the Seattle Federal Home Loan Bank. He was not openly contemptuous of people he considered rather foolish, but his high expectations of his staff and everyone he depended upon to do his job was readily apparent. He was also effusively proud of what he had accomplished at the S & K Housing Authority, reasonably so. He was equally proud of the innovative and entrepreneurial successes of S & K Industries, the business arm of the tribe that successfully developed a resort on the Flathead Reservation as well as a diversified Defense Department contractor that was one of the largest employers on the reservation. Bob does not have a quintessential "Indian" look physically, one of his parents was non-Indian, but he is as dedicated and devoted to the cause of Indian rights as anyone who might have been more identifiably Indian.

There were promising discussions with Bruce Brensdal, the manager at that time of the tax credit division at the Montana Board of Housing (MBOH), the state's allocating agency. No issues arose prior to the MBOH meeting and we were promptly awarded all the credits that we had applied for. The ease of this award belied the almost Kafkaesque problems we would have in the future with the MBOH, but I was blissfully unaware of the lingering mistrust of tribes at the state's allocating agency. Had I known of the problems we would encounter in the future, we might have given up on Montana before we ever got started.

The Flathead Reservation in western Montana encompasses all but a tiny fraction of Flathead Lake, the largest fresh water lake west of the Mississippi. It is home to the Confederated Salish and Kootenai, two tribes that historically shared hunting grounds and were mostly friendly to one another, but not always. The reservation includes the Mission Mountains and is heavily forested but also has very fertile agricultural lands within the boundaries of the reservation. It is one of the most "checkerboarded" reservations in the nation. Thousands and thousands of acres of the tribe's lands were declared surplus in the early years of the twentieth century thanks to the Dawes Act.

Most of the very best grazing and fertile bottom lands ended up in the hands of white settlers through nefarious misdeeds.[80] The tribes have been trying to reclaim some of those lands but the fee land on this reservation is much more expensive than comparable fee land on most other reservations. This is mostly because the Flathead Reservation is very close to Glacier National Park and the Bob Marshall Wilderness Area. Most importantly, it has Flathead Lake within its boundaries. Tourism is a major source of income on the reservation, even if most of that income goes to non-Indians. It is nonetheless a much more prosperous reservation because of tourism and Flathead Lake, far more so than most other reservations, particularly those in Montana.

There is also far greater economic diversification on this reservation than on most other Indian lands. The confederated tribes own 204 ft. high Kerr Dam, now officially known as Se¿lis Ksanka Qlispe¿. (This is its Salish name. Don't ask me how to pronounce it, I had a hard-enough time figuring out how to type it.) The dam generates 194 megawatts of power annually and is a major source of revenue and a very significant sustainable power generator for the reservation and surrounding lands. It is the only tribe in the US that owns a hydroelectric dam of this magnitude. S & K Industries has for years enjoyed multi-million-dollar contracts with the Defense Department and other major corporations. The tribe also owns and operates the KwaTaqNuk Resort on Flathead Lake in Polson, the largest town on the reservation.

Flathead, by the way, is a misnomer. The tribes comprising the reservation were never known to have practiced skull alterations. No one knows for certain why the name was applied to this reservation in error, but it mostly likely came from a mistranslation of sign language.[81] While the Salish and the Kootenai Tribes were relatively friendly and cooperated with one another, the traditional enemy of these tribes was the Blackfeet, whose reservation is now north of the Flathead Reservation directly to the east of Glacier National Park. There is a stark contrast between the two reservations, with the Blackfeet Reservation being far less prosperous for a variety of reasons I will chronicle later.

The nearby Bob Marshall Wilderness Area is a vast, roadless area consisting of over one million acres. It's a favorite hunting, camping, and hiking area for Montanans and out-of-staters. It has

Grizzly bears, black bears, wolverines, mountain lions, and every other North American predator with the ability to kill and eat human beings. Moose are prevalent in "The Bob" as it is affectionately known, and they are extremely truculent and dangerous animals, too. Because they are herbivores they won't eat you after they run you down and stomp you to death. People sometimes find out, to their great surprise and sometimes their demise, that real moose, in the wild, are not at all like Bullwinkle from the cartoon. They may look goofy, but they are churlish, fast, can be bigger than horses, and just as dangerous as some of the carnivorous predators you will find in the Bob Marshall Wilderness Area.

The Bob has a special place in my memory. Just prior to the award of credits for the S & K Housing Authority project, I was asked to speak at a meeting of the Community Bankers Association of Montana in Helena. I was giving a dandy speech, exhorting the bankers to invest in tax credits just like their colleagues in Virginia had done for City Light. I heaped flattery on the presence of so much wilderness in Montana giving the state its unique quality. I told the assembled bankers just how much I was looking forward to hiking the Bob *Marley* Wilderness Area. I saw a bunch of blank stares and a few guffaws and then I realized what I had said. "Indeed, the Bob *Marshall* Wilderness area is unique, but a Bob *Marley* Wilderness Area, now that would really be special," was my attempt at a save. That drew a pretty big laugh out of the crowd, but I never succeeded in getting any of those bankers to invest in tax credits. Perhaps they concluded that anyone who confused Bob Marshall with Bob Marley could not be trusted.

A Chicken in Every Pot and a Car in Every Garage

Avoiding further reference to the Bob Marley Wilderness Area, I sought opportunities everywhere I could connect with the tribes. There seemed to be greater interest from tribes that had heretofore been afraid of the program, but nothing from the investors that I wanted and expected to see. It was about this time that the US Congress passed a new law that returned to the tribes most of the control over their housing programs that had been lost through the 1937 Housing Act.

In 1996 Congress authorized the Native American Housing Assistance and Self-Determination Act, known as NAHASDA, reorganizing the systems of housing assistance provided through the Department of Housing and Urban Development by eliminating several separate programs of assistance and replacing them with a block grant program. It provided a direct grant to tribes and gave them, with some very significant limitations, the ability to determine what was best for their individual tribe. Prior to NAHASDA tribes had to compete tooth and nail for limited grant funds and had to essentially build what HUD demanded. This law, flawed as it may be, was enacted specifically to recognize the sovereignty of tribes. It reduced, but did not eliminate, HUD's oversight powers. Right away tribes began to complain that HUD systematically abused its oversight role and too often ignored tribal rights and obligations.

However, like so much that happens in Indian Country, the drafters of the law did not understand the unintended consequences of enacting NAHASDA, mainly because nobody bothered to ask the right people or the right questions. The failure to consider how this new law might conflict with the LIHTC program regulations perfectly exemplified why there was a housing crisis in Indian Country.

Despite its lofty aspirations for self-determinism, the new law included language that implicitly kept tribes dependent on the federal government to solve its growing housing problems. The new law mostly kept the old law's protocol for HUD oversight, but without any explicit language to limit or define how that oversight was to be implemented in light of the law's explicit assertion on self-determination. Any student of government, particularly of government bureaucracies, knows that once an agency has certain powers, limiting those powers becomes extraordinarily difficult. Absent specific instructions in NAHASDA, HUD had little incentive to restrain itself in its oversight responsibilities and naturally would resist efforts to rein in its powers. Nothing in the law prevents the retention of its long-held role as "big brother" to its Indian clients. The intent of the law was to encourage tribes to seek out funding from sources other than the federal government. There is, however, no provision for the seamless integration of public funds to leverage private funds in order to overcome the scarcity of public dollars, to stretch the public dollars to fill the gaps left from ever smaller public outlays.

Being silent on the mechanisms that would encourage the blending of public and private funds implicitly suggested that tribes had no interest in the very program that was the lifeblood of affordable housing everywhere else in the country—the LIHTC program. It was nothing short of assuming a hungry man would only eat at the local diner and had no interest in the grandest restaurants in town offering the greatest assortment of delicious foods. Well, tribes do want to eat at the Café de Goldman Sachs. They just needed some help and some time to get used to the private financial market. We found ourselves working with HUD, sometimes fighting with HUD, to give tribes the flexibility they needed to take advantage of the full menu of funding sources. It was arduous at times, but deeply satisfying when we had infrequent big victories, like granting tribes the right to lend NAHASDA funds to partnerships in which they were the general partners, and more frequent small victories, like allowing tribal subsidy dollars to be included in basis, an accounting tool crucial to a project's financial feasibility.

Good Intentions and Bad Outcomes

Housing & Community Development, Inc. was indeed descriptive of what we did, but it was a boring and forgettable moniker. We needed something memorable and catchy, without being cute or too clever. I began looking at Indian words, but there are few that are widely understood and at the same time not tied to a specific tribe or Indian nation. I settled on *Travois* because it is a word that evokes Indian Country. It was a perfect metaphor for the Tribes helping themselves rather than some non-Indian business doing something for them without their direct involvement. The tag line: *You know where you want to go; Let us pull some of the weight for you* really spoke to what I wanted to do with my tribal customers. It evoked Elizabeth's earlier tag line for City Light, "We build 'em, you live in 'em."

Few people outside of Indian Country know how to pronounce Travois (tr*uh*-**voi**), but that did not bother me. It was a word with an evocative meaning that was clearly "Indian" without making us look like Indian-wannabes. It was also not a "New Age" or trendy name that might change its meaning over time. It has since become a name that people immediately associate with our company, and it has proven to be enduring.

After four years in business, our company was becoming more and more successful, but it was still mostly just me. I was becoming overwhelmed with the time-consuming diversions to fight with the state allocating agencies, to meet with various committees of the US Congress, or to convince HUD that what we were doing was within the rules they were forcing on the tribes. I had to commit time to these diversions to preserve the tribal use of tax credits, which was inextricably linked to the success of my company. Also, as if things weren't complicated enough, we were unhappy with the offers we were receiving from investors. Despite the steps I had taken to reduce the inherent risk of a tax credit project, investors continued to look at Indian Country as a "one-off" sort of investment. And they were paying less for my Indian Country project tax credits than they were for non-Indian projects. None of the investors saw the tribal deals I was offering as something to which they wanted to devote enough time to generate a level of expertise or level of comfort that I thought was warranted. For me, every day began with the same fear — would today be the day I failed to find an investor for a project and a tribe would go without?

Of all the headaches and hoops we had to jump through, the investors posed the biggest problem. None, even the ones that had done a deal or two, was willing to commit to Indian Country to the degree needed. Enterprise Social Investment Corporation (ESIC), my old friend from Winchester, believed they already understood Indian Country, but they had a deeply flawed perception.

The parent of ESIC, the Enterprise Foundation, now known as Enterprise Community Partners, was a powerful force at HUD and in the US Congress. Jim Rouse, the founder of the Rouse Company and a true visionary, had created the foundation to bring more fairness into the housing market. He had hoped to achieve a semblance of that fairness with the new town of Columbia, which the Rouse

Company had developed out of the farmlands of Howard County, Maryland. The foundation hired very capable people and was accomplishing great things nationally, but the plaudits they were receiving, well deserved as they might have been, gave them the notion that they could master anything they set their sights on, including Indian Country. The foundation embarked on an initiative to assist tribes in New Mexico and had some modest success, but nobody on their staff had developed the required depth of knowledge. Nobody had spent the hours, weeks, months and years listening to tribal elders and tribal leaders describe the nature of Indian life. They felt that they could bring the same techniques that were working in urban areas, the same models for success that were even working in some rural areas, to Indian Country. They were dead wrong, but they would not listen.

The Enterprise Foundation in my eyes suffered from an abundance of hubris and exemplified the arrogance of good intentions. They advanced ideas for Indian Country that reflected ESIC's underwriting requirements in other regions that had no hope of succeeding in Indian Country: greater use of debt, aggressive collection of rents, remorseless enforcement of rules—including evictions—in order to bring Indian Country into what they considered the mainstream of housing management and finance. As an overarching strategy, that might succeed in any other community that had such bad business practices, but not in Indian Country.

It takes more than a strong track record of successful housing development; Indian Country requires cultural competence. The Enterprise Foundation and ESIC definitely wanted to do good, but they did not take the time to learn how Indian Country really functions and what stands in the way of progress. I tried on several occasions to collaborate with Enterprise and ESIC, but their preconceived ideas about the use of debt, their failure to fully grasp the depths of poverty and the underlying causes of poverty and hopelessness left me frustrated.

Nonetheless, we were not without investors. We just didn't have the right ones. Most investors were looking at Indian Country as something they might occasionally do, but it would never become a big part of their portfolio. I was losing hope that we would find an investor who would devote time to learning about tribal interests and accommodating the special needs of tribal families. Then in 1998 Raymond James Tax Credit Funds, a subsidiary of the massive Raymond James Financial Services company based in St. Petersburg, Florida, showed up.

Our record of winning awards of tax credits for our tribal clients was finding purchase among a small group of investors, including ESIC, Morgan Stanley, and Raymond James. Representatives from these potential investors came out to Red Lake to discuss the details of our newest deal. Scott Simone, representing Raymond James, seemed to fully understand the steps we had taken to minimize risk and to make the Indian Country deals better than deals outside of Indian Country. Scott is a New Jersey boy, a little rough around the edges, but thoughtful and decidedly sensitive to tribal interests. He immediately grasped what I had been preaching for years—that Indian Country deals have less risk than non-Indian deals. Indeed, Indian Country deals are better. The other investors I had spent months, even years courting, either didn't believe me when I described how Indian Country deals were better, or decided the projects were more subject to failure than non-Indian deals.

It was maddening to see all the other investors nod in agreement, but then offer a price for our projects that was well below what they were offering other deals, even rural deals that looked much like ours but were not sponsored by an Indian tribe. This pricing differential was inherently discriminatory, but investors have the right to price according to risk and they persisted in believing Indian Country deals were riskier.

But Scott Simone believed.

Chapter 13

There is No Such Thing as No Risk, But We Come Close

I MUST DRAG you deep into the tax credit weeds now, so bear with me. All housing tax credit projects other than the ones I was doing in Indian Country have basically the same risk profile. Most non-Indian Country housing projects are done in urban or suburban settings and generally have "hard" debt. That means that the money these projects borrow must be paid back in regular, agreed-upon intervals, just like your house mortgage or your car loan. The absolute expectation of payments on the debt, by its very nature, puts those projects at risk of default and foreclosure. Oddly enough, the risk from foreclosure isn't the foreclosure itself, rather, it comes from the fact that the IRS deems a foreclosure to be a change of ownership. That means that potentially all of the tax credits, generally including the credits previously awarded and already used to offset income tax liability, would be subject to recapture. (This is probably more than you need to know, but it relates to how investors consider risk.) Remember, the credits are paid out over a 10-year period, so if the project gets into trouble in year five, for example, the IRS could recapture the previous five years' credits and disallow the next five years' worth of credits. Recapture means that the IRS takes the tax credits back and they also levy a penalty for incorrectly employing a method to reduce tax liability. It's like somebody has stolen the wheels from your car and then you get a ticket for not moving your car.

What makes these non-Indian projects riskier is that every project also has some risk of vacancy, especially if there is hard debt on the project. If a project has hard debt it must, naturally, make periodic payments to cover interest and principle. And while the rents might be "affordable" in the eyes of the law, they can still sometimes be very hard for low-income households to pay. If the rents are high or the amenities are lackluster, and a competing project pops up nearby, some of your tenants might prefer the new place and leave when their lease is up. That is a significant risk. Or if the economy softens or some situation arises such that some of your tenants struggle and fail to pay the rent on time or at all, the project can quickly get into financial trouble. Mortgage payments can get missed. This is a risk that investors understand and routinely account for in the pricing of a project. They believe they can assess this risk, account for it, and do the deal. They were not as sanguine about Indian Country projects.

To lessen the foreclosure risk and give more predictability to rent collections, some non-Indian Country projects have the benefit of federal subsidies to cover the situation described above, at least in part. These subsidies are subject to a variety of circumstances in which they might not be renewed or might not last throughout the life of the project. Things might be going fine for the first three to five years or so, but if the subsidy is not renewed and there is no subsidy to replace it, tenants might not be able to make the rent payments. Then there is that risk of foreclosure looming over the project. Outside of Indian Country, this rental subsidy risk was understood and accounted for, but it was a risk nonetheless. Stay with me, I will get to the good stuff now.

We designed our Indian Country projects to eliminate all of these risks. The way we avoided the standard risks of foreclosure is in part by having only "soft" debt. That is, we had debt that only had to be paid back if the project had the money to pay it back. If there was not enough cash, the debt would be rolled over indefinitely and foreclosure was thereby essentially eliminated. This is called *Cash Flow Only* debt. Also, our Indian Country projects had permanent rental subsidies guaranteed by the tribes that could not be withdrawn. Unlike the federal subsidies afforded to some non-Indian projects, tribal subsidies would last throughout the life of the project. It was far better than the federal subsidies used on non-Indian deals. But investors discounted this reality and continued to offer less per credit dollar than what they were offering on non-Indian projects. Those non-Indian deals had the standard, which is to say, *higher* risk profile.

Furthermore, and this is a sad commentary on life in Indian Country, it was far less likely, indeed almost impossible, for our projects to run into a situation in which a competing project would pop up and steal tenants away. First of all, because the land is held in trust by the US Government and the reservations are typically a great distance from employment centers, there is virtually no private real estate development on reservations. There is some development on white-owned land, remember the checkerboard metaphor, within some reservations, but they do not target Native Americans. Secondly, the tribes control their own environment and simply can refuse the approvals needed for a competing project. Why would they allow a new project if it might put an existing project out of business? More importantly though, and more to the point of the tragic reality of life in Indian Country, there are so many low-income families on Indian reservations – our projects routinely had hundreds of families on our waiting lists -- that even in the unlikely event of a competing project rising nearby, there would most assuredly be an abundance of other low-income families waiting in line to move into any vacant units. Nobody else could offer such risk-limiting characteristics. But nobody seemed to get it until Scott Simone of Raymond James came along.

Things Were Looking Up, For a While

In my negotiations with Raymond James, I insisted that pricing must change. Each of the projects to date had had investors paying less for credits than they were for other projects. Part of this was because most tribes did not have banks on or near the reservations, and banks seeking Community Reinvestment Act (CRA) advantages would pay more for projects that gave them greater CRA "credit." I argued that the banks, by now the primary investors for most syndicators, were misreading the CRA regulations, as indeed they were, but my arguments were not winning the day. The Community Reinvestment Act specifically allowed banks to invest outside their direct service area, so long as it was done in a state or region that did contain one or more primary market areas. But too many banks refused to acknowledge this provision in the regulations.

With Raymond James though, I had someone who was listening and taking into account my knowledge and experience at the Federal Reserve Bank. Raymond James agreed to work with their bank investors to seek higher pricing, pricing that better reflected the lower risks of Indian Country projects.

Thanks to the greater commitment and flexibility of Raymond James, we were able to nearly double the number of tribal projects we could complete in a year. But that number was still too small; the need was too great. I could demonstrate to the tribes that not only was Raymond James paying a better price for the credits, we could show that it was becoming easier to close the deals.

Over the next couple of years, from 1999-2002 we were able to move into other states and win awards of credits for projects in New Mexico, North Dakota, and Wyoming, in addition to repeat customers in Arizona, South Dakota, Montana, Minnesota, and Wisconsin. Then another big problem arose that threatened to bring everything crashing down.

The relationship with Raymond James was working so well that I did not spend precious time cultivating relationships with other syndicators. I could continually monitor the pricing other syndicators were paying on non-Indian Country projects simply by calling around to project sponsors to see what their investors had paid for tax credits. I did this surreptitiously to keep Raymond James honest in their pricing for our Indian Country projects. But I stopped looking for new investors. This was a big mistake.

In my attempts to make sure that the prices we were getting for our Indian Country projects were competitive, I learned that the average price investors were paying for tax credits was rising dramatically. That meant that the yield expectations by the top investors were dropping. Remember, there is an inverse relationship between the price paid for tax credits and the Internal Rate of Return (IRR) the investor receives from those purchases. The more they paid for tax credits, the lower the yield. While this seems at first glance to be a good thing since higher pricing for credits means more capital for the projects, it was in fact very destabilizing. It was destabilizing because a single very big investor was driving the IRR in the tax credit market down to very low, indeed unstainable, levels. The average yield was now so low, around 3% or 4%, that very few non-bank investors, the so-called economic investors, were left in the market. That meant that rural projects with few nearby banks were seeing much lower pricing to compensate for the very high prices paid in CRA-rich environments. This put our Indian Country projects at greater risk, despite the promises to the contrary, because Raymond James, like every syndicator, had CRA-motivated banks as their primary investors.

Fannie Mae is No Candy Company

The culprit in this downward spiral was the Federal National Mortgage Association, more commonly known as Fannie Mae. By the late 1990s the single largest tax credit investor in the country was the then mortgage-giant Fannie Mae. Fannie was routinely buying a billion dollars or so in tax credits every year. Fannie Mae bought so many tax credits that it had relationships with multiple syndicators, including ESIC and Raymond James, among others. And Fannie Mae insisted that syndicators like Raymond James and ESIC include other investors (now almost exclusively commercial banks) along with Fannie Mae in what are known as multi-investor funds. They didn't want to be the only investor, but they were always the big dog, controlling where the money went and what the terms were.

Surprisingly, Fannie did not have CRA as a motivating factor in its decisions. It could and did buy credits anywhere it wanted, without regard to the CRA "credit" it would have received had they been regulated like a commercial bank. But they weren't regulated like a commercial bank, they were regulated by the US Congress, sort of. It was mystifying to everyone why they paid such high prices for credits. The only plausible explanation is that it was their attempt to demonstrate to Congress that they were doing their part for the production of affordable housing. In essence they were saying, "Look at what we are doing for affordable housing, now leave us alone as we dominate the highly profitable mortgage business."

Fannie was so powerful (and powerfully arrogant, too) it could dictate what was acceptable and unacceptable to them. Fannie Mae demands on project quality, Fannie Mae expectations on the terms of LIHTC deals, and most importantly, Fannie Mae's sometimes distorted view of the marketplace, essentially became the *only* view of the marketplace. Irrationally, what was acceptable and unacceptable, favored and disfavored, to Fannie Mae became the norm among virtually all the syndicators. A single corporation exerted virtual control over an entire industry.

A herd mentality had taken root. Richard Thaler and Cass Sunstein in their 2008 book *Nudge*, corroborate my view that narratives drive economic behavior. The narrative that Fannie Mae was perpetuating, a narrative that seemed inscrutable to everyone but them, was driving an entire segment of the economy. In *Nudge*, Thaler and Sunstein write:

> The best account has been given by Robert Shiller, who emphasizes the role of psychological factors and herd behavior in volatile markets. Shiller contends that "the most important single element to be reckoned with in understanding this or any other speculative boom is the social contagion of boom thinking, mediated by the common observation of rapidly rising prices.[82]

And suddenly, in 1999 Fannie Mae, inexplicably, out of the blue, and without justification, said no to Indian Country and every investor followed suit, just like a herd following the lead cow.

We had grown dependent on Raymond James and Raymond James had grown dependent on Fannie Mae. Now Fannie Mae pulled the plug on Indian Country projects. They never explained why. They gave no advance notice. They sprang this on us like a home invasion by nasty little quants. They made the decision to no longer invest in Indian Country and since Raymond James had essentially built its multi-investor funds largely through leveraging Fannie Mae capital, meaning that they had no funds without at least some Fannie Mae money in them, none of its funds could invest in our Indian Country projects. But this wasn't limited to just Raymond James. Fannie decided that their moratorium on investing in Indian Country would extend to all of their syndicator relationships. That effectively meant that nobody would invest in Indian Country. That is the kind of control that Fannie exerted on the market.

We never found out why Fannie Mae made the decision to stop investing in Indian Country. We never found out if they cared that their decision to abandon Indian Country meant that the poorest people in the entire country would be left out of participation in the single most important affordable housing tool ever deployed. The fact was, we were sunk. Raymond James decided to wait it out and essentially told us, "Hold your breath as long as you can, might be a while." It would have done us no good to shop around for another investor, since none would buck the dictates of Fannie Mae.

This was an untenable situation, but stopping what we were doing meant that dozens of tribal tax credit projects were in jeopardy. Travois would soon run out of breath and be out of business. All this because Fannie Mae and the herd mentality of other investors that Robert Shiller so aptly described, had dictated that there would be no Indian Country projects.

The larger implications of the decision by Fannie Mae were not lost on me. Fannie Mae, though a private, stock-held company, was also a GSE—a government sponsored enterprise. It enjoyed the full faith and credit of the federal government as a backstop, even though that full faith and credit was implied rather than explicit. It was a multi-billion-dollar corporation that exerted outsized influence on the tax credit market and it was making a decision that would have outsized effects on the lives of Indians. What was missing was an understanding that they had a special obligation to take care with their decisions, to ensure that those decisions were fair and just.

Unlike most private corporations that presumably have an obligation to maximize shareholder value—where the public good might even be in conflict with that goal—Fannie Mae had an obligation to both maximize shareholder value and to protect the interests of the broader community. It enjoyed the protection of the federal government but ignored the explicit, demonstrable needs of Native Americans, despite the likewise demonstrably lower risks and higher yields that accompanied investments in Indian Country. They did this, I think, because Indian Country was not "mainstream." Indian Country was little thought of and even less understood. Indian Country could be ignored because nobody would know the difference, and few would even care. Indian Country remained invisible.

Our challenge was to convince Fannie Mae that their decision to back away from investing in Indian projects was a mistake. Fortuitously, by 1999 Travois had established itself as the market-maker for Indian Country tax credit investments. Every year more and more tribes were joining the party. We had created the templates that made our projects almost foolproof. We had worked hard to establish relationships with tribes who would otherwise mistrust white consultants offering "too-good-to-be-true deals." We had worked diligently to overcome the initial hurdles like waivers of sovereign immunity and resolving disputes in tribal court versus state or federal court. We had gone to the US Congress and to HUD to successfully lobby for modifications to the law and the regulations to make sure that Indian Country was treated fairly. And more importantly, our forty Indian Country projects were flawless. None had lost credits for non-compliance, and none were in default or even remotely close to default.

In short, we had created a robust market out of whole cloth that worked and was delivering millions of dollars for affordable housing for the poorest families in the US. Furthermore, our projects were successfully delivering the yield (or a higher yield) than had been promised to their investors, and that market had now been shut down for no good reason other than what amounted to what seemed to be the whim of a massive semi-governmental organization.

I was not about to give up after we had put so much time, energy, and passion into Travois. Too much was at stake and not just the survival of our small business. To compound the travesty of this decision, NAHASDA was now in full swing, but the Congress was getting stingy. The appropriations for Indian housing had not been increased to keep up with inflation, even as the old HUD homes were aging and becoming ever more obsolete. Need was increasing in Indian Country and the only real solution to the dilemma of increased need and decreased funding was to use the Low Income Housing Tax Credit program and that was being yanked away. This was just wrong. Maybe Fannie Mae was a private, stockholder-owned business, but it was also a proxy for government action and once again Indians were about to be screwed by the government.

Well, not on my watch.

Storm Windows and Palestinians

I was not about to surrender, to let Fannie Mae leave Indian Country high and dry. I was determined to muster all the help I could. I protested to the leaders at Raymond James, those above Scott Simone, to no avail. Their advice was to wait until Fannie Mae changed their minds and once again agreed to invest in Indian Country. It seemed that our fate was in my hands and no one else's. I decided to call each of my tribal customers and start a letter-writing campaign to the Congress and Fannie Mae to protest their decision. Jane Barrett at Red Lake was willing to implore her tribal chairman, Bobby Whitefeather, to write Senator Paul Wellstone, a strong advocate for the Minnesota tribes. I then asked the Menominee Tribe's chairman, Apesanahkwat, to likewise send a letter to Senator Herb Kohl, also a strong advocate for Indian tribes. Apesanahkwat is an actor who was a regular on the long-running TV show, *Northern Exposure* (he played Lester Haynes), and most recently can be seen in the movie *Wind River*. He had a practiced and natural eloquence. Each of my customers at the Yankton Sioux Tribe, the Cheyenne River Sioux Tribe, White Mountain Apache, the Confederated Salish & Kootenai Tribes, the White Earth Band of Ojibway, and every other tribe I had done business with and who had already developed a successful LIHTC project wrote letters to their senators and members of Congress. I then asked each of my customers to write directly to the president and CEO of Fannie Mae, Franklin Raines, protesting the decision to cease investing in Indian Country.

The folks at Raymond James Tax Credit Funds weren't happy with our campaign. They did not want to confront Fannie Mae and felt that we could wait it out. Maybe they could wait—their corporate parent was a multi-billion-dollar conglomerate. We could not. And our letter bombing program worked. Within a matter of a few weeks, Fannie Mae changed its mind, but they added an insulting requirement. Fannie Mae would invest solely through its syndication relationship with ESIC, cutting Raymond James out of the process. This also meant that no other syndicators would gain any experience in Indian Country. I would be dependent on a syndicator who I already believed had a flawed perception of Indian Country.

ESIC did not understand the harsh realities of poverty on the reservations and I feared they would severely limit the tribes they would agree to do business with. I again protested and instituted a new letter-writing campaign from my tribal customers. This time Fannie Mae came back with a compromise that I had to accept, grudgingly. They proposed that all of Fannie Mae's Indian Country investments would be made jointly through ESIC and Raymond James.

There were two problems with this compromise. First, each syndicator would want to be paid and that meant that pricing for tribes would decline even more. Syndicators impose a "load" on tax credit investments, just like a mutual fund charges a load on the money they invest on your behalf. Unfortunately, the double load between Raymond James and ESIC would ultimately result in the pricing to the tribes going down to a level below what we were used to getting with Raymond James as sole syndicator. How was this fair? The second problem was that I still had no faith that ESIC understood Indian Country and that we could successfully work together. I learned, in quick succession, just how bad this new arrangement would be.

Like a Really Bad Blind Date

My old antagonist, he of the big, wide, ugly ditch routine, was the designated representative between ESIC and Raymond James. He began to exercise an unwarranted level of scrutiny and a far too strict level of selectivity for the tribes he considered suitable, just as I had feared. In one unforgettable encounter, it became clear that he and I would not play well together. I had been talking to the tribal council, the housing board of commissioners, and the executive director at the Leech Lake Reservation Housing Authority in Minnesota for over a year. I had been visiting frequently, carefully cultivating them, and providing training to their staff on the intricacies of the tax credit program. I believed Leech Lake would be a good sponsor and would meet the federal and state expectations, as well as the expectations of any investor.

We submitted an application to the Minnesota Housing Finance

Agency and we won an award of credits for a project to rehabilitate 30 units of old, rundown, but fully occupied houses. When the time came to present the project to a joint committee of ESIC and Raymond James, the ESIC rep objected and said that he would recommend that Fannie Mae turn down the project. His objection stemmed from a meeting he had had with Harry Entwistle, the executive director at Leech Lake. Harry had told him, reasonably, that they would not replace the windows in each unit of the project, but instead would install old style storm windows over each existing double hung window, at a considerable savings. He also mentioned that the maintenance staff at the housing department had experience replacing broken storm windows and given the number of windows that were broken every month, storm windows were much more cost effective. They were cheaper to repair than new, thermal pane windows.

Our putative investor explained that his rationale for turning down the Leech Lake project was because Leech Lake was "empowering the bad behavior of its tenants." He believed that by replacing the storm windows rather than installing new energy efficient windows, the executive director was enabling the bad behavior of tenants who abused the units, who broke the windows. He insisted that they were not being strict enough managers, willing to evict problem tenants, and that they should insist on installing the more problematic and difficult to repair, but more energy efficient new windows. Because the housing authority would not agree to do that, he opposed the project.

Exasperated, I sighed heavily and dramatically, and asked him how many times and for how long he had visited the Leech Lake Reservation. He admitted that his only experience was a single two- or three-hour meeting at the reservation. I thereupon stated, with sarcasm oozing out of me like toxic ectoplasm, that he must be the smartest guy in the world. Who else could assess the capabilities of an Indian housing authority in such a short time but the world's most astute judge of character and competence. I told everyone on the call, which included several officials from Raymond James, that I was in awe of our supposed investor's superior powers of observation; it was astonishing that he could assess the suitability and capabilities of a tribe after a single short meeting when it takes me well over a year to do such a thing.

I didn't let up and may even have disparaged his mother's ancestry. Finally, someone from Raymond James mercifully suggested a compromise in which a team of underwriters from Fannie Mae would go to Leech Lake and determine for themselves if the reservation could successfully develop and manage a tax credit project. I objected saying that who knew if these underwriters had any knowledge of Indian Country and could possibly understand and appreciate the difficulties of Indian life. I insisted that it was unreasonable to turn down a project based on such a flimsy rationale. But I was overruled and the Fannie Mae team was sent to Leech Lake. I was more than a little surprised and gratified when they reported back in favor of the project and it proceeded to a closing with an investment from Fannie Mae.

The ESIC rep was certain of his assessment of the management capabilities of the Leech Lake Reservation Housing Authority despite the paucity of time spent studying the housing authority's records or even time spent getting to know the executive director or any of his staff. Just like the illusion of validity that infused the promoters of exotic financial instruments (remember SIVs and other derivatives that were supposed to offer greater protections against risk but did not), he was convinced that he could accurately judge the risks at Leech Lake. Indeed, he could do it in a matter of a few hours. He did not bother to look for more evidence and he certainly gave no credence to my own due diligence with Leech Lake; he had seen enough. While I should have been more courteous and polite, I was ready to rumble. It was a good thing this discussion took place over the phone.

To be sure, there are management problems in Indian Country. Our erstwhile investor was parroting the belief that Indian housing authorities could not be counted on to be tough but fair managers. The mistaken assumption by people with a passing knowledge of public housing was that tribal housing was generally poorly managed and that things looked bad because the families did not take care of the units they lived in, breaking windows and such. That is the story that is shared among government agencies. That is the myth that he was retelling. The perception was that tribal housing authorities could not, or simply did not want to evict tenants who would be routinely sent packing by other, more professional, that is to say, non-Indian housing authorities.

To make matters worse, Fannie Mae was alarmed because the Standing Rock Sioux Tribal Council had recently passed an ordinance prohibiting the housing authority, or a tribal judge for that matter, from evicting any tenant during the months of December through February. Fannie Mae and ESIC saw this as a "free lunch" for tenants to avoid rent during those months, to feel free to abuse the units knowing, by ordinance, that they could not be evicted. But there is a very good reason that Standing Rock passed this ordinance. In North and South Dakota, during the winter months, temperatures can reach well below zero and stay there for weeks. The snow and the wind on the Standing Rock Sioux Reservation is life threatening to someone who is simply caught out in the cold, much less a family that is homeless. And there are no alternatives. There are no shelters for the homeless in Ft. Yates, North Dakota. There is no ample supply of vacant units where a recently evicted family can move.

Families did abuse this. There are examples of thoughtless people damaging their only source of shelter and never being held accountable on Standing Rock and other reservations. But these examples are the exceptions to the thousands of desperately poor households who do not abuse the units they live in. These bad examples stand in contrast to the efforts tribal housing authorities make to keep in operation housing units built during the HUD years with two-by-four walls rather than two-by-six walls, meaning that the insulation value is 20% or less of modern standards. These bad examples stand in contrast to maintenance staff who keep plumbing lines open despite 10-, 20- or 30-degree below zero weather. Some things just have to give and sometimes evicting lousy tenants is what gives.

Tribes make other bad decisions, too. They sometimes elect and reelect to their governing councils men and women who have consistently stolen from the tribes themselves. They mismanage their finances. They send staff on junkets when they are needed at home. They hire unqualified family members to fill crucially important tribal government jobs. They fire qualified staff because of some perceived slight. They fight among themselves over which tribal district will get a new community building when what they need to do is invest in promising economic development opportunities or needed infrastructure projects. Abba Eban, speaking of the Palestinians some 45 years ago, said, "They never miss an opportunity to miss an opportunity."[83] The same can be said of Indian tribes. But the same can also be said of Chicago and Philadelphia. The same can be said of Illinois and Mississippi. But for some reason, these deficiencies are not overlooked when it comes time to invest in Indian Country. They are explained away when it comes time to invest in Chicago, Philadelphia, Illinois, and Mississippi.

Why is Indian Country held to a different standard? Is it because so few people understand Indian Country? Is it because the tribes are remote and sometimes inaccessible? Is it because tribal lands were systematically reduced to the barest sustainable lands and have been forgotten? Is it racism? Is it a general inability to place oneself in the shoes of someone else? Perhaps it is all these things.

In my experience, the people making these judgments have very little actual experience with Indian people, but they have heard the stories of mismanagement and incompetence. Their data set is limited and what they have heard about Indian Country is uniformly bad. As Kahneman and Tversky say, "They tend to extract more certainty from the data than the data, in fact, contain."[84] I had to combat these intractable perceptions every time I had a tribal project in hand. Our greatest weapon was the success we were having. Our tribal clients were diligent and uncompromising in meeting the expectations of the investors and the state allocating agencies, despite having had no prior experience with the private capital markets and nearly zero experience with state government agencies. It put the lie to the prophecies of doom we had been hearing.

Part III
Slowly Becoming Mainstream

Chapter 14

Grim Reality Check

GOOD DECISIONS ARE made when they are based on facts. Your mother's delicious chocolate cake calls for two eggs, not one. Your car either has enough oil or it does not. The same is true for housing policy. If you want to know if there is a need for affordable housing, do a market analysis. We did.

There had always been a requirement for market studies to document the need for the housing credits. An amendment to Section 42, the governing statute for the tax credit program, eventually made it mandatory to have a third-party prepare those market studies. Since I had a background in market analyses I was the one preparing these studies for my customers in the early years. Not to put too fine a point on it, but the indigenous people of this country are not getting much out of the land deals they made with our forefathers.

Indian Country has far worse housing conditions than you will find anywhere else in the nation. What shocked me most was that when we presented the market study, in state after state for tribe after tribe, its disturbing findings almost never struck a chord. I never once heard a state allocating agency board member say to me, "My God, how have we let things get so bad?" I never heard anyone, not once, suggest that conditions were so deplorable that tribes deserved extra special consideration. And make no mistake, special consideration is warranted.

Bear in mind, as a general practice, tribal housing authorities, unlike their non-Indian brethren, will offer a housing unit to their most vulnerable families irrespective of those families' ability to make monthly rent payments. The Pueblo of Pojoaque in New

Mexico had a four-bedroom house available and dozens of large families on their waiting list. It also had a single mother with a disabled child and virtually no income. She could not pay even the minimum rent for this three-bedroom house, about $75 per month, without sacrificing something precious. There would either be less food or less care for her child in need. She was moved into this too-big house, without objection, even from the families who had in some cases waited years for an affordable house. To most people this makes no business sense. Indeed, it does not, it leaves tribal housing authorities gasping for money. But it is a cultural imperative. They cannot and will not turn away an elder in need, even if by doing so they leave themselves financially vulnerable. That is the Indian way. It means that tribal housing authorities do more with less, under the most deplorable conditions. But I never heard any state agency or investor applaud or even acknowledge the noble, honorable, charitable, and humane manner in which tribal housing authorities operate. Not once.

The deplorable conditions are manifest. The incidence of houses in which there are problems with plumbing in general and problems with kitchens in particular is 10.2% in Indian Country as compared to 3.0% in the U.S. as a whole. But that is among all Indians. If you look at the statistics for just low-income Indians, the number of households with incomplete plumbing and kitchens jumps to 19%, nearly one out of every five households. Indian households report being overcrowded at a rate of 10.8% of all Indian households versus the national average of only 2%. But again, if you look at just low-income Indian households, the percent that is overcrowded soars to 15%.[85] In one form or another we presented data specifically delineated for each of our tribal customers not unlike the chart below.

While we were winning awards of credits for our customers, at no time did anyone at any state agency suggest that more should be done, that this was not nearly enough. And more needed to be done, much more. We purposefully and strategically delayed tribal projects in some states because we knew they could not win an award that year, either because another tribe had been awarded credits or the tribe we were working with had not finished a previous project and would be seen as moving too fast. We could easily

HOUSING PROBLEMS COMBINED % with problem	AIAN in Tribal Areas	Total US
	Percent	Percent
FACILITIES/CONDITIONS PROBLEMS		
Plumbing/Kitchen	10.2	3.0
Other Heating/Electrical/Cond.	13.0	2.0
Subtotal	23.0	5.0
LOW INCOME HOUSEHOLDS (<80% of median income)		
Physical Problems		
Plumbing/Kitchen Deficiency	19.0	2.0
Other Overcrowded	15.0	5.0

Chart 1. Housing Needs of American Indian and Alaska Natives in Tribal Areas – US Department of HUD, 2017

have done far more, but we were discouraged by both state agencies and investors who thought they were doing enough. Remember the official in Winchester who thought there was no need for us to move so quickly in the North Kent Street neighborhood? Sound familiar?

Ironically, despite enduring housing conditions that are the worst in the U.S., young Indian men and women serve in the military in greater proportion than any other ethnic group. And they have done this for years. According to Kevin Gover, former director of the Bureau of Indian Affairs and current director of the National Museum of the American Indian, "I was raised with stories of friends and family members' bravery on the battlefield. Native Americans served in World War I even though they were not citizens of the United States. In fact, it was not until after World War II in the 1965 passage of the Voting Rights Act that all states were required to allow Native Americans to vote on the same basis as any other American. Despite decades of persecution and broken promises, despite being dispossessed of, and often forcibly removed from, their ancestral homelands, American Indians have served and continue to serve in our nation's armed forces in numbers that belie their small percentage of the American population. They step forward when duty calls."[86] It's hard to imagine how Indian people keep signing up to protect the "homeland" given the number of broken promises in the Ft. Laramie Treaties, or the Robinson Treaties, or the Treaties at Fort Carlton and Pitt, or any of the more than fifty other treaties that have been abrogated and unilaterally nullified. I cannot think of a more dramatic example of this country's disservice to its native sons and daughters.

According to the American Indian Relief Council: "American Indians are 600% more likely to die from heart disease than other Americans, 226% more likely to die from diabetes, and 600% more likely to die from tuberculosis. Disparities related to rates of cancer and cancer treatment are also higher than for any other Americans." [87] Indian Country has all of the social pathologies associated with poverty stricken communities, only worse, including rates of alcoholism and drug abuse that far exceed the rate for the nation as a whole. In a study of persons who needed treatment at a specialty facility for substance abuse over the period 2003 to 2012, 17.5% of Native American and Alaskan Natives needed such treatment, as compared to 9.3% of all other races and ethnicities.[88] According to studies conducted for the Centers for Disease Control and Prevention (CDC), incidences of Fetal Alcohol Syndrome per 10,000 total births for different ethnic groups showed that Asians had the overall lowest rate at 0.3 per 10,000 live births. Hispanics had a rate of 0.8 per 10,000, whites 0.9, and Blacks 6.0. Native Americans had a wretchedly high rate of 29.9 per 10,000 live births.[89] There is a lower rate of high school graduation in Indian Country than anywhere else in the nation. According to the US Department of Education, students are graduating from high school at a higher rate than ever before. The nation's high school graduation rate hit 82 percent in 2013-14, the highest level since states adopted a new uniform way of calculating graduation rates five years ago. But in Indian Country the rate is only 69.6%.[90]

Different but similar biases victimize African American households and Native American households, but the result is the same: diminished wealth, hopelessness, discrimination in employment, and social pathologies. People in the South have heard the mean-spirited stories for decades and they attribute the disparity in wealth and achievement to personal characteristics and individual failings. Majority populations in the South steadfastly refuse to put any stock in the data that points to discrimination and legal restrictions that date back to slavery and Jim Crow as the determining

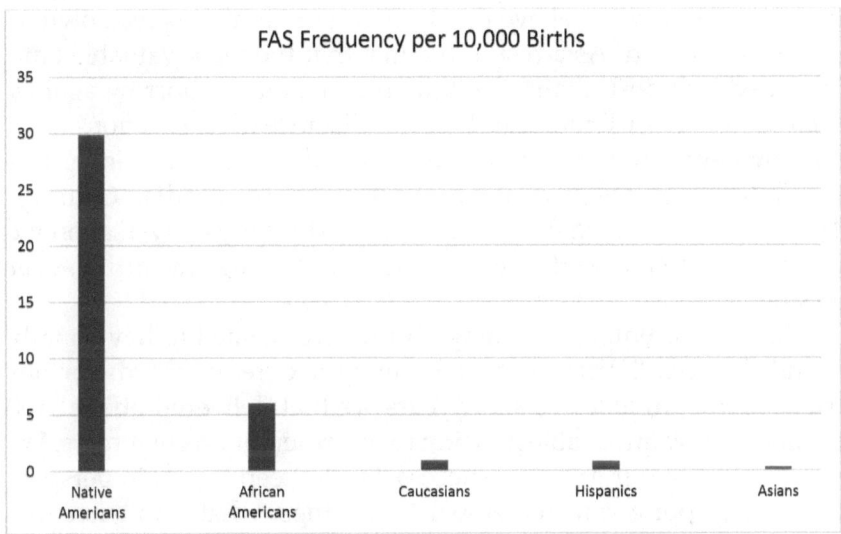

Chart 2. Fetal Alcohol Syndrome Frequency in Indian Country

factor in the disparities in wealth between white households and Black households.

The biases against Native Americans have a different source. First, there are far fewer Native Americans than African Americans and they are concentrated in the Southwest and the Great Plains states that have generally smaller populations. White people in the west rarely see American Indian people who are isolated on distant reservations, and the ones they may notice are homeless in places like Billings, Montana, or Rapid City, South Dakota, frequently suffering from drug and alcohol dependency. Furthermore, there is a generalized confusion as to whether or not Indians even receive "welfare" or food stamps or have some other mysterious government assistance that is peculiar to Native Americans. As a result, bias takes a dissimilar, qualitatively different form. Whereas a Black person might be stereotyped as lazy, an Indian is labeled drunk, careless, and abusive. There is the common misapprehension that Native Americans are poor stewards over capital assets like houses and office buildings, even schools. These presumptions fuel the tendency to believe that Indians shouldn't be given ownership of their land. As a result, the fact that the most valuable land is owned by non-Indians, the Indian's inability to borrow against their land held in Trust, and the great distance of reservations from employment centers are rarely understood as the determining factors in the disparity in wealth and achievement in Indian Country. That was the toxic fog that hung over nearly every conversation we had with investors and state agencies, but the fog was lifting, ever so slowly.

As Travois entered the new century we seemed to have finally found the secret ingredients to winning tax credit awards for our tribal clients. In just five short years we had delivered about $100 million in new affordable housing to our reservation customers. We were proud of our growing success, but to keep things in perspective it is important to remember two things: what a pittance this $100 million was relative to the need, and just how bad things were and continue to be in Indian Country.

By the year 2000 the tax credit market was about $10 billion per year. We were averaging just over $20 million per year for our tribal customers or about 0.2% of the capital deployed every year. That would grow dramatically in the years to come, but it would never reach a level adequate for the Native American population. Worse than the paltry percent of capital were the unpardonable and unrelenting housing conditions on reservations.

Still, Travois continued winning credit awards for tribal clients. And, predictably, the investment advisor at ESIC recommended against them for reasons that defied logic or imagination. He objected to an investment in a project with the Northern Arapaho tribe on the basis that this tribe shared the Wind River Reservation in Wyoming with its historic enemy, the Eastern Shoshone Tribe.[91] He had never visited the reservation nor talked with the housing authority executive director, yet he was certain that a project on the Wind River Reservation would fail because of the historic hostilities between the two tribes. He was the poster child for the illusion of validity: what little he knew about Indian Country was enough, in his mind, to make judgments without any consideration of the far-reaching implications for Indian families.

Sometimes Hollywood Gets It Right

The Wind River Reservation in Wyoming is a vast landscape of more than 1.8 million acres, hemmed in by the red rocks of the Owl Creek Mountains, the majestic Wind River Range, and the pine studded Absaroka Mountains and includes part of the spectacular Wind River Canyon. This canyon is a sort of mini version of the Grand Canyon, though it was formed by geologic up-thrust rather than erosion by a thunderous Colorado river. Strategically placed signs on the 2,500-foot sheer cliff walls that line either side of the highway tell passersby how old the granite or sedimentary stone is and which prehistoric period the stone represents. Parts of the canyon are more than 2.9 billion years old and date from the Precambrian prehistoric era. Also, included in the total acreage of the reservation is a wilderness area of almost 200,000 acres. From this wilderness area adjoining the Yellowstone ecosystem, Grizzly bears sometimes wander onto the reservation. Sometimes Grizzlies show up in Lander, one of the largest cities on the outskirts of the reservation. It is a lovely, if mostly dry and windswept place with the Wind River cutting through the reservation. But it is also almost unimaginably bleak. Single-wide trailers dot the landscape, with the obligatory sad corral containing an Indian pony or two. On almost every trailer, teepee poles lean against an outbuilding or the trailer itself. The distances on the Wind River Reservation, like Pine Ridge, Cheyenne River, Standing Rock, Crow or Ft. Peck are immense. You can drive for hours, you can see for hundreds of miles. There is nothing there. (The movie *Wind River* staring Jeremy Renner will give you a look it.)

In one of my visits, I remarked to Frank Armajo, the executive director of the Northern Arapaho Tribal Housing Authority, that I had come to Ethete, the headquarters of the housing authority, via Crow Heart Highway. I told him that it was interesting that the Arapaho or the Shoshone tribes would honor the Crow Tribe with the naming of a highway. He laughed and said, "It does not honor the Crow Tribe. It honors the Arapaho warrior who killed a Crow raider and cut out his heart to display to his Arapaho kinsmen." I had an entirely different feel for that highway on my way back home.

Frank Armajo was a tragic figure for me. I worked with Frank for nearly 2 years before we completed the first project. He was always thin and quiet, walking carefully and deliberately. I thought he was simply that – careful and deliberate. While he may well have been naturally unhurried and thoughtful, it turned out he was also very ill. Over the time that I worked with him he became progressively sicker and sicker. He was awaiting a liver transplant when he died. He had related to me the story of his disease being misdiagnosed for several years by the on-again, off-again peripatetic doctors of the Indian Health Service, who never seemed to provide any sort of continuity of care. His liver disease, so long misdiagnosed, led to heart disease and he eventually became too weak to hold out for the transplant that he should have had years earlier.

Our ESIC investor was certain that the enmity between the Northern Arapaho and Eastern Shoshone tribes, which was quite real, would lead to disaster if one tribe won an award of credits and the other did not. We countered that despite the historic animosities between the two tribes, each would see the benefit of cooperating with the other to ensure that the Wind River Reservation would see some new affordable housing and some outside investments. As it turned out, the Northern Arapaho Tribal Housing Authority became a very successful tax credit developer, undertaking, with Fannie Mae funds, its first project, Airport Road, then following with Beaver Creek I and Beaver Creek II. They sought approval from the Eastern Shoshone Business Council for these projects and it was granted. (Eventually, we would win for the Eastern Shoshone Housing Authority its share of tax credits too, but not with Fannie Mae as an investor.) We were settling into a pattern in which ESIC would object to a tribal project, I would strenuously, stridently and sometimes profanely, defend them, someone from Fannie Mae would visit, and our project would be approved. Every time. The last straw was an innovative project on the Standing Rock Reservation in Fort Yates, North Dakota.

Too Much Horse for the Harness

The sprawling Standing Rock Sioux Reservation sits astride the border between North and South Dakota. We had long worked with them, having completed seven projects between North and South Dakota, but this time our customer was Sitting Bull College, not the tribal housing authority. The College needed new housing, single family units to fit the needs of married students or students with young children. ESIC was stunned that we would entertain the idea of a housing project composed entirely of students. The LIHTC program has an ostensible prohibition against housing that will be occupied by full time students and it seemed foolish for us to even think about a project that would seemingly be in violation of that very clear rule. But the rule was not written for the circumstances in Indian Country and we argued that we had a solution.

Specifically, the rules stipulate that if a household is composed of married students who are not dependents on someone else's tax return, or single parents with children who were also not dependents on someone else's tax return, or students who are enrolled in certain job training programs or, finally, students receiving assistance through Social Security, then they are exempt from the "no student housing rule." Well, the typical student in a tribal college is older than the typical student enrolled in Iowa State University or Stanford, or virtually any other college in the U.S. Tribal students at tribal colleges are typically married or single parents and many are indeed enrolled in qualifying job training programs. And Sitting Bull College was full of students that fit the exceptions. They needed someplace to live. The president of the college at that time, Ron His Horse Is Thunder, a lawyer and the great-great grandson of One Bull, nephew of Sitting Bull himself, assured us that the College would restrict the units to households that fit the student exceptions. He wanted this project.

Ron His Horse Is Thunder is a formidable character. Long, glossy black hair flowing over his lean shoulders, he has the demeanor of someone you do not want to cross. His face is taut, leather stretched tight over bone. There is no excess, there is no fat. As a rancher, lawyer, and a college president who eventually became tribal chairman at Standing Rock, Ron is someone who finishes what he starts, no matter the hardships. In addition to his leadership of Sitting Bull College, Ron had for years led the Annual Chief Big Foot Memorial Ride from McLaughlin, South Dakota on the Standing Rock Reservation to Wounded Knee on the Pine

Ridge Reservation. Every year this ride begins on December 14th, in the dead of winter, with temperatures sometimes falling well below zero. It brings together dozens of young Indian men, women, and children, all on either horseback or horse-drawn wagon, who ride together to commemorate the struggles of their Lakota forebears. Now known as the Future Generations Ride, it starts in Ft. Yates, ND and ends at Wounded Knee Creek, on December 29th every year, following the same route as the ill-fated 191-mile trek that ended with the murder of Chief Big Foot and the massacre at Wounded Knee December 29, 1890.

If our investor had just thought it through he would never have challenged Ron His Horse is Thunder. But following his same pattern, he opposed the project. Considering what was at stake, Ron His Horse is Thunder simply called Franklin Raines, chairman and CEO of Fannie Mae. He made the case that this project was worthy, and the CEO of Fannie Mae was convinced. We overcame the so-called student prohibition and eventually completed projects with Sitting Bull College, United Tribes Technical College and Little Priest College, all tribal colleges and all projects that nobody else would consider doing.

After this last uncomfortable encounter, Fannie Mae was finally convinced that ESIC was not needed in the mix and we got back to working solely with Raymond James. I no longer had to contend with ESIC. If only he was the last person who was too quick to believe the stories he had heard. Sadly, there would be many more to come. That brand of willingness to believe something simply because it sounded plausible was a trait shared by too many people with outsized power. If we had failed to overcome this bias, Leech Lake, Sitting Bull College, and the Northern Arapaho tribe would have been denied something they desperately needed. The question became, for me, how many other people will do this in the future and what will we be able to do to thwart it.

In the meantime, I was wary of having a single source of capital and our success was, happily, leading more investors to see Indian Country as a viable place to do business. A breakthrough that led the way to new investors came with some help from a tribal attorney.

Mike Swallow was a practicing attorney licensed in North and South Dakota and with the Standing Rock Sioux tribal court. We needed a solution to the issue of where disputes, if any arose, would be resolved. The fear of tribal court by non-Indian investors and business people was and remains a laughable barrier to development. Banks and institutional investors were happy dealing with foreign nations like Saudi Arabia or Argentina, readily subjecting themselves to the laws and courts of those nations, but these same banks and investors were wary of working in courts serving Indian nations. Go figure. But Mike Swallow made a compelling case that tribal courts were mature, independent venues for adjudicating disputes, were in fact the "courts of competent jurisdiction" in the jargon of the law. Through his advocacy we fashioned a compromise in which tribal court would be the ultimate place for resolving disputes. Our alternative dispute resolution model has never had to be used since we have never had a dispute rise to this level, but it was a landmark compromise authored mostly by Mike Swallow and Angela Christy and it has stood the test of time.

This Should Be a Hollywood Moment

By this time, Marianne had resigned from the Ramsey County Library System, at the top of her game, to come work with me at Travois and we had added a few more employees. We had done what we set out to do--to build a business that was consistent with our core values, the values we cherished. Whenever someone or something tried to injure those values, by denying credits to a worthy tribal project, by paying less than a fair price for the credits, by putting barriers in the way of equal access to decent and affordable housing, we fought back. I was seen as pugnacious and arrogant, sometimes pushy and intractable. We stood up for our clients and for our company at so many forks in the road; it's hard to believe that we would have survived if we had not fought and fought hard.

But I was paying a price for our success physically and emotionally. All the travel on small commuter airplanes and in rental cars for hours-long rides on interstates and gravel roads had left me with constant back pain, sometimes debilitating pain. Contentious meetings with state agencies, emotional ups and downs when investors jerked our clients around and some difficult employees increased the pressure. I was also away from home as much as three or four nights a week and I was missing some of the most important moments in both my daughter Elizabeth's and son Greg's lives.

We had moved to Luther, Montana, an unincorporated town west of Red Lodge in the front range of the Beartooth Mountains to be closer to our tribal customers and in partial fulfillment of my lifelong quest to be a cowboy. My time spent away from home underscored the personal price I was paying for my business. I had been my son Greg's little league baseball coach. Marianne and I both logged long hours traveling to games played all over Montana. Greg was dedicated to baseball, eventually playing what was known as Senior Little League, Montana's equivalent to high school baseball. (Montana has such long winters, baseball is not played in the high schools so this top-notch version of Little League and American Legion Baseball are played instead.) Once, while Marianne and I were at a meeting on the Flathead Reservation, Greg's Red Lodge team was in a playoff game. His team was behind five to two in the bottom of the ninth inning with two outs. The bases were loaded, and Greg came up to bat. As was his exasperatingly consistent strategy, Greg nursed the pitcher to a full count. It was Greg's casual strategy all season long to let a strike go by because he preferred a full count. He said it focused his attention. It may have focused his attention, but it raised my blood pressure. It must have frustrated the pitcher in this playoff game. Unable to strike Greg out, he brazenly and foolishly asked Greg where he wanted the next pitch. In a variation on the iconic Babe Ruth gesture to the right field bleachers, Greg put his hand out waist high. The pitcher complied, sending a fastball directly to Greg's sweet spot. He was sure he would overpower Greg with his commanding heat. Greg crushed it, a walk off grand slam to left center to send them deeper into the playoffs. This was a once in a lifetime triumph and Marianne and I had missed it. Our daughter Elizabeth was there and gave us the account of the game, but we missed in person the single greatest athletic accomplishment of his young life, something that few kids and their parents get to experience. I sat in my hotel room and quietly cried that I had not been there to share this moment with my son.

In my modest despair at missing this iconic event it occurred to me that baseball was an apt metaphor for so many of my Indian friends. In everyday life we expect to win more than we lose. We expect that if we work hard and do the right thing that more often than not, good things will come our way. Instead, Indian Country is more like the journeyman baseball player, batting .250 or .265. If you were successful 30% of the time, if your batting average was .300, you were a star. You were not discouraged if you struck out 70% of the time. White people would be outraged and furious if circumstances beyond their control led them to a failure rate of 70%. Indians are as persistent and stoic as the batter who walks back to the dugout with his head held high, knowing that .300 was pretty good.

The pace of awards for our tribal customers had picked up and we began seeing greater and greater interest from more and more investors. We were seeing the kind of commitment from the investors that our clients deserved. We began adding more employees to meet our goals of assisting tribes with their reporting and compliance obligations, creating Travois Asset Management, LLC as a subsidiary. In the first seven years of business we had delivered just under $150 million to our tribal clients, a pace of around $20 million per year. Over the next two years we delivered another $50 million, more than doubling our business. In the two years after that we delivered another $75 million. The year 2005 was the year that we began to realize just how much business we could do, just how much housing we could deliver to the neediest families in the country, so long as we hired the right employees and continued to listen to our tribal customers and continued to be true to our values. Things were looking rosy, but there were foreboding clues that we were heading into troubling times in our adopted state of Montana.

A little less than half--about 40%--of the projects we finance in Indian Country are projects in which housing units already exist, are almost always occupied, but are in terrible shape. These projects include the complete rehabilitation of these typically old, utterly out of date, obsolete and almost completely dysfunctional dwellings. Remember the Ft. Peck units where the bathroom sink is in the hallway outside the bathroom? The units in these projects typically had no insulation to speak of, even though our tribal customers often live in areas where the weather is dangerously cold or vexingly hot and sometimes both. These units have windows that allow the cold in and the heat out-- not in a good way. These units often have floors that lean in or lean out, leaving doors unmatched to their openings. These units have bedrooms without closets or bedrooms the size of closets, take your pick. Mostly, these units were unimaginatively designed, without any ornamentation or reflection of the culture and ethos of the people expected to live in them, thanks to the Federal Department of Housing and Urban Development. When these units were built they were under what is known as the 1937 Housing Act, which allowed for virtually no flexibility in the design and construction of the buildings. HUD dictated to the tribes what was to be built, how big they would be, how many bedrooms and bathrooms they would have, and how much could be spent on each unit, which was virtually always insufficient. These units are affectionately known as the "HUD box." They literally look like the boxes that nice houses should have come in.

Asthma and Other Amenities Added Without Charge

One of the most perplexing cases Travois ever came across was with the Blackfeet Housing Authority, in Browning, Montana. They had over 150 houses built in 1979 with wood foundations in Northern Montana where 100 inches of snow might fall in any normal winter and where 100 MPH winds are not uncommon. HUD did not mandate that these units be built with pressure treated, wood foundations, but the Blackfeet Housing Authority had immense pressures to build houses to meet the needs of a growing tribal population, and had the choice of poured concrete, masonry, or wood foundations. It chose poorly. The tragedy really was that the Blackfeet Housing Authority should never have been put in a position to make such a Hobson's choice. Poured concrete or masonry was and remains prohibitively expensive in remote Browning, Montana. Because of their grossly limited funding, if they had used concrete, the gold standard for foundations, it would have reduced the number of dwellings they could build. Instead, without an awareness of the dangers, the housing authority chose to use wood that, in order to resist rot, had been treated with formaldehyde and arsenic. Over time these wood foundations deteriorated and the off-gassing from the treated wood sickened dozens of men and women, little girls and little boys, in some cases with conditions that are life threatening.[92] These houses were supposed to be homes the residents would own, through a program known as Mutual Help. Families put up the land in some cases, put in long hours helping to build the houses and made other deep concessions to become the owners of these houses. They did this, reasonably, without the expectation that some years later the foundations would off-gas poisonous fumes, leech out toxic heavy metals, and allow the infiltration of sewage into the basements, and other pretty undesirable things. They were built in good faith and they were bought in good faith. Where do people of such limited resources turn for help?

Lawsuits were brought against the Blackfeet Housing Authority, the tribe, and HUD on behalf of the residents, but the courts have determined that the Blackfeet Housing Authority and the tribe, not HUD, were liable for the damages and injuries from the gases emanating from the wood foundations, the instability that resulted from the foundations' failings and the houses in some cases being totally uninhabitable.[93] The Ninth Circuit Court of Appeals was unambiguous in its determination, but the lawsuit did not and the judges on the Court of Appeals were not asked to consider the real crux of the matter. The undeniable fact is that tribes and tribal housing authorities have been left with few reasonable options. Federal funding for Indian housing has never been sufficient to meet the challenges of housing the poorest people in the nation in some of the toughest environments imaginable. Too many tribal families wait too many years for a decent place to call home. Sometimes, seeking only to provide shelter for their members, tribes choose quantity over quality. Who fixes this? Why are tribal people left, not just holding the short end of the stick, but holding a stick that makes you sick?

The executive director of the Blackfeet Housing Authority, Chancy Kittson, a youthful looking and clearly resolute Blackfeet member, has had to deal with over 150 families living in houses that were simply a mistake to have ever been built, and he does not have the means to make amends. HUD has accepted no responsibility to help rebuild or replace the houses and the courts have agreed that legally they were not obliged to do so. And to make this even more dreadful, if the Blackfeet Housing Authority tore down these units and somehow came up with monies to replace them, they would get no help in maintaining the new houses and would lose a portion of their NAHASDA allocation in the process because the new houses would not be included on their NAHASDA rolls.

NAHASDA replaced the old funding under the 1937 Housing Act. That was the funding that provided the paltry funds for the Blackfeet Mutual Help project. Under the new rules, if a tribe divests itself of one of these old, worn out units by simply tearing it down or somehow selling it, even if it was replaced with a modern new unit, the tribe's NAHASDA allocation is reduced by a mysteriously determined but not insubstantial pro rata amount. They are financially punished for replacing dilapidated housing. As a result, tribes can only maintain their NAHASDA allocation amount, which is too small but desperately needed, by carefully nurturing their existing stock of dwelling units. They must maintain them even when they have long outlived their useful lives, even if they were built with wood foundations that no longer function as supports to hold up a house. To make things worse, if a tribe adds to its stock of dwelling units, as we do with 60% or so of our tribal projects, and as the Blackfeet Housing Authority wants to do to replace these worsening houses, their NAHASDA allocation does not increase to reflect the additional costs of managing and maintaining these new units. It is a gloriously, incomprehensibly, inane provision of the law. Tribes have fought this provision for years, but HUD and the Congress resist.

Our customers have a balance to strike between improving the houses that already exist on their reservations--improving the lives of families already housed, with the need for new houses to satisfy the needs of new families. Statistically, Native Americans are younger, poorer, more likely to be unemployed and to have larger families on average than the U.S. population in general. The median age of a Native American household residing within the boundaries of a reservation is close to ten years younger than the US median age. They are also four times more likely to be unemployed and have an average household size that is a full person higher than the U.S. average.[94] That means that reservations have a greater incidence of household formation than the U.S. as a whole yet these new households have less capacity to pay for the housing they need than does the average non-Indian household. Our goal was to help our tribal customers strike that balance just right, sometimes alternating a new construction project one year with a rehabilitation project the next. While Travois financed six projects to date with the Blackfeet Housing Authority, nothing we or they have done can make a dent in the tragic case of 150 toxic houses that should never have been built to begin with.

Chapter 15

A Wobbly Stool and Driving While Black

EVEN THOUGH WE didn't have to work with ESIC anymore, by 2002 Fannie Mae had nonetheless become increasingly troublesome. We knew that we needed to have more than just Raymond James as an investor for our tribal projects. Raymond James now became one of several investors competing to win our Indian Country projects. Years earlier I had met Margaret Yung, the director of tax credit investments for the then giant but soon to be defunct, Washington Mutual Bank, known as WaMu. Margaret was very well-known in the tax credit housing field and had a reputation of being direct and business-like. She was born in China and spoke Chinese-accented English. Whether it was her experience as an immigrant or some other unknowable reason, she caught on immediately to the special needs of tribal tax credit projects and embraced what we were trying to do. With Margaret's guidance by 2006 WaMu had become an enthusiastic and energetic investor in Indian Country. Her heart was with us. Margaret had a small staff, was overworked and nearly overwhelmed, trying to find ways for her employer to meet its CRA obligations. Her top assistant, Deloris Clarke, did most of the heavy lifting with respect to the underwriting and Deloris, likewise, became a strong advocate for working in Indian Country. In short order, WaMu became a steadfast investor for our tribal projects. But WaMu had chosen to only invest in a few states--Arizona, Oregon, Washington, and Idaho. We had many projects in Arizona, but we were struggling to find tribal customers in Oregon, Washington and Idaho.

Knowing that WaMu would be a good investor, but had a limited range, I embarked on an effort to find yet another investor who would see our deals for what they were--the lowest risk, highest yielding (from a social impact perspective as well as IRR) projects in the marketplace. Like the effort to land WaMu, a few years earlier I had contacted SunAmerica, a subsidiary of AIG, one of the largest insurance conglomerates in the world and a company that would be partly blamed for the 2008 financial crisis. After landing them as an investor I thought I was the smartest guy in the room. I now had a three-legged stool of investors for our Indian Country projects. The first leg of the stool was Raymond James, whose largest investor continued to be Fannie Mae. The next leg of this wonder-stool was WaMu. The last leg was SunAmerica, a subsidiary of AIG. In two years' time all three of these investors would be in the throes of the deepest recession since the Great Depression, indeed, they helped to create the mess. But I thought having these three massive financial giants gave me the kind of investor diversity to protect our company and the tribes we were working with. I could not have been more deluded.

WaMu invested in projects in Arizona and Washington and in our first project with the Nez Perce Tribe of Idaho. An incident with Deloris Clarke, the workhorse project manager for WaMu, reminded me how far we have yet to go in this country to be truly color blind. When Deloris and I drove together from Seattle to Lapwai, ID to meet with the Nez Perce Tribal Housing Authority I learned a startling lesson. Deloris is African-American and when we reached the mountains of Idaho on our long drive, in a stretch of switchbacks that necessitated a slow pace in the rental car, I passed an Idaho state trooper going the opposite direction. The speed limit was 55 mph but I was being cautious and was going no more than 45, at the fastest. When the trooper passed us I distinctly remember him staring at us as he went by. We were on a windy stretch and going slow enough for me to make out his features. Within a minute or so that same trooper had turned around and had come up behind us with his lights flashing. He pulled me over.

When he came up to my window, the trooper curtly demanded my license and registration and I told him that it was a rental car, that we were driving from Seattle. I was very courteous, but a bit stunned at his posture and his tone of voice. He was visibly angry and I could not imagine why. He said that I was going way over the speed limit and I politely protested that I could not possibly have been going as fast as he said given the winding nature of the road. That set him off and he started lecturing me about the precision of his equipment and the care he takes in safeguarding the good citizens of Idaho from dangerous drivers like me. He was getting red in the face and sort of fidgeting outside the driver's side door, agitated and puffed up, looking for all the world like I was keeping him from a much-needed visit to a bathroom. As he bent down to look at us I could see that he was much more interested in Deloris than me. He was talking to me but staring at her. I decided that it was no use arguing with this tall, well over six-foot, blond-haired, blue-eyed sack of ticked off humanity. Plus, he was armed.

After I got my speeding ticket the trooper drove away in great haste.[95] I pulled back into the lane and we drove on our way. I turned to Deloris and said, "What the hell was that all about?" She very nonchalantly told me that I had just been caught "driving while Black," or as close to it as a white boy from Virginia could come. It is unfair to cast aspersions on the beautiful state of Idaho and on the fine state troopers of that mountainous place, but it was 2005 in Northern Idaho, a time when there was a disturbing number of white supremacists and hate groups openly espousing a return to segregation and other more ridiculous notions. Could this state trooper have been an adherent of such nonsense? It is a reasonable hypothesis I am afraid. There is no other explanation except perhaps he was just having a very bad day and needed someone to take it out on, but the evidence suggests there is more to that story.

I was understandably chastened by our confrontation with the inexplicably furious trooper and drove even slower from that point on. We eventually made it to Lapwai without further incident. Deloris just smiled at the lesson I had learned but I remain disturbed by this close encounter with what must be an all-too-often occurrence for people of color. The memory has never left me.

More Broken Promises and Broken Hearts

Lapwai, Idaho, is a small, forgettable village in a territory of pristine rivers and dense forests and it is the heart of the Nez Perce Reservation. Early in the nineteenth century, the Nez Perce befriended Lewis and Clarke as they made their way to the Columbia River basin. The tribe generously fed and clothed them. At that time the Nez Perce were perhaps the best horse breeders among all of the tribes, going so far as to geld the lower quality male horses so as to prevent unwanted traits being passed on to their breeding line. The Appaloosa horse was first developed by the tribe and was considered one of the finest and most durable breeds found in the west and became a great source of wealth for the tribe. But the Tribe's hospitality to Lewis and Clark was not reciprocated in the years to come.

The Nez Perce, for decades after the visit from the Corps of Discovery, had compromised and acquiesced to the ever more excessive demands of white settlers and the U.S. Cavalry. But eventually they had had enough of compromise. The US government demanded that the Nez Perce settle on a small reservation and their leader, Heinmot Tooyalaket (Thunder Rising to Loftier Mountain Heights), better known as Chief Joseph, made a break for it in 1877. The US Cavalry, led by General Oliver Howard, outraged at the killing of four soldiers by some Nez Perce warriors, attempted to force the tribe's 300 men and over 500 women and children onto the pitiful lands set aside for the tribe. But Chief Joseph and these 800 tribal members, carrying all their possessions, brilliantly escaped while being chased by 400 well-trained and well-equipped soldiers. Chief Joseph led his people across eastern Idaho into what is now Wyoming, including crossing through the newly designated Yellowstone Park, on their way to the Bitterroot Mountains of Montana. They had hoped to find refuge with the Crow, but learned that the Crow had become the scouts for the US Cavalry and would provide them no quarter. The 1,700-mile journey evading the US Cavalry is considered one of the great military maneuvers of all time. But time ran out just 40 miles south of the Canadian border, where Chief Joseph had hoped to find deliverance.[96] Upon his surrender to General Howard, Chief Joseph said:

> ...It is cold and we have no blankets. The little children are freezing to death. My people, some of them, have run away to the hills, and have no blankets, no food; no one knows

where they are – perhaps freezing to death. I want to have time to look for my children and see how many of them I can find. Maybe I shall find them among the dead. Hear me, my chiefs! I am tired; my heart is sick and sad. From where the sun now stands I will fight no more forever.

Chief Joseph had been promised that he and his followers would be returned to the reservation in Lapwai, but they were lied to. Chief Joseph and the surviving men, women and children were instead shipped, like cattle, to swampy bottomland in Fort Leavenworth, Kansas, where nearly 100 perished. In the fall of 1878 Chief Joseph protested this betrayal and was allowed to go to Washington to plead his case to the "great chiefs of government," where he said:

I have heard talk and talk, but nothing is done. Good words do not last long unless they amount to something. Words do not pay for my dead people. They do not pay for my country, now overrun by white men…Good words will not give my people good health and stop them from dying. Good words will not get my people a home where they can live in peace and take care of themselves. I am tired of talk that comes to nothing…Let me be a free man – free to travel, free to choose my own teachers, free to follow the religion of my fathers, free to think and talk and act for myself – and I will obey every law, or submit to penalty.[97]

His appeals to the "great chiefs of government" in Washington were ignored and he spent the last years of his life fighting for the Nez Perce people. Some of his followers were eventually allowed to return to Lapwai, but not Chief Joseph. He was deemed a troublemaker and too dangerous. Instead, he lived out the rest of his life on the Colville Reservation in Washington State, dying in 1904, where the agency physician in Nespelem, WA, said he died of "a broken heart."[98] On the reservation in Lapwai, the Nez Perce people were forbidden from breeding the fine Appaloosa horses and instead were allowed only to have mules and Appaloosa and draft horse mix-breed horses, suitable for plowing fields and pulling wagons. That policy, a dubious requirement imposed upon them by government decree, left the Nez Perce in perpetual poverty since farming in that part of Idaho had little chance of success.

Travois eventually completed three projects with the Nez Perce Tribal Housing Authority, with WaMu as the investor for two of the deals. Every visit I made to Lapwai, I thought about the incredible strength of character of Chief Joseph. And every time it renewed my sense of purpose. Our tribal projects were more than just affordable housing. They were, in a small way, perhaps in a very small way, a penance for the grave mistakes of the past. I had argued for years that investing in our Indian Country projects was a moral imperative. No less than the tragedy of slavery, our treatment of Indians has left an enduring legacy of poverty and alienation. The slaughter and gross mistreatment of Native Americans and the persistent refusal to honor the terms of the treaties have left this country with an indelible mark of shame that stains all claims of what it means to be an American.

This sense of the moral imperative, and the well-documented wrongs done to Indian people left me bewildered when I was continually confronted with the obstinate refusal by those in a position to help to become a part of the solution. At the very least, they could give tribal applicants and non-tribal applicants equivalent access to tax credits. State allocating agencies could have conducted outreach to tribal communities and informed them about tax credits before Travois existed; none did. For the first ten years, I may as well have been an itinerant teacher, traveling from state to state to inform the tribes about this great new program. We were continuing to fight battles with the state allocating agencies. There were some bright spots, though. Arizona soon became a more thoughtful and reasonable judge of tribal needs and their Qualified Allocation Plan offered no distinct hurdles to overcome. Things were not perfect in Arizona and we periodically had to press the case for our tribal customers, but Arizona became a state that we could rely upon to judge Indian applicants fairly and evenly.

Will Someone Please Answer the Phone

For all of the heartless and needless barriers erected against Native Americans, I cannot deny that Indian Country is beautiful and beguiling and at times maddeningly backwards. Sometimes tribes were their own worst enemy. Poverty has a stranglehold on many Indian reservations not least because of government policy and simple geography. But it is also because of something as prosaic as the person who is supposed to answer the phone at the tribal administration building inexplicably letting it ring until the caller just gives up. Who knows who that caller might have been. Maybe it was Google looking for the perfect place to build their next server farm. Maybe it was someone who wanted to bring 20 or 30 visitors from Paris who was hoping to find a nice Indian interpreter to regale the French visitors with tales of Indian culture and life. But nobody answered the damn phone and we will never know.

Like the negligent inattention to letters from the Bureau of Indian Affairs, or the carelessness of missing public hearings, tribes often contribute to their own isolation and missed opportunities. I cannot count the times I made explicit plans to visit a tribal office, even confirming a day or two in advance, only to find when I arrived that nobody was there. In one case I flew from Minneapolis to Billings, MT, then drove two hours to Lame Deer on the Northern Cheyenne Reservation to meet a tribal official. After having confirmed the meeting the day before, when I arrived I found the office closed, without explanation. Being unable to find anyone who knew what was going on I simply drove back to Billings and caught the next plane back to Minneapolis. This was not a unique occurrence. Was it due to a lack of familiarity with standard business practices? Was it an utter lack of courtesy because I was not Indian? Probably some of both. These slipshod behaviors serve only to strengthen the bias too many people harbor against tribes. It is clearly also a result of the higher cognitive taxes paid by poverty-stricken populations, the overload, the depletion of cognitive resources that Anandi Mani and Sendhil Mullainathan describe in their *Science* article.

It could also be a result of the chronic stress of worrying about your job, whether or not your car will make it for another day, or whether or not you can make this month's heating bill that has caused you to lose sleep, that has worsened your blood pressure, and maybe made you just a bit forgetful. In his delightfully quirky book, *Why Zebras Don't Get Ulcers,* Robert Sapolsky has shown that the hormones released when you are in the classic "flight or fight mode" are also released when you are stressed out about making this month's rent. The difference is that after the zebra has outrun the lion his glucocorticoid levels return to normal, and he returns to blissfully eating grass in the Kalahari or the plains of the Serengeti, at least until the next time he has to run from a lion or leopard. Actually, there isn't much of a "flight or fight mode" distinction with the zebra. He knows he is unlikely to win a fight. So he runs. But it is hard to outrun the worry and stress that poverty imposes. Chronic stress keeps those glucocorticoid levels unnaturally high for long periods, causing a cascade of physical, emotional, and mental maladies.[99]

One of the reasons Travois has been successful is because we overlook the occasional lapse in businesslike behavior and we focus on the larger picture. As Winston Churchill once said, "Success consists of going from failure to failure without loss of enthusiasm."[100] He knew a thing or two about failure. Just because I have been snubbed does not negate the need and the opportunity, but other people, given the option, will take the path of least resistance, that is, simply avoiding Indian Country. Too few tribal people have the experience and the understanding to make sure the path of least resistance runs through Indian Country and not somewhere else.

Travois has prospered, no doubt, because we have been willing to walk the path of significant resistance, while trying to impress upon our tribal friends the need to clear that path, to make it as hospitable as possible. Tribes are indeed getting better. Calls are more often picked up now than 15 or 20 years ago, meetings are less often aborted now than 15 to 20 years ago. But even these deficiencies, while not inconsequential, pale in comparison to the barriers put up by states and by institutional investors.

Nobody Expects a SWAT Team to Come to Bingo Night

One state perplexed me more than any other--California. It had then and still has the highest Native American population in the country and it has more federally recognized Indian tribes than any other state, exclusive of Alaskan Native Villages, but it had never approved a tax credit project for an Indian applicant. We had tried, not less than eight times. In some states, we have a track record of nearly 100%. In the more troublesome states, Montana comes to mind, we had a track record of closer to 60%. Our national average, over the 12 states in which we were doing business over the first ten years or so, showed that about 75% of the time we won tax credit awards for our tribal customers. If this had been baseball we would already be in the Hall of Fame. But we were zero for eight in California.

I did everything I could think of, things that had worked in every other state, to get the allocating agency in California to come around. The Tax Credit Allocation Committee, known rather inelegantly as TCAC and pronounced Tea – Kack, was becoming an obsession for me. We wrote letters and memos, we went to see them, we testified at public hearings, all to no avail. British Prime Minister Lloyd George once said of Eamon de Velera, president of the Republic of Ireland, that arguing with him was "like trying to pick up mercury with a fork".[101] That is what it was like negotiating with the folks at TCAC. We could make no headway in the state that had some of the most remote Indian reservations in the nation, including the Round Valley Reservation, Hoopa Valley, the Yurok, and the Karuk Reservations. These reservations shared the same dismal income, poverty, and unemployment statistics as their brethren in Montana, Wyoming, and the Dakotas. I could not crack the code.

But that would end in the most accidental fashion.

In California, the intensity of the competition for tax credits was so great that suggesting changes to the state's QAP in order to benefit tribal applicants elicited groans and gripes from everyone except the mostly voiceless groups that stood to benefit the most from such changes. Resistance was strongest among for-profit developers who had learned to successfully adapt their proposed projects to the requirements of the QAP, cities with a vested interest in seeing these same private developers succeed, and the advisors and consultants who helped these private developers.

TCAC had learned over the years to acquiesce to the developers and made only very modest changes to their QAP, if any at all. They revised the rules and procedures only to the extent that such rules and procedures put no added burden on the groups and businesses that had learned how to use the QAP to their best advantage. Plus, the staff had labored over the QAP creating a document that they believed accurately reflected the needs of the state of California and it was, they believed, their best work. No data about the needs of tribes could overcome the loss they would feel in giving up their cherished document. They were not convinced that tribes really needed as much help as we said they did, and they worried that somehow changing the QAP might have unintended consequences. Damn, we had a fight on our hands.

Robert Shiller's Narrative Economics seems especially applicable in California. The narrative in California is that the 109 tribes in the state have become wealthy because of the healthy gaming economy. On a national scale, the most tribal gaming money in the nation is earned disproportionately by tribes in California. But even in California the revenue is not shared equally and that should have been widely known, but it wasn't. It is understandable that the small gaming tribes near San Diego, Los Angeles, and Sacramento are doing quite well, but the much larger tribes in remote northern California and in other remote areas, if they have casino gaming, barely break even. However, for most of its history, California has resisted tribal sovereignty and independence. Ironically, it was an unlawful action by California that jump-started casino gambling for tribes nationally.

It all started when Riverside County sheriff's department SWAT officers descended on a tiny trailer on the reservation lands of the Cabazon Band of Mission Indians. Imagine if you will, a trailer full of mostly elderly Native Americans, sitting quietly as the caller read the numbers and letters for a peaceful game of bingo. It must have been terrifying that still night in 1983. The sheriffs arrested every frightened person in the room for illegal gambling. After catching their breath, the Band sued, contending that the state had no jurisdiction.

California based its case on Public Law 280, a law that ostensibly gave the state the right to adjudicate criminal cases in state court. The law does not, however, give the state the right to regulate civil activity on reservation lands. The state lost and appealed to the Ninth Federal District Court of Appeals, where they lost again. California then took its case against the poor band of Indians all the way to the Supremes. They should have left well enough alone. The top court sang to the Band's tune and recognized that tribes are indeed sovereign nations and cannot be constrained in their proper functions as governments, at least to the extent that California was trying to constrain them. Where this might reasonably have been seen in California as a win by an underdog, the general statewide consensus seemed to be "Oh My God, illegal gambling and the mob are coming here to sunny California."

The media coverage, before and after the Cabazon case, was relentless with stories about law-breaking Indian tribes. The tone of the leaders in state government, including the governors over the last 30 years, had been uniformly dismissive of tribal rights and independence, with the exception of governor Jerry Brown. Remarkably little had been reported about the life of Indians in California. The lasting impression, the full-bodied narrative about California Indians was that they were uniformly rich and not paying their fair share of taxes. This is the backdrop that I believe influenced the attitudes of the staff at TCAC. It might not have been openly hostile, but there was no sense of obligation to do something to make life better for tribal people; they were assumed to be doing just fine.

We tried to disabuse them of this misrepresentation of reality, and we did finally succeed at that, but it took too long and was dependent on chance when we finally succeeded. Why was this happening in a state known for its progressive attitudes and liberal policies? One answer is contagion. As Robert Shiller says in his paper, "Narratives are major vectors of rapid change in culture, in zeitgeist, and ultimately in economic behavior. Spreading narratives, often many parallel narratives around a common theme, have been creating cultural change long before the Internet revolution, when the appearance of parallel phenomenon of computer viruses, which spread by computer to computer, popularized the virus metaphor."[102]

Shiller goes on to describe how a Scottish mathematician and chemist, William Ogilvy Kermack, and a British physician, Anderson Gray McKendrick, together devised a mathematical formula in 1927 for predicting the extent and duration of epidemics. The Kermack-McKendrick model postulated that in a population where people freely mix with one another, the rate of increase of people who become infected with a disease is equal to a constant contagion rate, times the number of the people who are susceptible to that infection, less the number of people who have had the disease and have recovered, times the number of people who have the disease and are able to infect others. Got it? You have to love economists. This is known as the SIR model, with "S" standing for the number of people susceptible to the disease, the "I" standing for the number of people who have the disease and are capable of spreading it around, and "R" standing for the number of people who have had the disease and are recovering or are recovered and not capable of spreading it. A bell-shaped curve results when the mathematical model is applied to contagious disease epidemics. You can manipulate the model by changing the numbers in any of the SIR functions to come up with fast or slow epidemics or narrow or wide epidemics. Shiller believes that the Kermack-McKendrick model might be useful in estimating the spread of social epidemics, the spread of ideas.[103]

This model might well explain how widespread the story became about the Indian who got a new house and promptly cut a hole in the bathroom wall for his horse. The relative narrowness of the spread of this toxic story relates to the number of people susceptible to the story, the people willing to suspend disbelief and then tell someone else about it. It was apparently started in North Dakota or South Dakota, places with small populations. If this same story had originated in California, and if California Indians had the same horse culture, I suspect that the Kermack-McKendrick model would have predicted a much wider epidemic for this narrative. Likewise, because California has such a large population, it seems to me quite plausible that the narrative of successful Indian gaming and the concomitant increase in rich Indians, as the story goes, spread quickly and widely in that state. The result, I believe, was a narrative that limited tribal access to the LIHTC program for 20 years, until we fortuitously met someone immune to the viral story.

Success Does Breed Success, Sometimes, Really

We had not come by our success easily. But for every new tribe willing to take a chance with us, we took a chance by hiring more and more capable people. One of those was my daughter, Elizabeth. And like many small companies, employees sometimes had to do everything; we were not yet at a spot where we could afford specialists. Elizabeth jumped in with a hard-wired sense of social justice, a work ethic she inherited from her mother and me, and a willingness to work wherever she was needed. She knew all of the functions of the company from housing development to compliance to advocacy. She had worked her way into de facto chief operating officer and it was time to make her the real thing. Now with a larger staff and Elizabeth taking on more and more of the day to day leadership responsibilities at Travois, Marianne and I had time to devote to what we hoped weren't lost causes. California was a lost cause I could not forsake.

I restarted a more concentrated effort to convince California that it was way past time for them to award tax credits to Indian tribes. I began another round of letters and calls to TCAC, only to be rebuffed once again. I decided to be a little more direct and maybe even a little more aggressive. In March, 2013, at a Socially Responsible Investment Fund conference in Huntington Beach, CA, the keynote speaker was the Treasurer of California, Bill Lockyer. The Treasurer had direct responsibility for TCAC. I decided that I had little to lose by confronting him at this conference. When he was leaving the ballroom following his keynote address I stood in the doorway, literally putting my hands on either side of the door frame and obstinately not moving, and as Bill Lockyer approached I said, "I am not going to let you pass unless you agree to hear me out." His bodyguard, or what I took to be his bodyguard, looked ready to shove me aside, and I felt like Gandalf in the *Lord of the Rings*, who said menacingly "You shall not pass", with a wonderful English accent that, try as I might, I cannot mimic. But because I smiled and because I don't look particularly menacing, the Treasurer offered to give me 5 minutes of his time. The bodyguard looked a little disappointed, perhaps lamenting the lost chance to dramatically knock me to the ground.

Bill Lockyer was true to his word and even gave me more than 5 minutes. I recounted for him the sad history of TCAC and Indian Country and the incongruity of the most progressive state in the nation willfully ignoring the needs of tribal people. He wanted to learn more and asked me to send him a detailed outline of what had happened in the past and what they needed to do to bring Indian tribes into the mix in California. I hurriedly drafted a detailed memo.

Chapter 16

The Dunning-Kruger Twins

WHEN NOTORIOUS BANK robber Willie Sutton was asked why he robbed banks, he reportedly replied, "Because that's where the money is." The goal of working in California with its high Indian population and the largest number of tribes was not only a good strategic business decision, it was a moral imperative. But getting into California was harder than robbing a bank. We realized something was amiss in 1998 when we first tried to apply for credits for the Indian Housing Authority of Central California in Fresno. We saw then that things were stacked against Indians and we began the first campaign to have the rules changed. In the succeeding 14 years, we met with each of the four succeeding directors of TCAC. We wrote memos and letters and made calls. Once we had the attention of the Treasurer of the great state of California, and he showed us his genuine willingness to listen, we had renewed enthusiasm. We supplied the detailed outline he had asked for in Huntington Beach. In fact, we began to inundate him and his Tax Credit Allocation Committee with data on incomes and housing on the reservations in California. We described the disparate treatment of tribes in the state. He could not find a suitable argument to explain why no tribe had ever won an award of credits. It had taken over a decade, but we had, it seemed, won the day.

We met with his staff and we became the power behind a task force composed of Travois, the tribes who were most likely to apply for credits, and a variety of non-profit organizations. We prepared the documentation to show how the state must change its criteria for distribution of credits and why the current plan unintentionally excluded tribes. Our secret weapon in this effort was my old mentor, Evan Becker. He is widely respected in California after running the San Diego Housing Authority and he gave us invaluable help as we finessed our arguments and crafted our strategy. After months of work, countless hours in Sacramento meeting with TCAC officials and with task force members, the State of California did the right thing and created a special set-aside just for tribal applicants.

Once those changes were made we delivered over $50 million to California tribes between 2014 and 2019 for housing that they would not otherwise have had. There will be millions more over the coming years, assuming TCAC does not follow the all-too-prevalent habit among states to periodically disregard the interests of Indians, as was playing out in Montana all the while we were making progress in California.

For years we had had only modest success in Montana, despite the huge need in the state. Montana has seven of the poorest reservations in the country. But even that modicum of success came at a steep price. Over a 13-year period, we had been awarded credits for four new projects on the Flathead Reservation, several projects on the Blackfeet Reservation, a couple for the Ft. Belknap reservation, and one each with Northern Cheyenne and Ft. Peck. But our relationship with the Montana Board of Housing (MBOH) was becoming ever more strained, to be generous. Our projects had about a six in ten chance of being awarded credits, despite always scoring high enough to be in the money. Always. But being in the money only matters if you could assume that the Board would follow the scoring and grant credits to the projects with the highest score.

The MBOH, unfortunately, engaged in a misbegotten misdirection. They believed they could craft an objective and transparent system for fairly determining the recipients of tax credits, as mandated under federal law, and then simply disregard that system, at their whim, excuse me, at their discretion. The Board believed that they had the latitude to ignore the scoring in order to overcome what they believed to be the inherent shortcomings of their own scoring process. By subjectively awarding tax credits, irrespective of the scores of those projects, they introduced uncertainty into the process. It opened MBOH up to influence by developers or lobbyists or whomever had an inside track with the MBOH. Whether that influence existed or not didn't matter. It could not be proved or disproved. The perception of influence and potential conflicts of interest, even if not widely held, nonetheless eroded the authority of the MBOH as a fair and unbiased arbiter of the public's interest. Even if they were not acting on behalf of preferred developers or other interested parties, they were acting as if they were.

Economists call the presence of undue influence and conflicts of interest "regulatory capture." All too often regulatory agencies, just like the MBOH, shift from their roles of providing transparent rules and procedures intended to protect the public to protecting the very groups from whom the public needs protection.[104] Rather than fix the shortcomings of the award process, which were many and easy to identify, the Board settled into a pattern of awarding credits to whomever they wanted, irrespective of the scores. And tribes were suffering. Our tribal clients were too often not awarded credits even when we scored higher than other projects. Once again, I was getting fed up. Was the MBOH exhibiting the symptoms of regulatory capture? It seemed so to me. If not, they were certainly engaging in a behavior that tended to foster a lack of trust in the Board's decisions.

We were no longer the sole practitioner who could be metaphorically patted on the head and then condescendingly ignored. By the end of 2007 we had grown to over 25 employees and we had delivered over $400 million in investor equity for our tribal clients. Travois was being recognized for the work we'd done. Surprisingly, I had even been named a Champion of Housing by the North Dakota Housing Development Authority. The car company, Volvo, had named me one of the finalists for its Volvo for Life Award. (Unfortunately, I did not win a Volvo for life. That would have been cool.) Travois was now a company to be reckoned with, an important force in the industry. But despite our hard-earned reputation and our suggestions to fix the scoring system, our protests every year to the Montana Board of Housing were met with outright contempt and were routinely ignored. The MBOH persisted in running the tax credit award process in an opaque fashion, indeed, in an utterly inscrutable fashion. Nobody could count on the scores in the competitive process to mean anything to the MBOH. It was becoming intolerable, and finally, in 2008, a year of remarkably bad things happening nationwide, Montana went too far.

There is an interesting psychological quirk known as the Dunning-Kruger Effect,[105] which is essentially the perception that highly incompetent people have of their own competence. They believe they are smarter and far more effective than they really are. These gloriously incompetent people:
- fail to recognize their own lack of skill
- fail to recognize the extent of their inadequacy
- fail to recognize genuine skill in others
- recognize and acknowledge their own lack of skill only *after* they are exposed to training for that skill.

There were two staff members of the MBOH who were responsible for scoring tax credit applications. They stunningly exemplified the characteristics described in the Dunning-Kruger Effect. It was made worse by a knowing and uncaring disregard for the impact that a loss of credits would mean on an Indian reservation. This combination of impressive incompetence and indifference to the needs of tribal people was exhibited with the scoring of our application for the Fort Peck Housing Authority.

I had come to know the two tax credit administrators at the MBOH, both since retired,[106] and both were basted in self-importance like a pair of over-cooked turkeys. I had grown to distrust them both. I had challenged them on numerous occasions, at public meetings of the MBOH and via letters and detailed memoranda taking exception to the MBOH award process. I was always courteous, if not deferential, but they apparently resented anyone who dared question their handling of an inherently contentious selection process.

In every state, some projects win and some projects lose and that means plans get dashed, communities go without, and some egos get bruised. MBOH made the process worse by stonewalling and bluffing. Both administrators possessed at best a shallow understanding of the complex interrelationships between developers, investors and the lawyers involved in structuring tax credit transactions. Both barely understood the transactions' governing documents that they themselves were supposed to review. To be fair, it is asking a lot to expect government employees like them to have the depth of knowledge that highly trained and experienced tax credit practitioners would have. My objection to them both and my verdict on their competence was not based just on their shallowness of knowledge, but rather on their unwillingness to admit or acknowledge that they did not know some things and an unwillingness to ask others to advise them and counsel them. They either did not know what they did not know, or they tried to hide the fact they did not know something by deceiving the board of directors and employing the age-old practice of obfuscation.

Who Knew Infinite Was a Small Number

Travois applied for credits for the Fort Peck Housing Authority, a tribal client for whom we had already completed one project, the one with units having bathroom sinks in the hallway. But this second project was denied credits, this time citing severe weaknesses in the financial structuring of the project. There were other mischaracterizations of our application in stark contrast to the non-tribal applicants, too convoluted to chronicle here, but for one potent example: They concluded that the project had an inadequate debt coverage ratio. Warning, we are going back into the weeds for a bit.

The debt coverage ratio is simply a ratio between the available income that a project generates that can be used for debt payments and the required debt payments themselves. Most states have both a minimum and a maximum debt coverage ratio. For example, if a project has $120,000 in net income available for debt service and the debt payment, its mortgage payment, is $100,000, the ratio is 1.2. (It is typically expressed as Debt Coverage Ratio = Net Operating Income Divided by Debt Service.) From a policy perspective, you don't want too much money available to pay off the debt because that would mean that your rents are higher than they need to be; the rents should be lower in order to serve lower income residents. Conversely, you don't want the rents to be too low and the resulting cash from operations to be so low that there is not enough money in reserve, which could lead to a default on the loan. What is important to remember here is that none of this existed on our tribal projects. Our debt coverage ratio was infinite, simply because there were to be no required debt payments at all. Dividing the operating income by zero yields a ratio that cannot be displayed—it is infinite. We had fully disclosed and explained this "cash flow only debt" at length and had employed it on all of our previously approved projects. They were no stranger to this financing tool. Somehow the MBOH staff, the Dunning-Kruger twins, concluded that infinite was not enough.

I was chagrined and upset when we learned of the scoring of our project and I knew that I had but one chance to appeal to the board at the public hearing in Helena. I had to convince them of the unfairness of the scoring of our tribal applicant and to change their minds and award credits to the project that should have been scored properly. It did not go well.

It was an embarrassment for me; it was a calamity for our tribal customer. We had but a single straightforward advocate on the board of the MBOH, and he was Native American himself. The former executive director of the Salish & Kootenai Housing Authority, Bob Gauthier, spoke up in defense of our application but he had only a single vote. He had influence on the board, but not enough to overcome the broadly held view that the MBOH staff was competent and should be honored by adhering to their recommendations. Even though the Board went against the staff recommendations on occasion, it was a rarity.

To complicate it further, the tax credit program itself is complicated. Over time the board had become comfortable with LIHTC lingo and had developed a basic understanding of how it worked, but they were not LIHTC professionals. They expected their staff to be. They were under the illusion, and wanted that illusion to be true, that their staff was not just competent, but had good intentions too. I was challenging the Board's perception that the professional staff knew what they were doing. They would not even consider the possibility that their intentions, at least with regards to Indian Country, were not honorable. This volunteer board, each member of which had outside jobs and outside interests, were dependent on the good will and competence of the staff at the MBOH. And the professional leadership of the MBOH was likewise dependent on the good will and proficiency of their staff. In this case, the dynamic was keeping people from seeing what needed to be seen. But this was partly my failure, too. I was angry, mystified, and I let them know it. I should have been more diplomatic and a bit less aggrieved. But the old saw about closing the barn door after the horse has left was beside the point. By now, the horse was galloping away and the barn was on fire.

To be fair, there were MBOH staff who had good intentions and were highly competent. But they had little or no influence on the two men guiding the board so poorly. Indeed, once the two had retired, not a moment too soon, the level of competence on the LIHTC side was elevated dramatically and the MBOH became, at least for a short time, an agency that could be counted on. But this came after we were forced to take the most dramatic step we could take; we were once again headed to court.

Since Travois is not a minority-owned company, not a protected class, and because the Ft. Peck Tribe was afraid to take on the MBOH for fear of reprisals, we could not file a Fair Housing Complaint. We had no choice this time, so in 2008 we filed a lawsuit in the US District Court of the District of Montana in Helena. It took two years to be resolved. It was a nightmarish time, made worse by the ushering in of the worst economic recession in our nation's history since the Great Depression. It was a bad time to embark on something that would require huge expenditures of my time, tens of thousands in legal fees, and a significant emotional toll.

Fortunately, it also came at a time of our greatest successes: an expansion of our staff, a corporate move to Kansas City, and a new office building where all our staff could be together, pursuing exciting new opportunities into economic development, architecture and design, and asset management. This was a time of real advancement for tribal access to equity capital and begrudging recognition of the rights of Indian nations to get their fair share of housing and economic development tax credits, and the cash that comes along. I made some big mistakes but had some big wins too.

The lawsuit against the MBOH, which was essentially a lawsuit against the state of Montana, was more difficult than any of the other legal maneuvers we had made in other states and came with a much bigger price tag and more modest results. Still, all the while I was fighting the Montana Board of Housing we were making progress on other fronts. The Great Recession of 2008, of all things, resulted in tribes finally getting some, at least a little, of what they were due. It was not a path to total justice, but it was a start.

What Does It Take To Get Some Attention Around Here

Carl von Clausewitz said that "Everything is very simple in war, but the simplest thing is difficult."[107] We were waging a constant war with syndicators and investors, trying to win the battle by making Indian Country projects as simple as possible. Why couldn't these investors and syndicators fully appreciate the lower risk and higher social impact of projects done on Indian reservations? This was not brain surgery. Of course, not every Indian Country deal was flawless, but ours were. A few notable tribal projects done by other consultants had a history of tax credit recapture and troublesome management. None of these projects followed our time-tested methods and none had advisors like Travois to guide them through the process and keep them from falling out of compliance. These shaky projects seemed to draw all the notice rather than our 100 plus projects without a single instance of credits being lost or non-compliant. Our Indian Country projects should have been highly sought after, but we were still fighting every day to convince investors that our projects were worthy of their attention.

Many large bank investors believed that they got greater CRA benefits from investing in projects in their urban and suburban primary market areas. What was missing was a recognition that Indian Country projects, while demonstrably lower in risk, also had demonstrably greater and more immediate impacts on the lives of families and the community in general on the reservations. That is what the LIHTC program is supposed to be about. It was maddening to talk to an investor, have them agree that our track record was impressive, acknowledge that Indian families were in desperate need of new housing, have them recognize that Indian projects undeniably had characteristics that lowered risk and raised the level of impact, then watch them put their money in downtown projects or suburban projects and walk away from ours.

To be fair, many of these investors had not taken the time to consider what an investment on an Indian reservation would entail. We were trying to make it easy. We had found a way to overcome investor misgivings about sovereign immunity and tribal courts. We had minimized the risks inherent in these sorts of deals by providing tribal subsidies; subsidies from tribes with the means to back them up. Sadly, we had an endless supply of poor families to fill the units. Most importantly of all, we had more than 100 projects successfully under our belt. Nonetheless, the path of least resistance remained somewhere other than Indian Country. Our constant effort to make Indian Country investments look and feel like mainstream, run-of-the-mill investments remained elusive.

We understood the reticence. After all, syndicators use "borrowed" money. They don't want to make a mistake and potentially lose an investor's cash, a clear fiduciary obligation. We got it and we worked with them. On the other hand, what was far harder to understand was the continued reluctance by states, who did not have a similar fiduciary responsibility, to advance Indian projects. Indeed, they had a federal obligation to administer the tax credit program fairly and honestly, and that should have been to our benefit. But getting some states to award credits to our projects was still too much like trying to pull a mule with a greasy rope. What is it about Indian Country that elevates skepticism to a high art? It is the entrenched narrative.

Why would the Montana Board of Housing go out of its way to deny credits to the poorest and most poorly-housed residents in the state? Indeed, why would any state, once confronted with the gross disparities between Indian and non-Indian communities, not do the right thing and redress this wrong, especially for a class of people historically so put upon, so denigrated, so abused? Why would California, of all states, refuse to acknowledge that Indians have been left out for too long and not make amends? Robert Shiller's Narrative Economics alone comes very close to explaining the willingness to disregard Indian needs and the refusal to pave a reasonable road for Indian applicants to drive down. But I think the combination of flawed decision-making along with toxic narratives so prevalent in Indian Country provide a more thorough explanation for the possible reasons that the tax credit authorities in Montana, California, Wisconsin, sometimes Arizona, and nearly always Oklahoma, follow policies that have a disparate and highly discriminatory impact on Indian people.

In Montana's case, the narrative of Indian indolence was emphasized. The MBOH put their faith in a system that allowed marginally capable people to administer their program, leaving them with diminished tools to make good decisions. This was abetted, I believe, by a willful ignorance of life on Indian Reservations to deny Indians their fair chance at the precious tax credits.

To make it even more complex, agencies like the MBOH, TCAC, the Oklahoma Housing Finance Authority (OHFA), and WHEDA in Wisconsin are held hostage by the complexities of the very practices they are created to regulate. This complexity makes regulatory capture an even more insidious force. The 2009 recession was an example of just this hostage situation. Banking regulators were ill-equipped to do battle with legions of Harvard trained "quants", quantitative analysts, sometimes PhD level mathematicians, arguing that their financial instruments were perfectly safe. We know how that worked out. In the case of the LIHTC program, volunteer boards are asked to make choices that they are almost always ill-equipped to fully understand. When you have incompetent and even just uninformed administrators, even when their leaders are well-intentioned, even when the likes of Bob Gauthier at the MBOH want to do the right thing, the good results you seek will all too often be defeated by the inertia of history and previous practice. In Montana and in a few other states, the historical status quo robs Indians of the decency, compassion, and understanding that they desperately need and richly deserve.

The MBOH and their state colleagues are mostly well intentioned. Their job is difficult. We get that too. But being well-intentioned is not enough.

You'll Be Alright, Just Walk it Off

When you consider that even NAHASDA had unintended consequences for Indians, think of the unintended consequences when Indians are not the direct focus of rules and regulations. A near perfect example is the contagious embrace of the concept of "Walkability." State agencies that administer the tax credit program, confronted with the ever more difficult task of differentiating projects one from the other, have included requirements that specify how far a development site can be from the nearest mass transit stop, grocery store, public library, medical center, public park, schools, and other important institutions. The closer a site is to these institutions and amenities, the less often a resident will have to get into a car to drive to these places, the higher the score in the competition for tax credits. It sounds reasonable and works well in urban and some suburban cases. It might even be good public policy most of the time. One unintended consequence, however, is that it immediately drives up the price of land near these amenities, thereby making affordable housing less affordable. Not such a good deal.

In rural areas, especially Indian Country, there are virtually no mass transit systems, not like the ones envisioned by the "Walkability" originators. By their very nature, Indian reservations do not have public parks, only a handful have public libraries, and they hardly ever have shopping centers with medical offices and the like, and they are certainly not within walking distance for anyone. To illustrate, I remember a phrase Gerald Sherman introduced me to. "Grazing the long meadow" is an ironic phrase (here is another example of Indian humor) to describe the practice of some tribal ranchers to let their cows graze the grassy median between the lanes of the highway traversing the reservation. It is inherently risky, but apparently the cows learn to stay out of the road. It is, of course, long and narrow and it is free. Anywhere where a rancher can take advantage of the "long meadow" is not a place where walking to the store, the office, the library, or the park is an option.

Without question, this scoring system automatically disadvantages Indian Country. It is akin to redlining in African American communities. But states have not been willing to add provisions granting exceptions for tribal applicants, even though we have lobbied intensely for the changes. Even Wisconsin, a state where nearly half the counties are considered "non-core,"[108] a state that is distinctly rural rather than having urban and suburban core areas, aggressively adopted the Walkability Standards. We protested and provided evidence of the disparate impact these standards have on Indian tribes. We argued that anywhere that "grazing the long meadow" was an option should be exempt from Walkability criteria. We were ignored. Why? Isn't it enough to know that Indian reservations are where they are because of federal mandates and restrictions beyond the control of the tribes? Isn't it enough to know that being with the people who share their heritage, their language, their life experiences, is worthy of preservation, notwithstanding the lack of "Walkability" development? Apparently not.

Each of the states with the highest barriers to tribal applicants had some common characteristics: none had included Indians in the analysis of existing conditions or need when they were first devising their systems for distributing tax credits. None had instituted special provisions to give tribal applicants an even shot at the credits. That seems like an obvious observation, of course. We would expect to have difficulty with the states who disregarded Indians. But more to the point, why were some states so resistant to making the kinds of changes tribes needed so that they would have a fair chance at succeeding in the competition? We thought there was a simple solution—demand that the states reach out to tribes and seek their advice and counsel. Ask that they never consider a rule or regulation to be final if it had not met a rigorous review by the tribes who, after all, will face the consequences of those rules and regulations. We were asking the states to be open to the possibility that their plans for the state as a whole might have a disparate and unfair impact on tribal people. We were not having much luck with this approach. It is a truism that the ones who don't count don't get counted. Too often, tribes didn't count.

Despite these failures, by the end of 2008 Travois had expanded to fourteen states and was providing ever more equity capital for homes for Indian families. We were a powerful voice for Indian Country, the market maker who investors had come to trust and even seek out, and a force that states had grown to respect, if sometimes grudgingly. We still had battles to fight and we had a lawsuit to press to make Montana more attentive to tribal needs. But still, tribes were not getting their fair share of tax credits. Indeed, while tribal people represent a little less than 2% of the total population, around five million souls, with the highest rates of housing need, tribes only account for about one quarter of one percent of the tax credit market, a grossly unfair distribution.

And then Lehman Brothers went bankrupt and the U.S. and the world's economy began to shudder. We weren't yet in the deepest recession since the Great Depression, but it was starting. All the progress we had made, all the capital that was now flowing to tribes, was soon to be shut off. The spigot was closing.

Despite my failure to find a Goldilocks investor, one that was not too big, not too small, we did have capital and we were being hired by more and more tribes. We were winning ever more tax credit awards. We were closely calculating and monitoring how many tribal tax credit projects could be awarded credits in each of the states that had large Indian populations. In addition to recalcitrant investors, some states remained difficult and obstinate, so we had to spend more time cajoling and talking to those states, fighting battles when we could, putting out fires when we had to. In some states, we knew we had but one chance to win credits for a tribal customer. In other states, typically the larger states, we knew that perhaps we could consistently win two or maybe even three tribal awards, so long as the projects were relatively modest in size and no single project ate up too big a share of the available credits. This was happening right when the economy began to sink inexorably into recession and equity capital began to dry up. Here we were, executing a carefully crafted strategy and our long-term efforts in Indian Country had begun to bear fruit, and all of a sudden, nobody wanted to buy our fruit anymore. Plus, there was our nasty lawsuit against the state of Montana, like an ill-tempered little dog nipping at our heels. So, to keep the string of difficult days going, to maintain an unbroken thread of infelicitous tidings, we decided to press our lawsuit against the Montana Board of Housing, to try to bring it to a resolution.

This Moose Was Gentle

The Fort Peck Housing Authority was an active participant, if not a named plaintiff. I had become friends with the executive director of the housing authority, Maurice "Moose" Lambert, a large and improbably even-tempered man who lived life from a wheelchair. Moose had been a good athlete as a young man, playing every sport on the reservation, and was an especially good basketball player. I never asked him how he had ended up in a wheelchair, but the story was related to me by the housing authority's lawyer. Apparently, Moose was in a car wreck on the reservation, not too long after he was married, and sustained a spinal injury. But the injury was misdiagnosed by the doctors at the local Indian Health Service hospital. Complaining of fierce back pain, he was nonetheless sent home the night of the wreck, only to have the injury to his spine worsen during the night, leaking spinal fluid and rendering him permanently paraplegic. In relating the story, the attorney told me that were it not for the negligent care from the Indian Health Service, Moose would likely have fully recovered.

Somehow, Moose never seemed bitter, never complained to me, and was full of equanimity and good humor. Moose died suddenly and unexpectedly on July 11, 2008, leaving a grieving wife and young grandchildren, only three months after the lawsuit was filed and after he had given me assurances of full cooperation that filled me with a sense of mission to redeem the Fort Peck Housing Authority's tax credit project and its prospects. He was sometimes unfairly criticized for the poor condition of the housing on the reservation, but he never struck back at that criticism, which sometimes even came from his own board of commissioners. After one mildly contentious board meeting during which a few of the commissioners blamed Moose for things over which he had virtually no control and no influence, he smiled and simply said that they meant well but did not know what he faced. Moose was four months younger than me and his death was a blow. As Marianne and I listened to the drum circle's mournful chorus in the shaded cemetery at his funeral, I vowed that I would do everything I could to make sure that Fort Peck received justice.

The state of Montana, as you would expect, aggressively defended itself against the suit, but failed at every turn. They filed requests for summary judgement, an effort to have the case thrown out because it was, they claimed, meritless. That failed. They filed requests to dismiss on a variety of other grounds and all were denied. They fought our requests for documents that we sought through discovery. Those ultimately failed. At every stage, we had to muster a counter argument to defeat their attempts to cast us as reckless provocateurs. It took two long years before we could even get to the point of depositions. It was becoming a burden I was less and less enthusiastic to bear. That is what defendants with deep pockets can do. They can stretch out the proceedings and put up endless and needless barriers, all of which we had to defend against, at great expense. It was becoming an unbearable emotional and financial loss for Travois to continue. We were asked, after the first round of depositions, if we would entertain a settlement. My first impulse was to say no and to go forth to trial. I wanted my day in court. But our attorney convinced me that talks could lead to a reasonable settlement and that that would be the safest and most cost-effective way to put this lawsuit behind us.

I knew that bringing the suit was going to be expensive. I would have to devote time to it without ever knowing for sure how the legal proceedings would advance. I had no control over when the defendants would respond or how they would respond. We already had so much uncertainty and so much ambiguity in our business; it was difficult to keep fighting the lawsuit. History had shown us that we could not control the investors we had lined up and we were under a constant fear that they would do what Fannie Mae had done and simply and inexplicably decide not to invest in Indian Country anymore. We lived with the uncertainty that at any time any of the states we worked in, like Wisconsin, might backslide and reinstate unreasonable policies. We lived with the uncertainty that even in states where we had fair chances to compete we might nonetheless still fail to win an award of credits for our customers. And our income was dependent, our very corporate life, and the lives of now 30 employees, depended entirely on our ability to persevere despite this ambiguity. The fate of so many families in Indian Country, families we had pledged to help, was in our hands and it was at times a terrifying responsibility. I lived with the constant fear that tribes would see us as part of the problem rather than part of the solution. We had to put this lawsuit behind us so that I could manage all the other uncertainties of our business and live to fight another day.

We decided to settle, a decision I would come to regret. In hindsight, I am certain we would have prevailed in a trial. But the circumstances were so complex and convoluted and the need to fully explain the tax credit program and then win the hearts of a jury were daunting enough that our lawyer urged us to settle. We settled, with the MBOH agreeing to have a third party, a highly-respected tax credit professional, review the MBOH practices and make necessary changes to the Qualified Allocation Plan. They further agreed to institute policies that would ensure that Indian applicants have an equal chance in the tax credit application process, without spelling out what they really meant by that. We were satisfied with the settlement, if not fully happy about the outcome. It was a moral victory even if I never had the satisfaction of seeing the two maladroit MBOH staffers on the witness stand acknowledging their errors. Common sense prevailed in the decision to settle, but it was not a courageous or noble decision. In the very least the lawsuit proved that tribal people cannot be ignored. It demonstrated that a state is at risk if it continues to disregard the special needs of tribes and tribal people. Nonetheless, I wish I had had greater fortitude, deeper pockets, a bit more insight, and had pressed on to trial. But there were other battles to fight and the recession was still hammering us and our tribal customers.

I miss Maurice Lambert. He would never have gloated at the victory, modest though it was. He simply would have gone to work each day persevering in the fight to bring better housing to his tribal family in a mostly bleak and desperate place. A place that the Indians of the Ft. Peck reservation call home, love dearly, and where they enduringly honor their ancestors.

Chapter 17

Swimming Pools and SMURFS

AT THE VERY beginning of the recession we were left with our three-legged investment stool. We had Raymond James, who was almost totally dependent on Fannie Mae investments, and we had Washington Mutual Bank, and of course, we had AIG-SunAmerica. Could there be a more star-crossed pool of investors for Indian Country? Between the end of 2008 and the beginning of 2009 WaMu went under and JPMorgan Chase picked them up for a song. Fannie Mae went into conservatorship, and AIG was both in bankruptcy and under indictment. Fannie Mae was being blamed by folks on the political right for the housing crisis and everybody, right or left, was ready for the top dogs at AIG to be put up in front of a firing squad. We needed some good news.

We got it from our newest division, Travois New Markets. The federal New Markets Tax Credit (NMTC) program was created in 2000, fourteen years after the Low Income Housing Tax Credit, and was designed to address economic development needs in economically distressed communities. We hired Elizabeth's husband, Phil Glynn, in 2006 to figure out whether tribes had a chance under the NMTC program, hoping to add jobs and economic diversification for our tribal housing clients. We miraculously received an award of $40 million from the Community Development Financial Institutions Fund, an arm of the US Department of the Treasury in 2007. Then Phil engineered yet a second allocation of $80 million in 2009. At long last capital was headed to Indian Country in amounts never before seen, thanks to the Great Recession. President Obama's stimulus package, designed to fight the effects of the recession, provided this new capital and we took advantage of it.

With these tax credits, we were able to finance a new electric substation on the Navajo Reservation through the tribally-owned Navajo Utility Authority. What made this new substation important and poignant was that it brought electricity to hundreds of families who had never had electricity before. It is nearly unthinkable that so many families in the US were without the most basic convenience that everyone else takes for granted in the developed nations of the world. This new substation also allowed millions of dollars in new developments to occur, and the jobs that came with them, that were previously inconceivable because of the absence of electricity.

Of course, this was only one relatively small enclave of unserved households on the Navajo Reservation. There remain thousands of families without electricity in the vast lands of the Navajo. How can this be and why do so few people even know about this? As I said before, the sad reality is that the ones who don't count don't get counted. Remember the Brandeis study on wealth that looks at the disparities between white households and Black and Hispanic households? Indian households were not a part of the analysis. Why? Travois was trying to make good on our promise to bring commercial and economic development, and good jobs, to Indian Country. But why does the scarcity of the most basic services on Indian reservations remain a mystery to so many people? It is one more example of the nearly invisible national tragedy that is Indian Country.

Our New Markets division also financed a salmon and halibut fish processing plant in the aptly named Goodnews Bay in Platinum, Alaska, on the Bering Sea coast. This fish processing plant put some 600 fishermen and women back to work who had had to abandon their lifelong occupation because of the exorbitant costs of bringing their catch to market. This plant processed the fish near where they were caught and allowed the fishermen and women to see their products heading to market, fresh and wild.

Phil Glynn and his ever more adept team members followed this with a financial package for a new tribal administration building on the Bois Forte Reservation in Minnesota. It replaced the tribal headquarters building that was obsolete and happened to burn to the ground during construction of the new building. We also financed new hotel developments to bolster nascent tourism programs, a wellness center on the Little Big Horn College campus on the Crow Reservation, and health and dental clinics to modernize medical care on several reservations. The New Markets division was adding luster to the task of building houses. It created a bit of hope for places that had so seldom seen anything newly built on reservations, Alaskan villages and even Hawaiian homelands.

In the years to come our New Markets division financed a waste water treatment facility on the Laguna Pueblo in New Mexico, broadband services in Alaska, community health facilities in Hawaii, a public school in North Dakota and an innovative educare center in Nebraska, among other similar public facilities. These types of services and facilities are routinely paid for out of tax receipts in states and cities all over the country. But not in Indian Country. Without the power to tax trust land, tribal nations lack the requisite revenue that cities, counties, and states use to meet critical public needs. Instead, tribes must rely on the federal government. The US government failed here, too.

The Hill Country Had Nothing on Indian Country

Think about it this way: in 1931 the US Congress passed comprehensive legislation for public works projects to combat growing unemployment and bank failures at the very start of the Great Depression. President Hoover vetoed the bill and there was not even an attempt to override his veto. After failing to consider an override the Congress basically gave up and adjourned for ten months. They went home and took a long nap. They did this in the midst of the worst economic catastrophe in our history.[109] For Indian Country the Congress may as well have never reconvened and the Great Depression lives on.

Robert Caro's *Lyndon Johnson: The Path to Power*, describes the years prior to the Great Depression:

> Electricity had, of course, been an integral part of life in urban and much of small-town America for a generation and more, lighting its streets, powering the machinery of its fac-

tories, running its streetcars and trolleys, its elevated trains and subways, moving elevators and escalators in its stores, and cooling the stores with electric fans. Devices such as electric irons and toasters (which were in widespread use by 1900), refrigerators (which were widely sold beginning in 1912), and vacuum cleaners, dishwashers, hot plates, waffle irons, electric stoves and automatic washing machines for clothes had freed women from much of the drudgery of housework. In the evenings, thanks to electricity, there were the movies, and by 1922, forests of radio antennae had sprouted on tenement roofs. By 1937, when Lyndon Johnson went to Congress, electricity was so integral a part of life that it was hard to remember what life had been like without it. It was not a part of life in the Hill Country.[110]

Electricity is also not a part of life to this day on parts of the Navajo Reservation, the Wind River Reservation in Wyoming, the Crow Reservation in Montana, and on many other reservations nationwide. Indian Country might as well be the 1937 Hill Country of Texas.

Swimming for Their Lives

Following the settlement of the lawsuit and no doubt in consideration of the successes we were having in other states, the Montana Board of Housing did indeed award credits to our next project with the Fort Peck Housing Authority. Abraham Lincoln, during the Lincoln-Douglas debates, said that "popular sovereignty," the underpinning philosophy of the Kansas-Nebraska Act, was "like a soup made from boiling the shadow of a pigeon that had starved to death."[111] This is how I felt about winning the award of credits for our Ft. Peck project from the MBOH. It was a modest project of 24 units of new houses, creatively conceived by our design and construction services division. But it didn't start out that way. The tribe wanted only 22 units. Importantly, they also wanted a swimming pool to be included in the project. One of the hallmarks of the LIHTC program is that it tries to break the mold of the old HUD programs of the past where the most banal "projects" are built with federal dollars, the boring and soulless places that did not meet the need for community. So, with uncharacteristic federal foresight the LIHTC program specifically includes an allowance for community spaces that can include common meeting rooms for events like graduation parties, wedding receptions and the like, as well as recreation facilities like basketball courts, ball fields, exercise rooms, and swimming pools. Especially swimming pools.

In every state, the emphasis was on the development of highly livable places that satisfy the yearning for community. But apparently, the folks at the Montana Board of Housing thought this was reserved for everyone except Native Americans. Montana had a provision in their QAP, which we were well-aware of, that prohibits "luxury" items from being included in any project seeking an award of tax credits. But they do not define "luxury." So, they awarded credits to our 22-house project with a community pool but insisted that the pool had to go. The MBOH justified this decision in part by concluding that the project could afford two more units if they did not build the swimming pool.

This pool was hardly a luxury. Luxuries would be if we had recommended whirlpool bathtubs, putting greens in the back yard, marble or granite countertops. This project of modest houses sought to include a community swimming pool because of the almost total absence of recreational facilities for young people on the reservation. And because the Fort Peck area is so profoundly low-income, it is designated a Qualified Census Tract or QCT. That meant that the community was so poor that under Section 42 rules, projects within QCTs could include more expansive amenities, up to a certain limit, that would be enjoyed by people other than just the residents of the housing project itself.

Tragically, in the year just prior to this project application, there had been six suicides by young Indian boys and girls on the reservation. The pain of that loss, the unnerving awareness that there is something desperately wrong on the reservation, left the leaders of the tribe seeking any way to add some semblance of hope and joy to the lives of the young people on the reservation. The tribe had been trying to find a way to build a community pool for years without success because pools are very expensive. But now we had a way to pay for a pool for the reservation by including it in the financial plan for the next tax credit project. The tribe offered to help pay for the pool if the cost of the pool exceeded the limits under the tax credit rules. But they could not pay for the whole thing. It was a way for the tribal housing authority and the tribe itself to cooperate in financing a much-needed community amenity that could provide children and families a respite from the brutal boredom of a remote and sometimes desolate place.

Indian tribes suffer a rate of teen suicide that is more than three times the national average. On some reservations, like Ft. Peck, it is ten times the national average.[112] We made our argument to the MBOH, we protested the denial of the pool, but were met with stern rebukes that "no such luxury items would be approved." Despite the evidence we showed that virtually every other state in the nation allowed pools in their LIHTC projects, and that this swimming pool was a desperate attempt to stem at least some of the hopelessness on the reservation, we lost at every stage. The MBOH told us that the governor, Brian Schweitzer, had insisted that state monies not be spent on luxury items. We never saw this mysterious memo. I doubt very much that the governor of Montana had the slightest clue how the Low Income Housing Tax Credit Program worked. But the board members of the MBOH were somehow convinced that the governor would be adamantly opposed to a swimming pool in a housing project on the Ft. Peck Reservation.

Coincidentally, Marianne and I had met Governor Schweitzer, an exuberant man and generally quite reasonable. We even had a fundraising event at our house in Red Lodge for him when he first ran, unsuccessfully, for the US Senate seat then held by Conrad Burns, before Schweitzer successfully ran for governor. I don't think he knew any more about the workings of the LIHTC program than did his dog, Jag, a border collie that the Governor brought to his office every day and even included in official occasions. I think the governor thought that bringing Jag everywhere gave him a touch of eccentricity, but eccentricity is not in short supply in Montana. We're talking about a state where, a few years earlier, the other senator from Montana, Max Baucus, ran for his Senate seat against a man who had turned himself blue by ingesting colloidal silver every day over a 12-year period. He looked like a smurf. I am not making this up.

If Governor Schweitzer had a policy against state funds being used to purchase luxury items, this should not have applied anyway since the LIHTC program includes no state monies. It made no sense. What explains the MBOH's unwillingness to consider the proscribed and limited existence of the men and women, boys and girls, on the Fort Peck Reservation? Why were we unable to overcome the MBOH opposition to this very modest amenity? We went so far as to have the president of the tribal council write a letter to the chairman of the MBOH requesting approval of the pool. This was a remarkable demonstration of the need for this pool. Tribal governments jealously guard their relationships with other government bodies and having the tribal president write to the board chairman of the MBOH was akin to the president of the United States writing a letter to a local city council asking for help.

At the final determining board meeting the sole voice of reason was once again Bob Gauthier, the only Indian member of the board (at least the only Indian member who attended meetings). Bob argued that the government to government relationship between the state of Montana and the Nation of the Assiniboine and Sioux Tribes on the Fort Peck reservation should have been given far greater consideration, that the request of the tribal council should be honored. But it was no use. We ended up with a 24-house project instead of 22 houses with a swimming pool. We hoped that the tragedy of young lives being lost figuratively and literally might overcome the parsimonious attitudes of the MBOH. We had faith that the MBOH would choose to be kind and generous. Our faith was profoundly misplaced.

A Slippery Slope to the Middle of Nowhere

What most disturbed me was the willingness of these public officials to disregard the deluge of despondency that engulfs families trying to make sense of the suicide of a teenager. Maybe a public swimming pool really would be little more than a Band-Aid on a gaping wound, but why was it up to the Montana Board of Housing to make that decision? The tribe had spoken, and they wanted this pool. They believed it would help. It cost the state nothing. But these officials stood on a misguided principal. They took a stand, but gained nothing. It was, after all, just a pool. But the pool represented the hopes of a community of deeply injured people that there might be something they could do, however small, to bring some measure of promise to a place with so little. By refusing to allow the pool the MBOH was effectively saying that reservation neighborhoods need not have the same level of amenities that white neighborhoods have. They need not offer the same respite from boredom, offer the same opportunities for community conviviality. Reservations by their very nature have a red line drawn around them, with our without the racist connotations of the color red. Refusing to allow such "luxuries" as pools relegates these neighborhoods to forever being barren of at least some of the attributes of vibrant and active communities.

To add just a bit more perspective, it is important to know just how far Ft. Peck is from nearly everywhere else. It is, in fact, in the middle of nowhere, literally. Consider a report from something called the Malaria Atlas Project at Oxford University's Big Data Institute, released February 2018. The purpose of the study was to find the most accessible and inaccessible places in the world. The analysis relates inaccessibility to vulnerability. The smaller your community and the farther you are from significantly-sized cities or towns, the higher the rate of mortality. The Washington Post used this data and spent "hours and hours of computer time to… find the one (data point) that best represents the "middle of nowhere."[113] According to the analysis, of all the towns with more than 1,000 residents in the continental US, the ones that are the farthest away from the next largest city of any size, which they defined as at least 75,000 people, happen to be Glasgow, MT, Scobey, MT and Wolf Point, MT. Wolf Point is within the boundaries of the Ft. Peck reservation and Glasgow and Scobey are just a bit north and west of the reservation. There are no towns with at least 1,000 residents on the reservation, so it did not count. The Ft. Peck Reservation was actually too remote to be counted as the most remote place in the US. Its remoteness increases its vulnerability, to teen suicide, to mortality from all variety of causes, but mainly to being disregarded.

Chapter 18

Demons and Prayers

AT RED HILL, Patrick Henry's farm in Brookneal, Virginia, hangs a famous painting by Peter Rothermel. It is a vivid scene of Patrick Henry addressing his fellow Virginia Burgesses, arm raised dramatically to the heavens. The painting presumably memorializes Henry's famous "Give me Liberty or Give me Death" speech. In the prominent foreground of the painting, to the left of Patrick Henry, sits Richard Bland, wearing the same flowing red cloak signifying membership in the House of Burgesses, the Colonial-era Virginia legislature. His white knuckles contradicting the calm look on his face, Richard was well on his way to becoming an advocate for independence, but on this day, he worried that maybe his friend Patrick Henry was going too far, too soon.[114] The British Crown had made foolish decisions, imposing such ill-conceived and onerous restrictions on the colonists as the nefarious and soon-repealed Stamp Act and the similarly contentious Townshend Acts. But the Crown followed these revenue-generating laws with the stupendously idiotic edict that men accused of treason outside the realm, that is, at one of the colonies, must be taken to England for trial. Under this new law there would be no trial with a jury of their peers. This was just too much for the Virginia colonials, to say nothing of the real hotheads up in the Massachusetts Colony. It seems almost that Richard Bland is asking, "Why would the generally insightful Parliament in London be so stupid and short-sighted"?

Sometimes it feels like I've been channeling my ancestor all these years, and if so, then I'm honored. Richard Bland introduced legislation granting slave-owners the right to free their slaves. He was promptly condemned by his own colleagues in the House of

Burgesses. But the short-sightedness and the flawed decision-making exhibited by both the British Parliament and the Virginia House of Burgesses is not consigned to the dustbin of history. It is displayed even today by state and federal agencies, in ways big and small.

To this day decisions are made based on too little information, with grossly biased and prejudiced notions about probity and justice, inflamed by the stories we hear and blindly believe. The narrative that food stamp recipients will almost surely cheat the system and therefore steps must be taken to prevent it continues to guide decisions. Stories inform the behavior of rule-makers and enforcers even though the stories are almost certainly untrue. The British Parliament was convinced that the colonists in America were pushovers and malcontents and should be shown who, by golly, was the real power here. In the Virginia House of Burgesses, Richard Bland thought it preposterous that the Crown should be the final arbiter on when and under what circumstances a planter could set free a slave. But the House of Burgesses believed the narrative that the "peculiar institution" of slavery was working just fine, common sense and decency be damned.

Most of us believe what we have been told time and time again. All too often what we have heard is hogwash intended to obscure the truth and to diminish the subject. Indian housing authorities are thought to be incapable of executing a complex financial transaction and cannot possibly follow a convoluted compliance protocol. But we make little or no effort to examine the circumstances of Indian life and the difficulties Indian housing authorities face every day. We ignore how they continue to honorably and capably deliver housing services to the poorest people in the country in the harshest conditions in the country, a complex undertaking if ever there was one. African Americans are assumed to be engaged in welfare fraud and food stamp fraud, bleeding billions from the federal budget. No concentrated and coordinated effort is made to advance the knowledge that neither of these assumptions is true. The nasty narrative is too comfortable and too persistent.

If we are ever to achieve equality for Black and Native Americans, somehow we must learn to question the narrative and to doubt the story. Einstein did not fail math in his early years, but the myth persists.[115] Food stamp fraud amounts to somewhere between 1% and 1.3% of the total expenditures,[116] far less than the fraud found in other government programs and likely a degree of fraud that is far less than the fraud found every day among major corporations. (We collectively forget the $7,600 coffee pot for that newfangled Air Force jet.)[117] We must be willing to change the narrative. It might be as easy as questioning the story teller. The next time you hear someone say that Black households "just need to get over slavery and get on with their lives," a not-so-gentle correction is in order. When you hear someone say, "Why don't Indians just leave the reservation if life is so bad," admonish them that there is a cultural imperative every bit as strong as the love of Mom, baseball, and apple pie that dictates against such a solution. The next time someone says to you that "Indians get special treatment that nobody else gets" (mythological monthly checks simply for being Indian, gaming revenues that make Indians rich) set them straight that it is just not so. The stories that seem to explain persistent poverty as the natural result of personal failings, as if "taking responsibility for yourself" will miraculously bring millions of families out of poverty, must be challenged. It is not too difficult to explain that red-lining, misguided zoning ordinances, holdover Jim Crow policies, lack of inheritances, cultural imperatives, the damn Dawes Act...all combine to limit the lives of Black and Indian households. We must stop telling the old stories and create a new narrative.

There are two schools of thought here. Some social scientists believe that we are unable to break the bonds of partisanship that lead us to disbelieve contradictory evidence, the fierce denial of climate change despite overwhelming evidence being an example of the strength of such partisan bonds. These social scientists are in the so-called "rationalization" camp. They believe that no amount of evidence, no headlines or news stories can overcome ingrained political or social beliefs. But there are others, like Gordon Pennycook and David Rand, who believe that we are simply being lazy when we disbelieve obvious evidence that contradicts what we want to believe. They believe that "people often just don't think critically enough about the information they encounter."[118]

They have conducted experiments that demonstrate that people who are more thoughtful, those "people who engaged in more reflective reasoning were better at telling true from false, regardless of whether the headlines aligned with their political views."[119] They believe that if we promote more rigorous thinking, if we demand a more thoughtful consideration of evidence, then we can overcome irrationality. I think they are on to something. If in our casual (or even not so casual) conversations with colleagues, friends, and relatives, crazy uncles notwithstanding, we insist on a closer examination of the evidence, a reasoned look at how things really are, then we can change peoples' minds. It will not be easy of course. But if we all commit to not letting the stereotype become destiny, if we insist on a more thoughtful and nuanced examination of evidence, perhaps we can make a difference.

More importantly, we must stop the public policies that are propped up by such lazy rationalizations. It is not enough to be big-hearted, kind, and more thoughtful in our interactions with friends and colleagues, though that is a pretty good start. We must also examine how public policy decisions are made and open the process to far more transparency and robust review. Decency and honor demand that we do more than we have done. The legacy of slavery, Jim Crow, and the Dawes Act cannot be overcome simply by well-meaning and thoughtful efforts. We cannot undo the lingering effects of the Indian wars, in all their manifestations, by just honoring the memory of Sitting Bull or Red Cloud. Public policy antecedents must be examined and scrutinized. Intended and unintended consequences are the conjoined twins of public policies and must be understood as if they are a natural law, like Newton's Third Law of Motion—for every action there is an equal and opposite reaction. For every zoning restriction intended to preserve value, there will be someone who has to pay the price. For every well-meaning Walkability Standard, there will be communities left behind. An effort to identify unintended consequences should become an imbedded feature of public policy formulations, at the local, state, tribal, and federal level.

Planning and zoning rules are complex. Housing regulations at the local and state level are shrouded in a complicated language that intimidates anyone not well-versed in the field. That means that the average citizen is at a distinct disadvantage if they want to make local and state rules, regulations, and ordinances more reflective of the real circumstances of life in poor urban and rural neighborhoods and on reservations. But what we can do, what anyone can do, is demand that these rules, regulations, and ordinances be reexamined regularly, in light of data that might indicate counter-productive and unintended effects and most importantly, disparate impact.

Did We Learn Anything

None of this will be easy. History tells us that we are all too inclined to backslide. 2018 was the 50th anniversary of the Kerner Commission Report. The Kerner Commission, more formally known as the National Advisory Commission on Civil Disorders, was authorized by President Johnson in 1967 following the riots of that long, hot summer. Detroit and Newark suffered the worst from the unrest, but other cities saw calamitous results from the rioting too, including the nation's capital. The Kerner Commission was a blue-ribbon, non-partisan committee charged with finding out just what was behind the seemingly coordinated civil disruptions. President Johnson, as well as many others, was convinced there was a conspiracy to foment the civil strife. Following months of investigation, the commission reported that there was no conspiracy, stating: "The Urban Disorders of the summer of 1967 were not caused by, nor were they the consequence of, any organized plan or 'conspiracy.'"[120] The report, remarkably, was unanimously adopted by the 11-member commission. Its most famous conclusion from the 1968 report was that "Our nation is moving toward two societies, one black, one white—separate and unequal."[121]

To see where the country stands relative to the findings of the Kerner Commission Report, Fred Harris and Alan Curtis, supported by the Milton S. Eisenhower Foundation, revisited the same data set, took a more recent look at the same cities and the same neighborhoods. Their new report, *Healing our Divided Society*, is a comprehensive look at the progress, or lack thereof, that we have made since the Kerner Report came out in 1968. The new report laments that while progress has been made, we have far to go. "Since the Kerner Commission, child poverty has increased in America. There are continuing high levels of wage, income, and wealth inequality."[122] Furthermore, the authors looked not just at economic conditions, but also at the institutions that define modern life. According to the authors, "Since the Kerner Commission, American public schools have been inadequately and inequitably financed. School segregation has increased."[123] Of course, they could not ignore the continuing crisis in housing nationwide. They conclude that "Dramatic reductions in funding for low-income housing over recent decades are especially indefensible, given America's history of unconstitutional court rulings and federal, state, and local governmental policies promoting racial housing segregation."[124] Nor did this report ignore Indian Country. It states:

> In many respects, tribal nations can be characterized as developing nations. They face many of the same challenges faced by developing nations on other continents: poverty, lack of infrastructure, and lack of investment.
> In light of these challenges, we cannot expect tribal government to provide instantaneous solutions to problems that developed over centuries. Over the long term, however, empowering tribes to address reservation problems related to public health and poverty, and even economic development, will produce significant improvements in economic opportunities for Native American people living on Indian reservations. Such efforts should remain the central strategy in federal efforts to address Indian Country poverty.[125]

To make the kind of progress that Fred Harris and Alan Curtis hope for, indeed that we all hope for, we must learn to overcome the inherent forces that lead us to do stupid things to begin with. To make progress we have to put aside the reliance on stereotypes and offensive narratives. We have to let facts that refute the suppositions guide policies, rather than the presumptions that have molded them for decades. The facts that interfere with what we prefer to believe are too easily ignored. And this ingrained habit of ignoring inconvenient facts is insidious. According to a study published in *Personality and Psychology Bulletin,* in sharp contrast to the findings of Gordon Pennycook and David Rand, Daniel Effron found that people do not necessarily confuse fact and fiction when faced with counterfactual statements, but nonetheless chose to come down on the side of the falsehood if it tended to support their political views. For example, in a large sample of 2,783 people who identified as supporters of Donald Trump and a similar-sized sample of people who supported Hillary Clinton in the 2016 presidential election "virtually everyone recognized the claims as false. But when a falsehood resonated with people's politics, asking them to imagine counterfactual situations in which it could have been true softened their moral judgments. A little imagination can apparently make a lie feel "truthy" enough to give the liar a bit of a pass."[126] I choose the more hopeful narrative from Pennycook and Rand, but Effron's study is compelling.

As if the findings of Daniel Effron and others of the rationalization camp were not bad enough, we may actually be hard wired to do stupid things. According to Dr. Nathan H. Lents, professor of biology at John Jay College of the City University of New York: "This is partly because our brains--powerful as they are--are also full of glitches. We commit cognitive errors in surprisingly predictable patterns and struggle to grasp the mathematics of large numbers, which limits our ability to learn important lessons and make good decisions."[127] Knowing this should help us recognize that perhaps we should step back, take a hard look at the evidence, seek help in looking at the data, before we blindly continue policies and procedures that have been in place for years, in some cases for decades. If our brains are on cruise control driving us over a cliff, let's apply the brakes. Let's look at the software and see where we can overcome our natural inclination to believe the things we should not.

Give Me a Fast Break

I wrote earlier about how important basketball is to Indian Country. The best way to describe it is to think of football in Texas, minus the multi-million-dollar stadiums. I have seen caravans leaving Lodge Grass, Montana on the Crow Reservation, or leaving Ponemah, on the Red Lake Reservation in Minnesota, heading to a basketball game in a distant town, cars and trucks on a seemingly endless and slow-moving conga line. Basketball is about more than just winning a game, it is about manhood, faith, and family. Indian ball, as it is known, means an exhausting full-court press on every change of possession. It is high-scoring, fast, and bewildering. But it is not about the individual. You are expected to pass the ball, to be generous with your teammates and honorable in your play. It is about the sport, the team as family. And basketball provides hope.

In a sort of slow-moving tragedy, between November 2016 and December 2017 there were 20 confirmed teen suicides on the Flathead Reservation in Montana. There were the teen suicides on the Ft. Peck Reservation, but there were also teen suicides on the Rocky Boy's, Ft. Belknap, and Northern Cheyenne Reservations in Montana. Basketball helped the grieving. In 2017, the Arlee High School Warriors on the Flathead Reservation were headed to the state championship. Just before one of the regional games, yet another teen took his own life and the team decided it had to do something. The leaders of the team got together and taped a video urging their fellow students and friends to be strong, to talk to one another, to reach out to their friends in pain to prevent more needless deaths. The video went viral and soon had been seen by more than a million people. It gave people hope. But the larger question is, what are we doing about the fact that young Native American men have a rate of suicide that is 38.2 per 100,000, *more than six times the rate of young white men.*[178] What school policies, community efforts and mental health evaluations could we institute to help these families?

We continue to demonize people in poverty. We have not come as far from the British response to the Irish Potato Famine as you might think. We have still not overcome the perverse need to describe the wall that separates the well-off from the destitute as a wall of moral strength on the one side and personal weakness on the other. We continue to write rules and regulations without regard to all the evidence and data available that ought to inform those rules and regulations. We continue to endow the processes and procedures we use to create these rules and regulations with more value than we should. We don't look deeper into the causes of inequality. We don't even look for the causes at all. We are content with the status quo and resist efforts to reform how we make decisions, how the rules are written, who benefits and who is hurt. We continue to tell stories that belittle the poor. We must decide to stop promulgating the poisonous stories, be kinder in our views of others, be more thoughtful and open in our decision-making. We must, each of us, become the agents of change that will lead to fairer, more equitable distribution of happiness and justice. Be mindful of Martin Luther King's words, "Shallow understanding from people of good will is more frustrating than the absolute misunderstanding from people of ill will."[129] Hold people to higher standards and force greater and deeper understanding not only of the lives others live, but the fault in our own perceptions and the depth of our own prejudices. Let the Lakota Great Spirit prayer guide you:

> Oh Great Spirit, whose voice I hear in the wind, whose breath gives life to all the world.
> Hear me; I need your strength and wisdom.
> Let me walk in beauty, and make my eyes ever behold the red and purple sunset.
> Make my hands respect the things you have made and my ears sharp to hear your voice.
> Make me wise so that I may understand the things you have taught my people.
> Help me to remain calm and strong in the face of all that comes towards me.
> Let me learn the lessons you have hidden in every leaf and rock.
> Help me seek pure thoughts and act with the intention of helping others.
> Help me find compassion without empathy overwhelming me.
> I seek strength, not to be greater than my brother, but to fight my greatest enemy—myself.
> Make me always ready to come to you with clean hands and straight eyes.
> So when life fades, as the fading sunset, my spirit may come to you without shame.[130]

Chapter 19

A Good Time to Go

THIRTY YEARS AGO, City Light Development Corporation picked a fight with a powerful opponent, a system and a city led by people who had closed their hearts to the African American community in its midst. Twenty-three years ago, Travois was born because a powerful marketplace remained inaccessible to Indians. The old dictum that nature abhors a vacuum was somehow not at work on reservations. Indian Country is and was a viable and profitable market for tax credits, both for housing and economic development. Travois filled the vacuum, or more accurately, we showed how the vacuum could be filled. Since our beginning, more than 5,400 families are better housed and have better access to schools, health care, education, and recreation than they would have had without us. Travois helped tribes win over $1.4 billion in housing and economic development funding. That money is investment capital, not loans that had to be paid back.

City Light and Travois exist because of the unmitigated, sanctimonious certainty on the part of too many political leaders and government officials that sloth and clever exploitation of government handouts have replaced industriousness and personal responsibility. Too many state and local agencies assume without a doubt that African American families and Native American tribes do not need any additional help, that casino-gaming money and HUD funding are more than sufficient. They believe with complete confidence that their employees would not mislead them, are highly competent, and are always ethical. They are all certain of the wisdom of their decisions to leave out Indians or to withdraw support to Black families. And of course, this misguided certainty is not limited to people with the power and the public authority to address common ills, but extends to other business and community leaders.

Certainty that is marinated in false narratives not only misleads rational thought, it derails more effective strategy and squashes hope. Certainty, however false, leads almost inevitably to mythologizing, and that inevitably leads to injustice. It is the ideologue who broaches no dissent who gives cover to unfairness. It was the certainty that God disapproved of race mixing and that Blacks were the lesser race that gave cover to slavery and then to Jim Crow. It was the certainty that Indians were savages that fueled first the massacres and then established the boarding schools where Native boys and girls were forced to cut their hair, forbidden to speak their language and made to be "civilized."

Why do people repeat the apocryphal stories that allow people to believe not just unsubstantiated claptrap, but downright ridiculous myths? When you look at the impact that stories about Native Americans have on bankers and investors in Indian Country you begin to see that capital is less available to Indians not just because of Indian trust land, but the lack of trust in Indians. Add in the insidious inclination to believe that we have all the information we need and you begin to understand that not just bankers and investors, but government agents contribute to the poverty and lack of opportunity in Indian Country.

The African American families across the U.S. suffer from the same delusional prejudices. Even when people know they have a bias and want to overcome that bias, they have great difficulty in doing so. The Müller-Lyer illusion--that phenomenon of two parallel lines of equal length that are perceived to be different, even after you know they are identical--is manifest every day in hiring choices and in lending and investing decisions.

A Ride Off Into the Sunset

Travois continues to have successes in both the housing development realm and in the economic development realm. One of our projects with the Housing Authority of the Confederated Tribes of the Colville Reservation in Washington was named the best rural affordable housing project in the nation in 2012, what is known as the Edson Award. That was the first time an Indian project had ever received such an award. It was not the last. In 2018 our project for the Pueblo of Acoma in New Mexico won the same award for its new 30-unit project. I was awarded the Hope Award[131] from the National Association of Realtors in 2011 and our New Markets Tax Credit project with the Coastal Villages Region Fund in Goodnews Bay, Platinum, Alaska, was named the top rural New Markets project in the nation. The awards and notoriety mean that our mission reaches more people as a result. The more our story is heard, the more hopeful I become that the old stories will change.

After more than thirty years of building and fighting and protesting, I will admit I am worn down. As they say in Montana, I have been rode hard and put up wet. Getting Travois into California was the high point of my career, but soon after that victory my health became something I could no longer ignore. I had turned prematurely grey during the ordeal with the Winchester Board of Zoning Appeals. I had lost a good deal of that hair during the fights with South Dakota. All those flights on small commuter planes and hours of driving on gravel roads deteriorated two discs in my back. When I developed Meniere's disease, I could no longer travel alone. Meniere's, exacerbated by stress, is a disorder of the inner ear that comes with progressive hearing loss and most annoyingly, an unnerving propensity for vertigo, an almost complete loss of equilibrium. It comes on suddenly and lasts for eight hours or more. Sometimes you have subtle hints that you are about to forfeit all semblance of balance, a weird sensation that the world is moving a few paces slower or faster than you are. Those hints, if you listen to your body, generally give you time to settle into a chair or bed and wait it out. Sometimes you only have minutes before you are overtaken by literally gut-wrenching nausea and a complete and debilitating loss of balance. The world spins around you and there is nothing you can do to stop it. Sometimes you can't tell up from down, much less right from left.

I remember one of my more harrowing adventures in Montana. I was driving from the Fort Belknap Reservation back to Red Lodge, about a five-hour drive. Somewhere between Fort Belknap and Roundup, on a lonely stretch of Rt. 87, on a bitterly cold early

December day, after the sun had gone down, I got a flat tire. It was well below zero, maybe 20 or even 30 degrees below zero, and it was windy. I had to work a little, get back in the truck to warm up, then go back out to work a little more to change the tire. It took over an hour. Not a single car came by during that time. If I had had vertigo, I would not have been able to drive, much less change the tire, and it is entirely possible that I could have ended up a human popsicle by the side of the road. That experience made me aware of my limitations. The company wisely decided that I could not travel alone anymore to visit our tribal customers. That became a burden on the poor employee who had better things to do but instead had to be my travel mate, anxiously waiting for me to puke in their lap like George H. W. Bush did to the prime minister of Japan. They might be called on to deliver my presentation to a tribal council or conference audience. It was not a sought-after posting.

Plus, I can't hear worth a damn anymore. In small rooms with reasonably low ceilings I can hear well enough, so long as I can also read the lips of the person with whom I am trying to converse. I cannot hear at all in the cavernous, high ceilinged rooms where so many conferences and meetings are now held. More and more as I took on the role of elder statesman at Travois, my responsibilities were to attend industry conferences and quite often be a speaker at those conferences. It was becoming embarrassing because I could not make out all of what the speakers before or after me said, could not hear some of the questions asked from the audience. I just could not keep up the pretense that everything was fine. The worst of it, though, is the inability to hear the little things I used to be able to make out. I had always been able to judge situations well, to know when someone is dissembling or being truly honest. I had always been able to gauge when what I was saying was working, when I was being persuasive or when I was losing my audience. Part of that skill was being attuned to the little sounds people make. A subtle harrumph in the back of the throat has meaning. An ever so slight "huh," or the tiniest chuckle gives you important clues. Now all I can judge is the body language; the roll of the eyes accompanied by that subtle harrumph means something quite different when it is just the roll of the eyes. A little smile without that little encouraging peep means something else entirely. It might be contempt instead of respect. It might be suspicion instead of faith. I now miss the clues that gave me insight into what my colleagues, friends, and antagonists are thinking. I hate this loss of nuance. It was part of who I am, and it is gone now.

It is embarrassing to have people in conversation with me ask entirely appropriate and pertinent questions, which I invariably mishear. At a restaurant recently while making small talk with the young waitress serving us, Marianne casually mentioned that we had walked to the restaurant through a very nice neighborhood. The waitress thereupon told us either that she was a doctor and had many clients in the neighborhood from which we had just walked, or she had said that she was adopted and had many clients in said neighborhood. Neither scenario seemed likely. She was quite young and could possibly have been a female version of Doogie Howser, MD, but why then would she be waitressing. On the other hand, why would she be volunteering to complete strangers that she was adopted and what sort of clients do adoptees have anyway. After she left I leaned into Marianne and learned that she was a "dog-walker" and had many clients in the neighborhood. That cleared that up.

I am grateful that Elizabeth and her husband Phil Glynn have filled out the company with superstars. Elizabeth is now CEO and Phil is president. Under their leadership Travois wins more tax credit awards for our customers than nearly any company in the U.S., even those ten or 20 times our size. Our compliance and asset management department keeps our tribal customers free of nasty notices from federal or state agencies and our investors don't have to worry that their credits will be recaptured. Our design team creates innovative, attractive and award winning houses and community facilities. We have delivered more capital to Indian Country for affordable housing and economic development than any organization other than the federal government, this scrappy little company that never took no for an answer.

Travois is in good hands and I am happy to say that I came to the mostly unaided realization that I was the human embodiment of the theory of diminishing marginal utility. This theory holds that the value of a commodity, its utility to a consumer, diminishes with each additional unit of that commodity. The first unit of consumption for any product is highest, with every unit of consumption thereafter holding less and less value, having less and less utility.[132] Think of a starving man given a loaf of bread. The first few slices of bread are very important, the next slices fill his belly. The rest of the loaf is nice to have, but no longer crucial to his survival. I had become the slices at the back of the loaf and every day I continued to work at Travois had less utility than the day before. To my relief, Elizabeth executed a skillful and easy exit for me in recognition of my diminishing utility to Travois and I am proud to have recognized that my contributions to the company are now most valuable in hindsight. Marianne and I remain Chairman and Vice Chairman of the board; we are asked for advice on occasion, we offer advice on occasion. The time had come for the family business to live up to its destiny and let family take over. It was high time they said to me, like we'd say to Elizabeth so many years ago, "We love you. GO AWAY!"

Acknowledgments

I have many people to thank for the help and encouragement they so generously gave while I obsessed over this book. My wife, Marianne Roos, never wavered in her support, never gave in to my discouragement, and was a constant source of inspiration. She provided reassurance that I did indeed have a story worth telling when I began to think that nobody would care. Her editorial guidance was invaluable. I cannot thank her enough, but I will keep trying.

Of course, this book was inspired by the courage and perseverance of the many friends I made in Winchester and Indian Country over the last 30 years or so. Judy Humbert continues to amaze me with her quiet determination. Bill Buckner continues to demand by example that I acknowledge the strength of the African American families that continue to live in neighborhoods disfavored and discounted in Winchester and throughout the nation.

I am blessed to count among my friends Gerald Sherman, Jane Barrett, and Linda McGraw-Adams. I would never have made progress in understanding the depth of the housing crisis in Indian Country without the special help and the patient assistance from Bob Gauthier, Chancy Kittson, and Ron His Horse Is Thunder, among the scores of others on reservations all across the country. They are the reason this story can and should be told.

I owe a debt of gratitude to the best high school teacher I ever had, Deborah Erskine (now Deborah Lankford). She taught me to love a well-crafted sentence and to appreciate the power of words. My mentor, first boss, and life-long friend Evan Becker deserves credit for showing me that working for affordable housing is more than an occupation, it is a passion.

I am grateful to my daughter, Elizabeth Glynn, and son-in-law Phil Glynn for so ably continuing the work of Travois and the fine men and women, dedicated and professional, who keep doing the job of bringing decent, safe, and affordable housing and critically important infrastructure to tribes all across the U.S. Special thanks to Eva Schulte for her suggestions and guidance.

Thanks also to my cousin and someone whose eccentricity I aspire to, Luther Carter, for reading a very early copy and making astute suggestions, to Jim Miller, Lance Morgan, and Dick Todd, for reviewing the next-to-final version of the manuscript and to Anna Lawton at New Academia Press for having confidence in my book. Wayne Koonce and Harriet Hentges deserve my enduring gratitude for recommending Hamlet's soliloquy as inspiration for the title.

This book would not have seen the light of day had it not been for the very considerable talents of Leeanne Seaver, my book doctor. She provided the kind of editorial ministrations and language surgery that my all too often un-well manuscript needed.

Thanks to the late Dee Brown for his heartbreaking history, *Bury My Heart at Wounded Knee*. My heart goes out to the families of Frank Armajo and Maurice (Moose) Lambert. Their untimely deaths paint in stark relief life on Indian reservations. I was lucky to have known them.

Notes

1. *Absalom, Absalom!* By William Faulkner, Random House, 1936. (Like every self-respecting Southerner, I keep an abundance of Faulkner quotes near at hand at all times.)
2. *The Courage to Act,* by Ben Bernanke, W. W. Norton & Company, 2015, page 35.
3. When describing unemployment rates in Indian Country I have incorporated the notion of "non-employment" in the unemployment rate. The official unemployment rate includes only people in the labor force and excludes people who have, for a variety of reasons, abandoned the labor force. Because jobs are so scarce on so many reservations many people have become so discouraged that they no longer seek work. It seems appropriate to me to include the non-employed with the unemployed to give a true picture of employment in Indian Country. A good explanation for this can be found in "Measuring Labor Utilization: The Non-Employment Index" by Marianne Kudlyak, in the Federal Reserve Bank of San Francisco's *Economic Letter*, March 27, 2017.
4. "Dead cat bounce" is a term used by securities traders and some economists to denote a pause in a bear market or an unsustainable and generally small uptick in economic activity. The meaning is derived from the notion that even a dead cat would bounce if it is dropped far enough and fast enough.
5. National Indian Gaming Commission, 2013 and 2014 Annual Reports
6. *Census of Housing, 2010*, US Bureau of the Census
7. *Thomas Jefferson, An Intimate History* by Fawn Brodie, W. W. Norton & Company, Inc. 1974 p. 91, *Thomas Jefferson, The Art of Power* by Jon Meacham, Random House, 2012 p. 49 and *Jefferson: Architect of American Liberty,* by John B. Boles, Basic Books, 2017, p. 28.
8. *Richard Bland: Conservator of Self-Government in Eighteenth-Century Virginia*, Robert Chester Daetweiler, 1968, University of Washington Press p. 101-102.

9. *Harry Byrd of Virginia,* by Ronald L. Heinemann, University of Virginia Press, 1996, pages 32-33.
10. Ibid, page 4.
11. *Return of the 'Welfare Queen,'* by John Blake, CNN Politics, 2012.
12. *What is Motivated Reasoning? How Does it Work?,* by Dan Kahan, Science & Religion Today, May 4, 2011.
13. *Narrative Economics,* by Robert J. Shiller, January 7, 2017, Chicago, IL, page 9.
14. *Foods Typically Purchased by Supplemental Nutrition Assistance Program (SNAP) Households,* Office of Policy Support Food and Nutrition Service, USDA, November, 2016
15. *The Bank Fees You Don't Even Know About,* by Lisa Servon, PBS News Hour Column, June 22, 2017.
16. Poverty Impedes Cognitive Function, by Anandi Mani, Sendhil Mullainathan, Hdar Shafir and Jiaying Zhao, *Science,* August 30, 2013, Vol 341, pages 976 – 980.
17. Ibid
18. *The Rich Boy,* by F. Scott Fitzgerald, Article in Redbook, January and February, 1926, Paragraph 3.
19. *Why Zebras Don't Get Ulcers,* by Robert M. Sapolsky, St. Martin's Press, New York, 2004, p.247.
20. *The Great Hunger,* by Cecil Woodham-Smith, Old Town Books, London, 1962, page 62, 63
21. Ibid, pages 64-65.
22. *The Immortal Irishman,* by Timothy Egan, Houghton, Mifflin, Harcourt, 2016, page 40.
23. Seebohm Rowntree *Poverty: A Study of Town Life, Centennial Edition,* Bristol: Policy Press 2000, pp. 133-134
24. "How Far it is Possible to Provide Satisfactory Houses for the Working Classes, at Rents Which They Can Afford to Pay", Seebohm Rowntree, Lectures on Housing, Warburton Lecture, 1914.
25. *Hero of the Empire* by Candace Millard, Doubleday, 2016, page 97.
26. Winchester *Star* Newspaper, August 14, 1989, Susan Abramson Staff Writer
27. *The Enigma of Reason,* by Hugo Mercier and Dan Sperber, Harvard University Press, Cambridge, MS 2017, page 9.
28. "If he can do it, so can they: Exposure to Counterstereotypically Successful Exemplars Prompts Automatic Inference," by Clayton R. Critcher and Jane L. Risen, Journal of Personality and Social Psychology, March, 2014 Vol 106 (3), pages 359-379.
29. *Mismatch and the Paternalistic Justification for Selective College Admissions,* by Michael Kurlaender and Eric Grodsky, Center for Demog-

raphy and Ecology, University of Wisconsin-Madison, CDE Working Paper No. 2013-06, May 2013 and *Sanding Down Sander*, by Emily Bazelon, Jurisprudence, April 29, 2005

30 Letter from James Q. Wilson to Joseph Califano, August 8, 1967, Box 6, Presidential Papers, LBJ Library, as described in *The Gifted Generation*, by David Goldfield, Bloomsbury Publishing, 2017, page 351, footnote 46.

31 "Rethinking the Risks of Poverty: A Framework for Analyzing Prevalence and Penalties," David Brady, Ryan M. Finnigan, Sabine Hubgen, *American Journal of Sociology*, Volume 123 Number 3 November, 2017, pages 740-786.

32 *White Privilege: An Insidious Virus That's Eating America from Within*, by Andrew O'Hehir, Solon, August 23, 2014

33 *Are Emily and Greg More Employable than Lakisha and Jamal? A Field Experiment on Labor Market Discrimination*, by Marianne Bertrand and Sendhil Mullainathan, National Bureau of Economic Research, NBER Working Paper No. 9873, July, 2003, and *The Benefits of Socioeconomically and Racially Integrated Schools and Classrooms*, The Century Foundation, February 10, 2016.

34 *Household Wealth in the U.S.: 2000 to 2011*, by Alfred Gottschalck, Marina Vornovytskyy, and Adam Smith, U.S. Census Bureau, Survey of Income and Program Participation, 1996, 2001, 2004 and 2008 Panels, and Survey of Financial Characteristics of Consumers 1962 (December 31), Survey of Changes in Family Finances 1963, and Survey of Consumer Finances 1983–2013, Urban Institute.

35 *The Asset Value of Whiteness*, by Amy Traub, Laura Sullivan, Tatjana Meschede, and Tom Shapiro, Institute on Assets and Social Policy, Brandeis University, February 6, 2017, page 1.

36 Ibid, pages 4 - 7.

37 *The Truly Disadvantaged: The Inner City, the Underclass, and Public Policy*, 2nd Edition, by William Julius Wilson, University of Chicago Press, 2012 (1987), page 6, 12.

38 "Housing Discrimination as a Basis for Black Reparations," by Jonathan Kaplan, Andrew Valls, *Public Affairs Quarterly*, Volume 21, Number 3, July 2007, pages 255-273.

39 "The Racist Housing Policy That Made Your Neighborhood", by Alexis Madrigal, *The Atlantic*, May 22, 2014.

40 *The Color of Law*, by Richard Rothstein, Liveright Publishing Corporation, 2017, page 65.

41 "Linking 'toxic outliers' to environmental justice communities," by Mary B. Collins, Ian Munoz, and Joseph JaJa, *Environmental Research Letters*, IOP Publishing, January 26, 2016.

42 Winchester *Star*, March 24, 1993.
43 "Greenspan Concedes Error on Regulation" by Edmund L. Andrews, New York *Times*, October 23, 2008.
44 *Thinking, Fast and Slow*, by Daniel Kahneman, Farrar, Straus & Giroux, 2013, page 216.
45 Ibid, page 212.
46 *Traders, Guns & Money*, by Satyajit Das, Prentice Hall, 2006, page 44.
47 *Promise Me, Dad*, by Joe Biden, CelticCapri Corp., Flatiron Books, 2017, page 129.
48 "Issues Relating to Leases on Native American Reservations," by Don J. Miner, Sarah Kubiak, Almira Torralba, Finnemore Craig, PC, April 24, 2007.
49 *Reconfiguring the Reservation: the Nez Perces, Jicarilla Apaches and the Dawes Act*, by Emily Greenwald, University of New Mexico Press, 2002
50 *A People's History of the United States, 1492 to Present*, by Howard Zinn, Harper & Row, 1980, Chapter 7.
51 North Dakota Studies Program, State Historical Society of North Dakota, *Final Garrison Diversion Unit Commission Report*, Appendix F, p. 57.
52 "For the Taking: The Garrison Dam and the Tribal Taking Area," *Cultural Survival Quarterly*, Terri Berman, June 1988.
53 "A Dam Brings a Flood of Diabetes to Three Tribes", by Lisa Jones, *Indian Country Today*, July 6, 2011.
54 "Federal Government Offers $270 million for Fractionated Blackfeet Land", by Justin Franz, Flathead *Beacon*, December 4, 2016
55 *Third World Islands in a Sea of Relative Prosperity*, David W. Bland, The Region, Quarterly Magazine of the Minneapolis Federal Reserve Bank, Volume 8, Number 2, June 1, 1994,
56 *Narrative Economics*, by Robert J. Shiller, January 7, 2017, Chicago, IL, page 9.
57 Ibid, page 10.
58 *Nudge: Improving Decisions About Health, Wealth, and Happiness*, by Richard Thaler and Cass Sunstein, Penguin Books, 2008, page 25
59 This saying has been attributed to Martin Luther King, Jr. but I have not found evidence for it. It has been suggested that he was inspired by *Past and Present, Thomas Carlyle's Collected Works, Vol. XIII*, 1843, in which he wrote "Only in times of great darkness can you truly see the stars."
60 "How Many Bison Originally Populated Western Rangelands," by James H. Shaw, *Rangelands*, Vol 17 (5), October 1995, page 148.
61 *Bury My Heart at Wounded Knee*, by Dee Brown, Holt, Rinehart & Winston, 1970. page 435.

62 *The Earth is Weeping: The Epic Story of the Indian Wars for the American West*, by Peter Cozzens, Alfred a. Knopf, 2016, page 428.
63 Ibid, page 453.
64 United States Court of Appeal for the District of Columbia Circuit, Navajo Nation, A Federally Recognized Indian Tribe, Navajo Nation Department of Justice, Appellant v. United State Department of Interior and Ryan Zinke, In His Capacity as Secretary, United State Department of Interior, Appellees (No. 1:14-cv-01909)
65 Poverty Impedes Cognitive Function, by Anandi Mani, Sendhil Mullainathan, Hdar Shafir and Jiaying Zhao, *Science*, August 30, 2013, Vol 341, page 976.
66 "California's Culture Bloom" by Bruce Bliven, The Rotarian, Volume 100, May 1962, Number 5, page 63.
67 Low Income Housing Tax Credit Short Summary, South Dakota Housing Development Authority, May 9, 1996
68 *Thinking, Fast and Slow,* by Daniel Kahneman, Farrar, Straus and Giroux, 2013, pages 27-29.
69 Complaint, filed with the Office of Fair Housing and Equal Opportunity on behalf of the Lower Brule Housing Authority, the Yankton Sioux Housing Authority, and Oti Kaga, Inc., October 8, 1996.
70 Census of Housing, 1990, US Bureau of the Census
71 The annual Bulwer-Lytton Fiction Contest, created and run by the English Department at San Jose State University, "honors" the purple prose of Edward Bulwer-Lytton each year with a contest to see who can write the worst opening line to the worst of all possible novels. Bulwer-Lytton's novel *Paul Clifford,* published in 1830, includes the opening line misquoted above. It is considered by some to be perhaps the worst opening line in history.
72 *South Dakota: Troubled Driving Record,* New York *Times,* July 1, 2004
73 *In the Spirit of Crazy Horse,* Peter Mathiessen, Viking Press, 1993.
74 *Neither Wolf Nor Dog,* by Kent Nerburn, New World Library, 1994, 2002.
75 *Review - Fort Apache, Directed by John Ford,* by Kelley L. Ross, 1997, The Proceedings of the Friesian School, Fourth Series
76 *Kinishba: A Classic Site of the Western Pueblos,* by James B. Shaeffer, Bureau of Indian Affairs, Branch of Education, November 29, 1956
77 *A Season on the Reservation: My Sojourn with the White Mountain Apache*, by Kareem Abdul Jabbar, with Stephen Singular, William Morrow & Company, 2000
78 *Apache Scouts Receive Medal of Honor for Service,* by Cynthia Palcich, Indianz.com, June 21, 2016.
79 Phrase originating probably in 16th Century Italy as a practical way to

protect buildings from bombardment and more prominently from *The Godfather* movies. The Phrase Finder, United Kingdom, 2016.
80 *Flathead Reservation Marks Century of White Settlement*, by Tom Bauer, Missoulian, September 26, 2010.
81 *Lewis and Clarke: The Journey of the Corps of Discovery,*, by Dayton Duncan and Ken Burns, Alfred A. Knopf, Inc., 1997, p.139.
82 *Nudge*, by Richard H. Thaler and Cass Sunstein, Penguin Book, 2008, page 66.
83 *The Jerusalem Post*, Richard Harris, July 19, 2011.
84 *Belief in the Law of Small Numbers*, by Daniel Kahneman and Amos Tversky, Psychological Bulletin 76, no 2, 1971, page 29.
85 Housing Needs of American Indian and Alaska Natives in Tribal Areas: A Report From the Assessment of American Indian, Alaska Native, and Native Hawaiian Housing Needs, US Department of HUD, Office of Policy Development and Research, January, 2017.
86 Blog Post, National Museum of the American Indian, May 22, 2015
87 American Indian Relief Council, now known as Northern Plains Reservation Aid, *Indian Health Disparities*, 2006 and *Native People for Cancer Control*, 2005.
88 *The NSDUH Report: Need for and Receipt of Substance Use Treatment Among American Indians or Alaska Natives*, Substance Abuse and Mental Health Services Administration, Center for Behavioral Health Statistics and Quality, November 2012.
89 *Leading Major Congenital Malformations Among Minority Groups in the United States, 1981-1986*, Journal of the American Medical Association, 261(2):205-209, 1989.
90 *US High School Graduation Rates Hits New Record High*, US Department of Education's National Center for Education Statistics, December 15, 2015.
91 The Eastern Shoshone Tribe originally occupied lands in Colorado, Idaho and Utah. In 1868, they were forced onto a reservation in Wyoming and occupied the territory now known as the Wind River Reservation. In 1878, the Northern Arapaho Tribe was allowed to settle on the Wind River Reservation, pointedly without the consent of the Eastern Shoshone Tribe. The United States Supreme Court has held that since 1878, the two tribes have been equitable owners and sovereigns in common of the Wind River Reservation.
92 *Blackfeet Housing on Shaky Foundations*, by Adam Weinacker, Native News, University of Montana School of Journalism, August 18, 2004
93 Marceau v. Blackfeet Housing Authority, United States Court of Appeals, Ninth Circuit, No. 04-35210, August 22, 2008
94 *The Demography of American Indian Families*, by Gary D. Sandefur and

Carolyn A. Liebler, National Library of Medicine, National Institutes of Health, 1996
95 *My Cousin Vinny*, 1992 movie starring Joe Pesci, Ralph Machio and Lane Smith. In the movie Lane Smith describes the two wrongly accused defendants, played by Ralph Machio and Mitchell Whitfield, when leaving the murder scene, as driving away "in great haste." I love that line.
96 *The Native Americans: An Illustrated History,* David Hurst Thomas, Jay Miller, et al, Turner Publishing, 1993, page 350-353.
97 *Bury My Heart at Wounded Knee,* by Dee Brown, Holt, Rinehart, Winston, 1970, page 330.
98 Ibid.
99 *Why Zebras Don't Get Ulcers,* by Robert M. Sapolsky, St. Martin's Press, New York, 2004.
100 Variously attributed to Winston Churchill and Grover Cleveland.
101 Éamon de Valera: A Will to Power, Ronan Fanning, Harvard University Press, 2016
102 *Narrative Economics,* by Robert J. Shiller, January 7, 2017, Chicago, IL, page 10-11.
103 Ibid, page 17.
104 Peltzman, Sam, 1993. *"George Stigler's Contribution to the Economic Analysis of Regulation,"* Journal of Political Economy, University of Chicago Press, vol. 101(5), pages 818-832, October, 1993.
105 *Unskilled and Unaware of It: How Difficulties in Recognizing One's Own Incompetence Lead to Inflated Self-Assessment,* by Justin Kruger, David Dunning, Journal of Personality and Social Psychology. Volume 77, number 6, pages 1121 – 1134, 1999.
106 I have chosen not to name them. There is little to gain by doing so.
107 *On War,* by Carl von Clausewitz, London, 1827, Book 1, Chapter 7.
108 *A Primer on Rural Poverty in Wisconsin,* Professor Katherine Curtis and Professor Leann Tigges, University of Wisconsin-Madison, Department of Community & Environmental Sociology, September 11, 2015.
109 *Lyndon Johnson: Master of the Senate,* by Robert Caro, Alfred A. Knopf, 2002, page 53.
110 *Lyndon Johnson: The Path to Power,* by Robert Caro, Alfred A. Knopf, 1982, page 502.
111 Abraham Lincoln, rejoinder in the sixth debate with Senator Stephen A. Douglas, October 13, 1858. *The Collected Works of Abraham Lincoln,* ed. Roy P. Basler, vol. 3, p. 279
112 Center for Native American Youth at the Aspen Institute, One DuPont Circle, Washington, DC 20036-1133, also *The Hard Lives – and*

High Suicide Rate – of Native American Children on Reservations, by Sari Horwitz, the Washington Post, March 9, 2014.
113 "Using the Best Data Possible, We Set Out to Find The Middle of Nowhere," The Washington *Post,* by Andrew Van Dam, February 20, 2018.
114 *Richard Bland: Conservator of Self-Government in Eighteenth-Century Virginia,* Robert Chester Daetweiler, University of Washington Press, 1968 p. 248.
115 *Making the Grade,* by Walter Issacson, Time Magazine, April 5, 2007.
116 *Stop Worrying About Food Stamp Fraud,* by Matt Bruenig, *The American Prospect,* August 19, 2013.
117 "Only the Pentagon Could Spend $640 on a Toilet Seat," by William D. Hartung, *The Nation,* April 11, 2016.
118 "Why Do People Fall for Fake News?", by Gordon Pennycook, Hill & Levine Schools of Business at the University of Regina and David Rand, Sloan School of Management, Massachusetts Institute of Technology, New York *Times,* January 20, 20019.
119 Ibid.
120 *Report of the National Advisory Commission on Civil Disorders,* March, 1968, page 202.
121 Ibid
122 *Healing Our Divided Society,* by Fred Harris and Alan Curtis, Eisenhower Foundation Books, Temple University Press, 2018, page 14.
123 Ibid, page 38.
124 Ibid, page 59.
125 Ibid , page 341.
126 Daniel A. Effron, New York *Times,* April 29, 2018, *Personality and Psychology Bulletin,* 2018, Vol 44(5) pages 729-745.
127 *Human Errors: A Panorama of Our Glitches, from Pointless Bones to Broken Genes,* Houghton Mifflin Harcourt. As published in the WSJ, April 14-15, 2018, page C4
128 "What the Arlee Warriors Were Playing For", by Abe Street, *The New York Times Magazine,* April 8, 2018.
129 *Letter from a Birmingham Jail,* Dr. Martin Luther King, Jr., April 16, 1963.
130 Author unknown but generally attributed to the Lakota Chief, Yellow Lark, 1887.
131 National Association of Realtors created the Home Ownership Participation for Everyone (HOPE) Awards in 2001 and the last awards were given out in 2011. I won the award for Leadership.
132 *The Fortune Encyclopedia of Economics,* Edited by David R. Henderson, Warner Books, 1993, p 797.

Photo Credits

Fig. 1: Lillian Somoza being crowned at the 1940 Shenandoah Apple Blossom Festival, courtesy of the Steward Bell, Jr. Archives of the Handley Regional Library
Fig. 2: Winchester *Star*, April 2, 1992
Fig. 3: Winchester *Star*, March 24, 1993
Fig. 4: Indian Land for Sale, Department of Interior poster, 1911, courtesy of the Library of Congress
Fig. 5: Gerald Sherman with Mohammed Yunus, 1988, Courtesy of Gerald Sherman
Fig. 6: AP photo by William Chaplis, of A. J. Krug, Secretary of the Interior and George Gillette, Chairman of the Three Affiliated Tribes, May 20, 1948
Fig. 7: Body of Chief Big Foot at the Massacre of Wounded Knee, courtesy of the Library of Congress - LC-USZ62-116812
Fig. 8: Angela Christy, courtesy of Angela Christy
Fig. 9: Chief Joseph, The Miriam and Ira D. Wallach Division of Art, Prints and Photographs: Photography Collection, The New York Public Library. (1903). *Chief Joseph*. Retrieved from http://digitalcollections.nypl.org/items/510d47da-82dc-a3d9-e040-e00a18064a99
Fig. 10: Travois on the Plains, Courtesy of the Library of Congress – 3a40649u
Fig. 11: Parade Magazine Cover from May 16, 2004, Courtesy of AMG/Parade.
Fig. 12: Chief Alchise (Alchesay), Courtesy of the Library of Congress–LC-USZ62-109711
Fig. 13: Funeral Bulletin, Maurice (Moose) Lambert, July 11, 2008
Fig. 14: Peter Rothermel Portrait of Patrick Henry, Patrick Henry Memorial Foundation
Fig. 15: Navajo Utility Authority Electric Substation, Courtesy, Travois Holdings, Inc.
Fig. 16: Colville Homes II project. Courtesy of Travois Holdings, Inc.

Bibliography

Almond, Steve. *Bad Stories: What the Hell Just Happened to Our Country.* Pasadena, CA: Red Hen Press, 2018.
Bernanke, Ben S. *The Courage to Act: A Memoir of a Crisis and Its Aftermath.* New York: W. W. Norton & Company, 2015.
Biden, Joe. *Promise Me, Dad: A Year of Hope, Hardship and Purpose.* New York: Flatiron Books, 2017.
Blackmon, Douglas A. *Slavery by Another Name: The Re-Enslavement of Black American from the Civil War to World War II.* New York: Doubleday, 2008.
Brown, Dee. *Bury My Heart at Wounded Knee: An Indian History of the American West.* New York: Holt, Rinehart & Winston, 1970.
Caro, Robert. *Lyndon Johnson: Master of the Senate.* New York: Alfred A. Knopf, 2002.
Caro, Robert. *Lyndon Johnson: The Path to Power.* New York: Alfred A. Knopf, 1982.
Colby, Tanner. *Some of My Best Friends Are Black: The Strange Story of Integration in America.* New York: Penguin Books, 2012.
Cozzens, Peter. *The Earth is Weeping: The Epic Story of the Indian Wars of the American West.* New York: Alfred A. Knopf, 2016.
Daetweiler, Robert Chester. *Richard Bland: Conservator of Self-Government in Eighteenth-Century Virginia.* University of Washington, 1968.
Das, Satyajit. *Traders, Guns, and Money: Knowns and Unknowns in the Dazzling World of Derivatives.* Harlow, UK: Prentice Hall, 2006.
Desmond, Matthew. *Evicted: Poverty and Profit in the American City.* New York: B/D/W/Y Broadway Books, 2016.
Diangelo, Robin. *White Fragility: Why it's So Hard for White People to Talk About Racism.* Boston: Beacon Press, 2018.
Drury, Bob and Tom Clavin. *The Heart of Everything that Is.* New York: Simon & Schuster, 2013.
Duncan, Dayton and Ken Burns. *Lewis & Clark: The Journey of the Corps of Discovery.* New York: Alfred A. Knopf, Inc., 1997.

Egan, Timothy. *The Immortal Irishman: The Irish Revolutionary Who Became an American Hero*. Boston: Houghton Mifflin Harcourt, 2016.

Fanning, Ronan. *Eamon de Valera: A Will to Power*. Cambridge, MA: Harvard University Press, 2016.

Harris, Fred and Alan Curtis, ed. *Healing Our Divided Society: Investing in America Fifty Years After the Kerner Report*. Philadelphia: Temple University Press, 2018

Heinemann, Ronald L. *Harry Byrd of Virginia*. Charlottesville: University Press of Virginia, 1996.

Henderson, David R., ed. *The Fortune Encyclopedia of Economics*. New York: Warner Books, 1993.

Jabbar, Kareen Abdul with Stephen Singular. *A Season on the Reservation: My Sojourn with the White Mountain Apache*. New York: William Morrow & Company, 2000.

Kahneman, Daniel. *Thinking, Fast and Slow*. New York: Farrar, Straus and Giroux, 2011.

Keltner, Dacher. *The Power Paradox: How We Gain and Lose Influence*. New York: Penguin Books, 2016.

King, Thomas. *The Truth About Stories: A Native Narrative*. Minneapolis: University of Minnesota Press, 2003.

Lewis, Michael. *The Undoing Project: A Friendship That Changed Our Minds*. New York: W.W. Norton & Company, 2017.

Mann, Charles C. *1491: New Revelations of the Americas Before Columbus*. New York: Vintage Books, 2005.

Mathiessen, Peter. *In the Spirit of Crazy Horse*. New York: Viking Press, 1993.

Mercier, Hugo and Sperber, Dan. *The Enigma of Reason*. Cambridge, MA: Harvard University Press, 2017.

Millard, Candice. *Hero of the Empire: The Boer War, a Daring Escape and the Making of Winston Churchill*. New York: Doubleday, 2016.

Nerburn, Kent. *Neither Wolf Nor Dog: Our Forgotten Roads with an Indian Elder*. Novato, CA: New World Library, 1994, 2002.

Riis, Jacob. *How the Other Half Lives: Studies Among the Tenements of New York*. New York: Charles Scribner's Sons, 1890.

Sapolsky, Robert M. *Why Zebras Don't Get Ulcers*. New York, St. Martin's Press, 2004.

Rothstein, Richard. *The Color of Law: A Forgotten History of How Our Government Segregated America*. New York: Liveright Publishing, 2017.

Sharftstein, Daniel J. *Thunder In the Mountains: Chief Joseph, Oliver Otis Howard and the Nez Perce War*. New York: W. W. Norton & Company, 2017.

Rowntree, Seebohm. *Poverty: A Study of Town Life, Centennial Edition*, Bristol: Policy Press, 2000

Thaler, Richard H. and Cass R. Sunstein. *Nudge: Improving Decisions About Health, Wealth, and Happiness.* New Haven: Yale University Press, 2008.

Thomas, David Hurst and Jay Miller, et al. *The Native Americans: An Illustrated History.* Nashville, TN: Turner Publishing, 1993.

Woodham-Smith, Cecil. *The Great Hunger,* London: Old Town Books, 1962.

Young, Kevin. *Bunk: The Rise of Hoaxes, Humbug, Plagiarists, Phonies, Post-Facts, and Fake News.* Minneapolis: Graywolf Press, 2017.

Zinn, Howard. *A People's History of the United States, 1492 to Present,* New York: Harper & Row, 1980.

Index

A
Abdul-Jabbar, Kareem 17, 182, 289, 295
aboriginal title 170
Affirmative Action 58, 59, 75
African American (See also Black) 14, 25, 28, 31, 33, 44, 46, 58, 62, 64, 66, 91, 182, 214-215, 253, 268, 277-278 ,283
AIG (See also SunAmerica) 230 259
AIM (See also American Indian Movement) 125
Alaska 213, 260-261, 279 290
Alaskan Native Villages 237
ALTA (See also American Land Title Association) 145
alternative dispute resolution 221
American City Corporation 12
American Indian Movement (See also AIM) 125
American Indian Relief Council 214, 290
American Journal of Sociology 60, 287
American Land Title Association (See also ALTA) 145
American Legion Baseball 222
Apesanahkwat 203
Appaloosa 232-233
Arizona Department of Housing 183-184, 186
Arizona Inter-Tribal Council 185
Armajo, Frank 217-218, 284
arsenic 225
asset value of whiteness 91, 287
Autry National Center 87

B
Badlands 79-80, 146
Banks, Dennis 125
banks/banking 3-4, 17-18, 23, 37-38, 47-51, 53, 68-69, 72-73, 75, 82-88, 91-103, 110-112, 116-117, 125, 197, 199, 221, 243
Barrett, Jane 167-170, 172-173, 175, 179, 203, 283, 286
basketball (See also Indian Ball) 17, 177, 182-183, 255, 263, 273-274
bathtub for horse to drink from 101, 141
Baucus, Senator Max 264
Bear Comes Out, Herman 17
Becker, Evan viii, 11, 244, 283
Beige Book (See also Current Economic Conditions by Federal Reserve District 109
Belcourt, ND 20
Bemidji State University 168
Bernanke, Ben 17
BIA 91, 97, 141
Big Data Institute, Oxford University 266
Billings, MT 19, 215, 235
Black, 4, 5, 11-12, 14-15, 25-26, 28-31, 35, 37, 53, 58-59, 60-69, 75, 87, 90, 121, 127, 177, 182, 189,

215, 219, 229, 231, 260, 268-269, 271, 277, 287, 294
Black Hills 121, 177
Blackfeet Community College 17
Blackfeet Housing Authority 224-227, 290
Blackfeet Reservation (See also Blackfeet Tribe) 17
Blackfeet Tribe 95-96
Bland, Elizabeth 10, 25-26, 74, 191, 222, 241, 259, 281-282, 284,
Bland, Gregory 10, 25, 74, 185, 222
Bland, Haywood Gilbert, Sr. 23
Bland, Richard 23-24, 26, 162, 267-268, 285, 292, 294
Bland, Roos and Associates 9, 13, 15
Bland, Theodoric 23
Board of Zoning Appeals (See also BZA) 56-58, 82, 139, 279
Bob Gauthier 173, 175, 186-187, 248, 252, 268, 283
Bob Marshall Wilderness Area 188-189
Bois Forte Reservation 260
Borgstrom, Richard (Borgy) 169
Brady, David 60, 287
Branch Dividian 116
Brandeis University 63, 91, 260, 287
Braunstein, Sandy 110-112
British Parliament 267-268
Brown, Dee 124, 126, 284, 288, 291, 294
Browning, MT 224
Buckner, Bill 66-67, 283
buffalo 2, 79-81, 105, 212, 182
Bulwer-Lytton, Edward 147
Bureau of Indian Affairs (See also BIA) 19, 91, 97, 125, 129-131, 213
Bureau of Labor Statistics 109
Burgesses, Virginia House of 23, 162, 267-268

burning newly bought car 99
Bury My Heart at Wounded Knee 124, 127, 284, 288, 291, 294
Bush, George H. W. 280
Byrd family 9, 11, 23-24
Byrd machine 14, 24
Byrd, Harry Flood, Sr. (See also Byrd family) 9, 24, 30
Byrd, William 23
BZA (See also Board of Zoning Appeals) 56-58,

C
Cabazon Band of Mission Indians 238-239
Califano, Joseph 59-60
California 19-20, 53, 117, 136, 170, 237-244, 251, 289
Cannon Ball 17, 128
Caro, Robert 261, 291
Carson, Dr. Ben 58-59
Carter, Luther 284
cash flow only debt 196, 248
casinos (See also Indian gaming) 19-20, 238, 277
Castillo, Dave 185
Catch 22 54, 56
Catch the Bear 126
Cavalry, US 123-124, 126-127, 180, 182, 232
CDOs (See also collateralized debt obligation) 85-86
CDSs (See also Credit Default Swaps) 85
Center for Indian Country Development 117
Centers for Disease Control and Prevention 214
Charles Edson Award 163, 279
character loan 88
Charles Edson Award for Excellence in Affordable Housing (See also Edson Award) 163

checkerboarded 89, 187
Cheyenne 2, 4, 123
Cheyenne and Arapaho Reservation 4, 179
Cheyenne River Reservation 120, 126, 138, 203, 217
Chief Alchesay 182, 293
Chief Alchise (Alchesay) (See also Chief Alchesay) 160, 293
Chief Big Foot 126-127, 155, 219-220, 293
Chief Big Foot Memorial Ride 219
Chippewa 113, 168, 171
Choctaw Nation Aid to Irish 41
Christy, Angela 134-135, 145, 147, 156, 165, 184, 221, 293
Churchill, Winston 45, 58, 236, 291, 295
City Council 28, 32, 36, 38, 69, 72, 74, 82
City Light 9,11,14, 29-31, 43-51, 65-66, 69, 71, 73-74, 82-84, 113, 189, 191, 277
City Light Development Corporation (See also City Light) viii, 14, 28, 30, 277
City University of New York 273
Civil Rights Act of 1964 60, 62, 67
Clarke, Deloris 229-231
Clausewitz, Carl von 250
Clinton, Hillary 273
Coastal Villages Region Fund 279
Cobell lawsuit 96
Cobell, Elouise (See also Cobell lawsuit) 95, 96
Code Talkers 180
Coen, Cindy 184
cognitive capacity 39, 131, 289
cognitive errors 273
collateralized debt obligations (See also CDOs) 85
colloidal silver 264

Colville Reservation (See also Confederated Tribes of the Colville Reservation) 4, 163, 233, 278, 293
Community Affairs 1-4, 72, 82-83, 102, 110, 112, 117
Community Bankers Association of Montana 189
Community Development Financial Institutions Fund 259
Community Reinvestment Act (See also CRA) 50, 51, 53, 62, 83-84, 113, 197
Confederated Tribes of the Colville Reservation (See also Colville Reservation) 4, 278
Consumer Expenditure Survey 109
Corps of Discovery 232
Corps of Engineers 94, 128, 132
CRA (See also Community Reinvestment Act) 50-51, 53, 83-84, 110, 197, 199, 229, 250
Creator (See also Wakan Tanka) 179
credit default swaps (See also CDS) 85
Crow Tribe 123, 217
cultural deference 88-89
Current Economic Conditions by Federal Reserve District (See also Beige Book) 109
Curtis, Alan 271-272, 292
Custer, General George Armstrong 123, 127

D

Dakota Access Pipeline (See also DAPL) 17, 128
DAPL (See also Dakota Access Pipeline) 17
Dances with Wolves 81
Dawes Act (See also General Al-

lotment Act of 1887) 93-95, 121, 168, 187, 269-270, 288
Dawes, Henry L. 93
de Velera, Eamon 237
death by broken heart 233
debt coverage ratio 247
Denver Museum of Art 87
Department of the Interior (See also Interior Department) 95
Department of Housing and Urban Development (See also HUD) 36, 100, 190 ,224
depositions 256-257
diminishing marginal utility 281
ditch, big wide ugly 178-179
Dodge, Colonel R. I. 121
due diligence 144-145, 206
Dunning-Kruger Effect, vi, 243, 245-249, 251, 253, 255, 257, 291
Dunning-Kruger Twins vi, 245, 247, 249, 251, 253, 255, 257

E

Eastern Shoshone Tribe 216, 290
Eban, Abba 208
Edson Award (See also Charles Edson Award for Excellence in Affordable Housing) 279
Effron, Daniel 272-273
Einstein, Albert 73
Elks Lodge 54, 66-67
Energy Transfer Partners (See also ETP) 128, 132
Enigma of Reason 57, 286, 295
Enterprise Foundation 48, 192-193
Enterprise Social Investment Corporation (See also ESIC) 48, 177, 192
Entwistle, Harry 205
Erickson, Kathy 1-2, 73, 83, 87
Erskine, Deborah 283
ESIC (See also Enterprise Social Investment Corporation) 48-49, 192-194, 199, 203-207, 216, 218-220, 229
ETP (See also Energy Transfer Partners) 128, 132

F

Fair Housing 61, 140, 143, 185, 249, 289
Fannie Mae 71, 199-207, 218, 220, 229-230, 257, 259
Fannie Mae Foundation 71
Faulkner, William 5
FDIC (See also Federal Deposit Insurance Corporation) 84
Federal Deposit Insurance Corporation (See also FDIC) 84
Federal Housing Administration (See also FHA) 64
Federal National Mortgage Association (See also Fannie Mae) 199
Federal Reserve Bank of Minneapolis (See also Minneapolis Federal Reserve Bank) 79, 83, 135
Federal Reserve Bank of Richmond (See also Richmond Federal Reserve Bank) 68-69
Federal Reserve Board of Governors (See also Federal Reserve System) 17, 72
Federal Reserve System 68, 72, 82-83, 87, 111-112
Fetal Alcohol Syndrome 214-215
FHA (See also Federal Housing Administration) 64-65, 75
FHA Underwriting Manual 64-65 ,75
fight or flight 236
Finnigan, Ryan 60, 287
First National Bank of Strasburg 49
First/Second Continental Congress 23-24, 265

Fitzgerald, F. Scott 40
Flathead Reservation 173, 186-188, 222, 244, 274, 290
fluid intelligence 39
Flying Fortress 146
food stamps (See also SNAP and Supplemental Nutrition Assistance Program) 31, 32, 35, 58, 215
formaldehyde 225
Fort Apache (See also Fort Apache Indian Reservation and White Mountain Indian Reservation) 16-17, 180-182, 289,
Fort Laramie Treaties 121
Fort Leavenworth, Kansas 233
fractionated land 95-96, 288
Frederick County 69, 72
Fresno, CA 243
Ft. Belknap 244, 274
Ft. Berthold Reservation 94, 154
Ft. Peck 172-173, 217, 223, 244, 249, 258, 262, 264, 266, 274
Ft. Peck Housing Authority (See also Ft. Peck) 172-173

G
Gandalf 241
General Allotment Act of 1887 (See also Dawes Act) 93, 95
George, David Lloyd 43
George, Prime Minister 237
German bwana 79-80, 105
Geronimo 81, 180, 182
ghost dance 126
Gillette, George 94, 154, 293
give me liberty, or give me death 24, 267
Glasgow, MT 266
glucocorticoid levels 236
Glynn, Phil 183, 259-260, 281, 284
good trade 54, 98,

Goodnews Bay 260, 279
Google 235
Goons (See also Guardians of the Oglala Nation) 125
Gover, Kevin 213
Grameen Bank 103, 138
great recession 17, 50, 86, 249, 259
Great Society 59, 60
Great Spirit prayer 275
Green, Graham (See also *Dances with Wolves* and *Thunderheart*) 81
Greenspan, Alan 72, 83-86, 110-111, 113
grocery store 35, 106-107, 110-112, 252
Guardians of the Oglala Nation (See also Goons) 125

H
Handley Library 14, 71, 82
handshake, significance thereof 88-89, 110-111
hard debt 195
Harris, Fred 271-272, 292
Healing Our Divided Society 271, 292, 295
Heinmot Tooyalaket aka Chief Joseph 232
Helena, MT 113-114, 173, 189, 248-249
Henry, Patrick 24, 162, 267, 293
Henry, Patrick 24, 162, 267, 293
His Horse Is Thunder, Ron 17, 159, 219-220, 283
Hoopa Valley Reservation 237
Hoover, President 261
horse/horses 9, 15, 80, 100-101, 141, 220, 232-233, 240, 249
House of Burgesses 23, 162, 267-268
Housing & Community Development, Inc. 122

Housing Act of 1937, 12, 189, 224, 226, 262
housing code enforcement 43, 62, 74
Howard, General Oliver 232, 295
Howser, Doogie 281
Hubgen, Sabine 60, 287
HUD (See also Department of Housing and Urban Development) 36, 59, 64, 90, 100, 117, 134, 140, 143, 145, 147, 171-172, 174, 185, 187, 190-192, 202, 207, 213, 224-226, 254, 262, 277, 290
HUD box 224
Humbert, Judy 30, 31, 135 ,283

I
Idaho 229-232, 234, 290
illusion of validity 206, 216
incompetence 41, 171, 208, 246, 291
Indian ball (See also basketball) 274
Indian Country viii, 4, 12, 15, 17-21, 26
Indian gaming 19, 20, 88
Indian Health Service 170, 218, 256
Indian Housing Authority of Central California 243
Indian Reorganization Act of 1934 125
Indian Self-Determination and Education Assistance Act 129
Institute on Assets and Social Policy 63, 91, 287
Interior Department (See also Department of the Interior) 129-130, 132
Internal Rate of Return (See also IRR) 49, 198, 230
IQ 39
Irish potato famine 40-41, 274
IRR (See also internal rate of return) 49, 198, 230

IRS 45, 47, 134, 147, 195
Isburg, Deb 120

J
Janklow, Bill (Wild Bill) 176
Jarboe, Mark 88, 102, 105, 141
Jefferson, Thomas 23, 285
John Jay College 273
Joseph, Chief 1, 81, 157, 232-234, 293, 295
JPMorgan Chase 259

K
Kahan, Dan 30, 58
Kahneman, Daniel 36, 85-86, 139, 208, 288-290, 295
Kansas City Federal Reserve Bank (See also Federal Reserve Bank of Kansas City) 83, 86, 111, 117
Kansas-Nebraska Act 262
Kaplan, Jonathan 64, 287
Karuk Reservation 237
Kermack-McKendrick model 240
Kermack, William Oglivy (See also Kermack-McKendrick model) 240
Kerner Commission (See also National Advisory Commission on Civil Disorders) 271-272, 295
Kerr Dam 188
King, Martin Luther 30, 114, 275, 288, 292
Kinishba 181, 289
Kittson, Chancy 225, 283
Kohl, Senator Herb 203
Kramerbooks & Afterwords 13
Kyle, SD 106, 135

L
Lakota 79, 104, 122, 124-127, 179, 220, 275, 292
Lakota Fund 103-104, 106, 120, 122, 133-134, 138-139, 142-147, 165

303

Lambert, Maurice (Moose) 161, 173, 255, 258, 284, 293
Lame Deer, MT 16, 19, 135, 235
Lander, WY 217
Lapwai, Idaho 230-231, 233-234
Last Chance Gulch 114
Lawton, Anna 284
Leech Lake 204-206, 220
Leech Lake Reservation Housing Authority (See also Leech Lake) 204
Lehman Brothers 254,
Lending in Indian Country 89, 100-101, 105, 113
Lents, Dr. Nathan H. 273
Lewis and Clark (See also Corps of Discovery) 120, 232
Library of Congress 13, 293,
LIHTC (See also Low Income Housing Tax Credits) 45-50, 53, 117, 120-121, 133-134, 143, 165-166, 184-185, 190-191, 200, 203, 219, 240, 248-250, 252, 262-265
limited liability companies (See also LLCs) 47
Lincoln-Douglas debates 262
Lincoln, Abraham 262
Little Big Horn 123, 261
Little Big Horn College 261
LLCs 47
Lockyer, Bill (See also Treasurer of CA) 241-242
Lodge Grass, MT 273
looking into eyes, significance thereof 89
Lopach, John 184
Lord of the Rings 241
Low Income Housing Tax Credit (See also LIHTC) 45, 113, 115, 177, 202, 259, 264, 289
Lower Brule Sioux Tribe 103, 120-121, 138, 142, 289

Luce, Clare Booth 13
luxuries 263, 266
Lyndon Johnson 262
Lyndon Johnson: Master of the Senate 291, 294
Lyndon Johnson: The Path to Power 261

M

Malaria Atlas Project 266
Malta, MT 2
Mandan, Hidatsa, and Arikara (See also Three Affiliated Tribes) 94
Mani, Anandi 131, 235, 286, 289
Manteo, NC 13
Massachusetts Colony 267
Massacre of Sand Creek 126
Massey, Dallas 186
massive resistance 14, 29-30
Maxwell Award for Excellence in Housing 71
MBOH (See also Montana Board of Housing) 187, 244-246, 248-249, 251-252, 257-258, 262-266
McGraw-Adams, Linda 168-170, 172, 283
McKendrick, Anderson Gray 240
McVeigh, Timothy 116
Means, Russell 125
Meniere's disease 279
Menominee Tribe 138, 203
Mercier, Hugo 57, 286, 295
Michel Associates 144, 146-147
micro-loan program 4, 103, 146
middle of nowhere 266
Miller, Jim 284
Miniconjou 126
minimum wage 31, 43
Minneapolis Federal Reserve Bank (See also Federal Reserve Bank of Minneapolis) 41, 73, 101-102, 109, 118 ,288

Minnesota 82, 101, 117, 134, 165-167, 169-172, 175-176, 198, 203-204, 260, 273, 295
Minnesota Chippewa Tribe 171
Montana 1, 2, 17, 19-20, 82, 95-96, 98, 112-113, 117, 120, 123, 172, 180, 186-189, 198, 215, 222-224, 237, 244-245, 249, 252, 254-256, 262, 264-265, 273-274, 279, 290
Montana Board of Housing (See also MBOH) 187, 244-245, 249, 251, 255, 263, 265
Morgan, Daniel 9
Morgan, Lance 284
Morris, Edmund 13
Morris, Sylvia 13
motivated reasoning 29, 58, 286
Mullainathan, Sendhil 131, 235, 286-287, 289
Muller-Lyer 139, 278
Murrah Building 116
Mutual Help 225, 226

N
NAHASDA 190, 191, 202, 226, 252
Narrative Economics 4, 27, 99, 102, 238, 251, 286, 288, 291
National Advisory Commission on Civil Disorders (See also Kerner Commission) 271-272, 295
National Gallery of Art 87
National Indian Gaming Commission 20, 285
National Museum of the American Indian 87
Native American Housing Assistance and Self-Determination Act (See also NAHASDA) 190
Native Americans viii, 4, 29, 81-82, 93, 98, 102, 124, 128, 180, 197, 201, 213-215, 226, 234, 238, 263, 278, 291, 296

Navajo Nation 129-131, 289
Navajo Utility Authority 260, 293
Neighborhood Reinvestment Corporation 12
NeighborWorks 12
Nespelem, WA 233
New Markets Tax Credit (See also NMTC) 259-261, 279
New Mexico 193, 198, 279, 288
Newton's Third Law of Motion 270
Nez Perce 230-234, 295
Nez Perce Tribal Housing Authority 230, 234
Ninth Circuit Court of Appeals 225, 239
Ninth Federal Reserve District (See Federal Reserve Bank of Minneapolis) 1, 82, 98, 104, 106-107
NMTC (See also New Markets Tax Credit) 259,
Nobel Peace Prize 103
Nobel Prize in Economic Sciences viii, 4, 36, 139
Nohwike' Bagowa 181
Norfolk Redevelopment and Housing Authority viii, 11
Norfolk, VA viii, 12, 21, 52
North Kent Court 68-70, 82, 152
North Kent Street 25-26, 28-29, 33, 36-38, 43-45, 50, 53-55, 58, 62-63, 65-66, 68-71, 73, 82, 152, 184, 213
Northern Arapaho Tribal Housing Authority 217-218
Northern Arapaho Tribe 216, 220, 290
Northern Cheyenne Indian Reservation (See also Northern Cheyenne Tribe) 2, 235, 244, 274
Northern Cheyenne Tribe 2, 123, 235, 244, 274
Not Help Him, Dani 17
Nudge: Improving Decisions About

Health, Wealth, and Happiness 102, 200, 288, 290, 296

O
Obama 96, 259,
OCC (See also Office of the Comptroller of the Currency) 84
Office of the Comptroller of the Currency (See also OCC) 84
Office of Thrift Supervision (See also OTS) 84
Oglala Sioux Tribe 79, 80, 120, 126
Oit Kaga, Inc. 120, 133-134, 138, 142, 289
Oklahoma 20, 117, 179, 251-252
Oklahoma City 116
One Bull 219
OTS (See also Office of Thrift Supervision) 84
overdraft 38, 51
Owl Creek Mountains 217

P
Paiute Indians 126
pass-through entities 47, 63
peer lending (See also solidarity lending) 4, 103
Pennycock, Gordon 269, 272, 292
Personality and Psychology Bulletin 272
Phase I Environmental Assessment 145-146
physical efficiency, Rowntree theory of 42
Pierre, SD 139
Pine Ridge Indian Reservation 2, 79, 81, 100, 103-107, 110, 112, 120, 124, 128, 138-139, 146, 176, 179, 217
Plains Indians 98, 158
planning commission 33, 38, 82
Platinum, Alaska" 260, 279

Ponemah, MN 273
popular sovereignty 262
poverty vii, 1, 4-5, 14, 17, 26, 30, 33, 38-39, 41, 43-44, 51, 59-60, 64, 75, 89, 96, 104, 108, 125, 131, 135-136, 178-179, 182, 184, 193, 204, 214, 234-237, 269, 271-272, 274, 278, 286-287, 289, 291, 294-295
Public Affairs Quarterly 64, 287
Public Law 280 239
Pueblo of Pojoaque 211

Q
QAP (See also Qualified Allocation Plan) 237-238, 263
QCT (See also Qualified Census Tract) 263
Qualified Allocation Plan (See also QAP) 234, 257
Qualified Census Tract (See also QCT) 263
quantitative analysts (See also quants) 252
quants (See also quantitative analysts 200, 252

R
Ramsey County 72, 82, 118, 221
Rand, David 269, 272, 292
Rapid City, SD 106, 177, 215
rationalization 269
Raven's Progressive Matrices 39
Raymond James Financial Services 194
Raymond James Tax Credit Funds 194, 197-201, 203-206, 220, 229-230, 259
re-sequencing 38, 39, 75
Reader & Swartz 56
Reagan, Ronald 28, 29
Red Cloud 270
Red Lake Band of Ojibway 101, 165, 168, 170-171

Red Lake Hight School 168
Red Lake Reservation 101, 166-168, 170, 172, 273
red lining 50
Red Lodge MT 222, 264, 279
regulatory capture 245, 252
Richmond Federal Reserve Bank (See also Federal Reserve Bank of Richmond) 69, 72
Riverside County, CA 238
Roane, Elizabeth Bland 23
Robinson Treaties 214
Rocky Boy's Indian Reservation 2, 113-114, 274
Roos, Marianne 9-10, 12-14, 20, 24-26, 71-72, 74-75, 82, 114-115, 132, 135, 221, 241, 256, 264, 281-282
Roosevelt, Theodore 13
Rosebud Indian Reservation 2, 176
Rothermel, Peter 162, 267, 293
Round Valley Reservation 237
Roundup, MT 279
Rouse Company 12, 13, 48, 71, 109, 135, 192
Rouse, James (Jim) 48, 192
Rowland, Dr. Annabelle 123
Rowntree, Seebohm 41, 42, 43, 286, 295

S

S & K Housing Authority (See also Salish and Kootenai Housing Authority) 186, 187
S & K Industries 187
Sacramento, CA 238, 244
Salish and Kootenai Housing Authority (See also S & K Housing Authority) 175, 178, 186-187
Sapolsky, Robert 40, 236, 286, 291, 295
Schulte, Eva 284
Schweitzer, Governor Brian 264-265

Science 39, 131, 235, 286, 289
Scoby, MT 266
scoring system for tax credits 245, 253
SDHDA (See also South Dakota Housing Development Authority) 137-143, 176
Seaver, Leeanne 284
settlement 96, 168, 257-258, 262, 290
Shenandoah Apple Blossom Festival 9-11, 151
Sherman, Gerald 102-106, 111-113, 120, 154, 179, 253, 283, 293
Sherman, Richard 79, 81, 105
Shiller, Robert viii, 4-5, 27-28, 33, 99, 101, 200-201, 238-239, 251, 286, 288, 291
Simone, Scott 194, 197, 203
Sinclair, Diane 30-32
single motherhood 60
Sitting Bull 81, 126, 219-220, 270
Sitting Bull College 219-220
SIV (See also Structured Investment Vehicles) 84, 86-87
slaves/slavery 23, 26, 33, 58, 182, 234, 267-268, 270, 278, 294,
smurf 264
SNAP (See also Supplemental Assistance Nutrition Program 35, 36, 286
social entrepreneurs 16
social pathologies 214
soft debt 196
solidarity lending (See also peer lending) 103
Somoza, Lillian 10
South Dakota 2, 20, 82, 100-102, 106, 110, 117, 120-121, 124, 127-128, 133, 137, 139, 141-143, 165-166, 177, 179, 185, 198, 207, 215, 218-219, 221, 240, 279

South Dakota Housing Development Authority (See also SDHDA) 137, 176, 289
sovereign immunity (See also tribal sovereignty) 99, 102, 202, 250
sovereign/sovereignty 88, 98, 128, 190, 238, 262
Sperber, Dan 57, 286, 295
St. Paul, MN 72, 73, 82, 173
Stamp Act 267
Standing Rock 131, 132, 169, 217
Standing Rock Sioux Reservation (See also Standing Rock) 17, 126, 128, 131-132, 169, 207, 217-219, 221
Standing Rock Sioux Tribal Council 207
state allocating agencies 135, 143, 173, 175, 192, 208, 234
Stegner, Wallace 136
Stern, Gary 83, 112
Stone Child 114
Structured Investment Vehicle (See also SIV) 86
SunAmerica (See also AIG) 230
Sunstein, Cass 102, 200, 288, 290, 296
Supplemental Nutrition Assistance Program (See also SNAP) 35, 286
Sutton, Willie 243
Swallow, Mike 221
swimming pool 263-265
syndicators 48-49, 197-200, 203-204, 250-251

T
Tax Credit Allocation Committee (See also TCAC) 237,243
tax credits (See also LIHTC) 46-48, 50, 117, 121, 133-134, 137, 142, 166, 169, 172, 168, 189, 192, 194-195, 198-199, 218, 234, 237, 241, 244, 249, 252-254, 260, 263, 277
TCAC (See also Tax Credit Allocation Committee) 237-239, 241-244, 252
teen suicide 264-266, 274, 291
teepees 1, 81
Texas Hill Country 261-262
Thaler, Richard 36, 102, 200, 288, 290, 296
Three Affiliated Tribes 94-95, 154, 293
Thunder Rising to Loftier Mountain Heights aka Chief Joseph 232
Thunderheart 81
Todd, Dick 284
Townshend Acts 267
travois 15, 258, 293
Travois, Inc. viii, 15-16, 20, 24, 191-192, 201-202, 216, 221, 223-224, 227, 234, 236, 241, 243, 245, 247, 249-250, 254, 257, 259-260, 277-282, 284
Treasurer of California 241, 243
treaties 93, 94, 121, 126, 173, 213-214, 234
Treaties at Fort Carlton and Pitt 214
tribal sovereignty (See also sovereign immunity) 88, 238
Trip from Hell 3, 73, 79, 105
Trump, Donald 273
trust land/land held in trust 18, 90-91, 95, 145, 183-184, 186, 197, 218, 261, 278
truthy 273
Tversky, Amos 36, 208, 290

U
Umatilla Tribe 119, 165
Urban Reinvestment Task Force viii, 12, 21

US Court of Appeals for the District of Columbia Circuit 130

V

Valls, Andrew 64, 287
viral narratives/stories viii 5, 27, 240, 274
Voting Rights Act of 1965 60, 62

W

Wahlstrand, Liz 1, 2, 105
Wakan Tanka (See also Creator) 179
walkability 253-254, 270
WaMu (See also Washington Mutual Bank) 229-230, 234, 259
Washington Mutual Bank (See also WaMu) 229
Water Protectors 128, 131
welfare queen 28-29, 286
Wellstone, Senator Paul 203
West, Jim 87-88, 97-98, 102, 105, 141, 179
West, Richard, Jr. 87
West, Richard, Sr. 87
Westover Plantation 23, 24
White Man Runs Him 123
White Mountain Apache Reservation 17, 181-183, 186, 203, 289, 295
white privilege 61
White, Susan 185
Whitefeather, Bobby 203
Whitside, Major Samuel 127
Why Zebras Don't Get Ulcers 236, 286, 291, 295
willful ignorance 15, 252
Willie Wonka 42
Wilson, James Q. 59, 287
Wilson, Richard 125
Wilson, William Julius 64, 287
Winchester City Council (See also City Council) 38, 82
Winchester Star 11, 28, 82, 152, 286, 288, 293
Winchester, VA 9-12, 14-15, 21, 23-25, 28-31, 33, 35-36, 38, 44, 50, 53, 57, 62-63, 65-66, 69-73, 75, 82, 135, 139-140, 152, 177-178, 184, 192, 213, 279, 283, 286, 288, 293
Wind River (See also Wind River Reservation) 16, 203, 216-218, 262, 290
Wind River Canyon 217
Wind River Range 217
Wind River Reservation (See also Wind River) 216-218, 262, 290
Winner, SD 2
Wisconsin 48, 82, 138, 198, 251-253, 257, 287, 291
Wolf Point, MT 266
World War I 213
World War II 64, 146, 180, 213, 294
Wounded Knee 16, 124-125, 127-218, 133, 155, 219-220, 284, 288, 291, 293, 294
Wovoka 126

Y

Yankton Sioux Tribe 120, 136, 138, 142, 203, 289
Yanktonai Sioux 120
York, England 41
Young Man Afraid of His Horse 123
Yung, Margaret 229
Yunus, Muhammad 103, 154, 293
Yurok Reservation 237

www.ingramcontent.com/pod-product-compliance
Lightning Source LLC
Chambersburg PA
CBHW021804220426
43662CB00006B/168